Zero
Tollerance

OTHER BOOKS BY TOLLER CRANSTON

The Nutcracker

A Ram on the Rampage

Zero Tollerance

An Intimate Memoir by the Man

Who Revolutionized Figure Skating

TOLLER CRANSTON

with Martha Lowder Kimball

Canadian Cataloguing in Publication Data

Cranston, Toller
    Zero tollerance : an intimate memoir by the man who revolutionized
figure skating

Includes index.
ISBN 0-7710-2334-0

1. Cranston, Toller.   2. Skaters – Canada – Biography.   I. Kimball,
Martha Lowder.   II. Title.

GV850.C73A3 1997   796.91'2'092   C97-931193-4

The publishers acknowledge the support of the Canada Council for the
Arts and the Ontario Arts Council for their publishing program.

Set in Berkeley by M&S, Toronto
Printed and bound in Canada

McClelland & Stewart Inc.
The Canadian Publishers
481 University Avenue
Toronto, Ontario
M5G 2E9

1 2 3 4 5   01 00 99 98 97

To Carol Anne Letheren and Michael Murnaghan,
two of the rarest and best friends
anyone could ever hope to have

T. C.

To my mother,
Marion Westlin Lowder,
whose love of skating was contagious,
and to my father,
Paul Adkins Lowder,
whose love of words became a living legacy

M. L. K.

Contents

Il y a toujours du courage à dire ce que tout le monde pense.

(There is always courage in saying what everyone thinks.)

– Georges Duhamel

Prologue: The Genesis of a Legend

I was born at Hamilton General Hospital on April 20, 1949, at 6:20 in the morning to Montague (Monte) and Stuart Cranston. Certain people seem to spring from their parents' ribs. I inherited my father's athletic ability and my mother's artistic sensibilities, yet even though they can be directly traced to those sources, they were and are a million miles from their roots. Instead of being a football player, the quarterback at Queen's University that my father was, I became a figure skater. While my mother painted bucolic landscapes – cows and haystacks in the Ottawa Valley – I painted dragons, magical queens, and fireflies. Even though I am the spitting image of my mother, I believe that I am a foundling, a mystical child left on the doorstep by folkloric creatures.

Through Grade 1, I lived in Swastika, Ontario, a hamlet outside Kirkland Lake. From earliest memory, I affected a role and lived in my own world. Whatever I became later in life, the seeds were planted from birth, and there was never any change of persona or vision. I had an understanding of the child that I was and a sense of my own destiny. Even though I was churning inside with a sense of my own unusual character, my own sense of aesthetics, I pretended to be a normal child. Over the years, I ran into the arms of assorted people, usually older spinsters, looking for someone who understood who I was.

At a very young age, I told my mother that I wanted to become a ballet dancer. How I discovered ballet, I do not know. I entertained the women at her tea parties with a spontaneous, uninhibited, technically incorrect but highly passionate form of dance – not dissimilar to the kind of skating I became known for twenty years later. It was innate. I was an instrument of another force, a child with an artistic volcano inside that had already started to erupt. Creative lava spewed all over the living room, but the women drinking tea didn't know it. I hoped that my father didn't know about it either.

My mother took me to a ballet studio when I was about six. As soon as I started to do the exercises, an alarm sounded in my head. "This isn't it! Ballet isn't for me." I made that decision right then and there at the barre.

Rebel with a Cause

I first skated on an outdoor rink with high snowbanks. While I glided around with my sister in a pair of hockey skates – my first and only – a girl named Barbara Jackson, on holiday from Ice Capades, appeared at the rink and told me that the little tricks and turns that I felt I had invented were called figure skating.[*]

In the same year as my only ballet class, I went to see my sister in the Kirkland Lake ice skating carnival. The second that the carnival began, I heard a magical click in my mind. I thought,

---

[*] Toller has an older sister, Phillippa, and younger twin brothers, Guy and Goldie.

"It's not dancing, it's *figure skating* that I'm supposed to be doing."

I asked my mother for figure skates, which were almost impossible to find for a male child. We sent away to a shop called Toronto Radio and Sports for my first pair of girl's white skates, which, of course, my father painted black.

There were five beginning groups in the figure skating school, followed by intermediate and senior. Within weeks I was in group four, then group five. My crowning glory was a two-minute solo in the carnival that year. There was a poetic twist. The music that was chosen for me was Khachaturian's *Sabre Dance*, the very same music with which I later won my first Worlds short program.

My mother always made me little woollen yarmulkes with pompons on top. That was my costume for many years. In Grade 1, I did a crayon drawing on manila paper of myself in a perfect split jump under spotlights with one of those yarmulkes on my head and a big S on the front of my costume traced in pink, red, yellow, and green. I told my mother that the S stood for skating.

The same year, I had after-school ski classes. The teacher told my mother, "This kid has got it. This kid is going to the top." I was an athletic, artistic child, a fact that numbers of people could see, but my parents didn't encourage me to develop very far along those lines.

My first skating teacher informed them that I was the kind of pupil one dreams about. She wanted to take me to a small town in Ontario for summer skating school. My mother refused. If that happened once, it happened twenty times in my life. I knew that I had to go. I begged. But my mother prevented me from achieving my destiny that summer.

In art, I had a different problem. I had a need, an obsession, a conviction about being different from everyone else, and I was punished for it – right up to university. If I were a teacher today, the first thing I'd look for is originality in anybody's work. Anything generic, regardless of how brilliantly it was done, would not interest me. In Grades 1, 8, 11, and even at the École des Beaux-Arts in Montreal, there were incidents in which I was condemned for being different. Why was I bucking the establishment? Why was I trying to make trouble?

The natural course of my skating career, of my painting career, of my life, has always been to run against the current. If others are going downstream, I'm going upstream, leaping over waterfalls and cataracts. That is the nature of the beast within me. If people think that I do it for effect, the truth, on the contrary, is that I'm following – and always have – my natural inclination.

In Grade 2, just after my family moved to Galt (now Cambridge, Ontario), we had an exercise in abstract design. Every child in the class drew intersecting black lines, then coloured the spaces in red, yellow, green, and other "normal" colours. My drawing was a paisley design in black, blue, turquoise, and purple. It stood out like a sore thumb, and I was not acclaimed.

Today perhaps it's funnier, because now I understand myself, and I understand the reasons. Then I couldn't understand why people didn't see who I was. Why didn't they recognize that I was different/better than the others? If I ever managed to snag someone who appreciated me, I entwined myself around her and held on as long as I could. Such people were my security, my confidence-builders. The support never came from my immediate family, friends of the family, or peers. It came from strangers.

Once, I competed against Neil Carpenter, the son of the president of the local skating club. Neil, whose parents knew much more about skating than mine, had an orchestrated program: one-two-three-split jump and one-two-three-spin. I simply stepped onto the ice and interpreted my music. The audience liked me better than Neil, but he won. That scenario occurred dozens of times in my skating career. I would flip on to automatic and rely on spontaneity; and I would score with the audience but strike out with the judges.

If I compared my first interclub competition to my last amateur competition in Göteborg, Sweden, there were many similarities. Göteborg was a magnification of the earlier competition, with identical results and strangely identical frustration, pain, and loneliness. Why didn't they understand me? Why didn't they like me? With each competition, the idiosyncrasies of my style became more pronounced, and each time they interested and irritated more people.

When I was eleven, we moved to Baie d'Urfé in the suburbs of Montreal. I skated in Lachine. Eva Vasak, who had students going to the Canadian championships, told my parents the first day she saw me that she didn't want them to pay for lessons. That was both good and bad. The positive aspect was that she saw my talent and took an interest in me. The negative was that, since she was a volunteer, I was never able to say, "Where's my lesson?" I received moments of free time.

Eva taught me many truths of life. One that I didn't learn very well was, "You can never be too popular, and you can never have too many friends." I understood but fell short.

Leaving the Nest

I was conditioned to believe that school and painting were important. Although, by the time I graduated from MacDonald High School, skating was winning the tug-of-war over art by a small margin, continuing my education was imperative, and my parents encouraged it. In 1965, there were perhaps one thousand first-year applicants for the École des Beaux-Arts, which accepted only fifty.

As part of the evaluation of applicants, the examiners set up a huge table of dozens and dozens of objects: bottles of dried flowers and utensils and ashtrays. In half an hour, each of us had to choose a number of them and compose a still life in crayon. We were being judged on our artistic conceptual powers. If we used crayons, we couldn't rub anything out. I was one of the fifty chosen from among the thousand. My technical abilities were inferior to those of many, some of whom could draw like Rembrandt. I thought, "I'll never make it." But I did.

By 1968, an Olympic year, my skating career had bottomed out. I was a has-been at eighteen. I had never been fully trained. I didn't know about conditioning. No pro in Montreal at the time knew that practising one's entire program was prerequisite to performing it well at competitions. You just went through it on the night and hoped for the best.

Beside the École des Beaux-Arts was a twenty-storey apartment building, the Colisée. Every day during my lunch hour, I ran up all nineteen flights of fire stairs. The first time, I fainted at the top. I conditioned myself, because I really believed that I could make the Olympic team. That was naïve. Anyone from Quebec was strychnine to the Toronto-based Canadian skating establishment.

At the national championship in Vancouver, I was the last to skate the free program. I had placed fourth in figures. The way the scoring was then, it was next to impossible for me actually to finish among the top three. Nonetheless, because of my conditioning and my desire – I could have died happy if I had made that Olympic team – I skated a flawless performance and had so much energy left that I ended with six split jumps. What happened next was the beginning of the end; the beginning of everything. The judges' marks came up. Mine ranged from first place to last. My first-place mark was 5.9, higher than the scores of Jay Humphry, the eventual champion. My last-place mark was 4.2. Although he denies it to this day, my memory is pristine: it was David Dore who gave me the 4.2.[*]

Tears rolled noiselessly down my face. It was the disparity of marks that confused me and induced the tears. Some judges liked me and some didn't. I couldn't understand it then, and I can't understand it now. What was I doing wrong? A national and subsequently international controversy that was to rage around me for the rest of my career started there in Vancouver.

Ellen Burka, who was to play a huge part in my life, appeared

---

[*] Dore today is director general of the Canadian Figure Skating Association (CFSA). Toller characterizes their long, stormy relationship as "the Dore wars." The CFSA has not preserved the records of individual judges' marks from that era.

from nowhere, ignoring her own student on the podium. She led me under the stairs and encouraged me to continue skating. Still, I went into shock. When I got home to Baie d'Urfé, I went to bed for a week. My mother didn't believe me when I said, "Mother, really, I was great." But many letters arrived, confirming my version of what had happened. I read in the *Vancouver Sun*, "The hit of the competition was fourth-placer Toller Cranston whose free skating the world has yet to see." That was a little nugget of hope I clung to.

After studying at the École des Beaux-Arts for almost three years, I failed sculpture. I told the teacher, Joan Essar, "Look, I'm not really a sculptor. It's not my thing. As a matter of fact, I'm having a painting exhibition in Toronto." She convened three other art teachers, two of whom were famous in their own right. My mother brought some paintings that had been newly framed. The teachers were impressed. They asked me, "What do you want to be, an art teacher or an artist?" I answered, "I want to be an artist." They told me, in essence, "Don't bother finishing school." I left a week before graduation and never went back.

In the summer of 1969, I left Montreal. I went to Lake Placid, New York, where I trained, lived alone in a garage, and worked as a groundskeeper at the Mirror Lake Inn. My payment included free board. As a result, I gained more than twenty pounds.

Lake Placid in the winter is a bit bleak, so one day I phoned Ellen Burka in Toronto and asked if she would coach me. Ellen was the one teacher in the world who was right for me. She said that she would have to ask the permission of Jay Humphry, the Canadian champion. Since I was so overweight and out of shape, Jay saw no reason to object. I arrived in Toronto with a pair of skates, a bag of paints and brushes, and fifty dollars in my pocket.

I was thrown out of two boarding houses for spilling ink: once in the sink and once on the floor. I told Ellen that I didn't really like Toronto. I was returning to Montreal. She said, "Let me see your work." Unbeknownst to me, Ellen had been married to an artist. After

I showed her my work in the lobby of the Toronto Cricket Skating and Curling Club, she told me two things: "I won't charge you for lessons. You can pay me in art" and "You can live in my house for one week until you find another boarding house." The one week became more than a decade. In some strange way, we needed each other. I don't think that she would deny that over the long period when she trained me, I was her most interesting and disciplined pupil.

One of the first things she told me was depressing (but, as it turned out, it was true): "You're so fat and out of shape that it will take me three years to get you into condition." That was a fair assessment. The first year, I went to the 1970 world championship in Ljubljana, Yugoslavia, and finished eleventh.

The Unorthodox Champion

In 1971, my second year with Ellen Burka, I won my first Canadian title. I was so thrilled to have won (when I saw all the 5.9s, I knew that I had) that I ran onto the ice and did an encore in the middle of the competition – twenty split jumps. That was highly unorthodox. I felt the hands of the commentator, Otto Jelinek, grab my back, but they slipped off my costume as I ran out to do my split jumps.

My skating career was full of terribly unlucky things; cruel, mean, and awful things; and extraordinary things. I was second in the 1971 North American championship. A month later, at Worlds in Lyon, France, I placed fifteenth in figures, near the bottom of the barrel, below all the people I had beaten weeks earlier. I told Ellen, "I just won't be able to skate the long program. I'm too ashamed." Nevertheless, when the music started, my mind said no but my legs said yes. I skated a dazzling long program and got high marks right off the top, the third skater out. I took sixth place in the free skating but should have won it.[*] Ellen and I thought we'd forget about skating, go to Morocco, and smoke hashish, but reason prevailed.

The post-Worlds tour traditionally featured the first five skaters in all disciplines. In 1971, for the men's complement, numbers one, two, three, four, five, and eleven were invited. Eleven was me. I was worried about skating first. The skater with the least impressive credentials performs first. But the longer I skated, the later I went in the running order. Eventually I was skating in the middle of the second half.

After I finished the tour, the Russian contingent asked me if I would skate with their team in eleven Siberian cities. In those days, the Soviet Union was the land of the evil wizard. I was afraid that if I went there, I'd never return. I didn't know any of the Russians, and none of them spoke English. It was all too scary. I said no. There are several great regrets in my life. That was the first.

---

[*] Toller's long program ordinals, numbers reflecting the order in which each judge placed him, ranged from eighth to twelfth. Among the skaters who finished below him was John Curry, with thirteenth-place ordinals for both phases of the event. (The short program had not yet been introduced.) Ondrej Nepela was the gold medallist.

Every Canadian and world championship I skated from then on was dramatic and controversial. With each moment, I thought I was breathing my last. I lived a desperate, passionate, historical existence. I felt more, suffered more, and tried harder than anyone. I was under a microscope. I lived by extremes. At the same time, I cultivated a persona that exemplified strength and confidence, but it was false.

I wasn't always a victim. Often I invited controversy. I was uninhibited in a day when lack of inhibition was virtually unknown: uninhibited in interpretation, original moves, and body language – which I felt was inherently neither male nor female. In the days when men dressed up as maître d's, skated their long programs in shirts, ties, and tiny matador jackets, and were not allowed to raise their hands above their shoulders, I was a renegade. I invented beads on men's costumes. I invented décolleté. Everything I did was new, different, and shocking to the Old Guard, and I was punished for it.

I admit that I was guilty as charged. I was guilty of individuality when the establishment disparaged it. I was guilty of clinging to a dream despite every obstacle. I was guilty of being a creative and experimental instrument. I was guilty of being multi-faceted, which went against me in both the skating and art worlds. I was guilty of being myself, and totally guilty of inventing myself.

Valentin Piseev, the head of the Soviet skating federation, told Ellen through an interpreter, "We recognize that Toller's the best, but when it comes to competition, you know what we have to do to him. You do understand that, don't you?"

The fact that I was ignorant of the corridors of influence and power was an advantage. If I had known what I was up against, I probably would have given up. Many times during my evolutionary crawl from fat little boy in a Lake Placid garage to Legend, I wanted to stop skating. My human voice said, "Quit!" But the spiritual voice that controlled me wouldn't allow it.

The Declining Canadian Champion

*I*t was a moment when the end was nigh, the beginning of the disaster that was to befall me at the 1976 Olympics in Innsbruck, Austria.

The Canadian Figure Skating Championships then were similar to, and no less than, what the American championships are today: virtually as important as Worlds. I had an arch-adversary, Ronnie Shaver, breathing down my neck. He was often described as the great athlete and technical skater of Canada, while I was the artist. I disagreed with that assessment, because I considered myself to be technically far more of a virtuoso, but the overriding feature of my participation in skating was its theatricality. Therefore, my technical side was often underappreciated.

The 1976 Canadian championship in London, Ontario, was to be my last. Lynn Nightingale told me that we were what was referred to by the then-reigning president of the Canadian Figure Skating Association (CFSA) as "the declining Canadian champions," a prime example of familiarity breeding contempt.[*] I believe that the CFSA (with which I have always had an estranged and somewhat vitriolic relationship) wanted me out. They wanted to give good old Ronnie Shaver a chance at the title that had eluded him for five years.

Ellen Burka and I set out for the championship in her ochre Plymouth Barracuda in a blinding snowstorm. London is in the middle of the Canadian snow belt. Whereas it might be snowing in a minimal way in Toronto, it could be beyond the Antarctic in London. At a certain point in that drive, the visibility dropped to nil, which thrilled me. Although Ellen didn't know it, I was desperately hoping for a major accident. I wanted to end up in the ditch.

Every time Ellen let out a yelp because we had almost hit a truck, I let out a corresponding yelp – but mine was one of pleasure. I hoped that I wouldn't have to compete. If only we could have come up with a wonderful excuse ("Oh dear, they had an accident!"), all would have been well. But 'twas not to happen. Somehow, we got to London.

That city could only be described as the seat of the Ronnie Shaver camp. Strangely enough, although the Shaver groupies weren't aware of it, I also came from that neck of the woods. I had been a beginning skater in Galt at exactly the same time as Ronnie.

There is an historical photograph of us dressed as polar bears with our claws reaching out towards one another as though trying to scratch each other's eyes out. I was eight and he was six. If we had gone eighteen years into the future, we still could have been dressed as polar bears, and we still would have wanted to scratch each other's eyes out – although I have never had a real enemy among my fellow skaters (which was to be my undoing and my curse). I have

---

[*] Nightingale was the Canadian ladies' champion from 1974 through 1977.

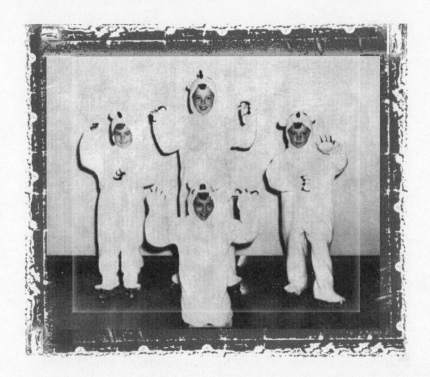

always liked everybody. All around us, one was either a Cranston fan or a Shaver fan, but Ronnie and I liked, supported, and appreciated each other. Never was there a mean word between us.

When Ellen and I arrived in London, there was already a certain pall over me. Like John McEnroe, whose strength was always to fight against the establishment, I had a lot to fight against. Ellen and I both sensed that the day of execution had dawned, and a new king would reign after the competition.

Unlike Todd Eldredge, who lost the 1996 U.S. national championship, then rallied and won the Worlds, in those days, if you lost the Canadian or American title, you might as well join the chorus of Holiday on Ice, because you were ruined. Your hopes of winning a medal or a world title had just been nipped in the bud. No one took you seriously. (I'm not absolutely certain that was true, but it was the truth we knew at the time.)

I was yesterday's news. I had been the Canadian champion for five consecutive years. There was a whole camp of Ronnie Shaver supporters, and they felt that it was his turn to win for a change. So it was one more Canadian title defence, one more hurdle to get over, one more trial by fire. Deep down inside, I had a crack in my confidence. I wasn't sure that I could do it just one more time.

Ellen had instilled a great inferiority complex in me.[*] We believed that everyone in the hierarchy was against us, no one wanted me to win, and we had to prove that we were the best. That was the hymn that was sung at every competition. It fuelled me with a certain energy, yet it also alienated me from people who could have helped. I was never popular with the CFSA. To this very day, the association and I are engaged in a cold war.

I was unusual on the ice, but Ellen was unusual, too. She had European breeding and was fluent in a number of languages. The two of us were, in the skating environment, as inseparable as Tweedledum and Tweedledee. Together we were a formidable pair, which intimidated and terrified most people. (At least, that's what I hoped.) We were very cool, very into our own thing. Ellen and I were joined at the hip – truly the skating world's oddest couple.

The thing that kept us in harmony as two people living together was the fact that we never discussed skating from the second we left the rink. We were more interested in Hieronymus Bosch or the early works of Edgar Allan Poe. It was two different worlds, two different personas.

Brian Orser and I hold the record for winning titles consecutively, something that many contemporary skaters cannot imagine.[†] I won six times. He won eight times. Winning consecutive titles,

---

[*] Ellen disagrees.

[†] Montgomery Wilson won nine titles: seven in a row, beginning in 1929; then two more in succession after Osborne Colson's two-year reign.

especially in Canada and the United States, is very difficult. People such as Robin Cousins, although uncontested as great skaters, won consecutively without running the gauntlet in their own countries; without number two and number three breathing down their necks. I sometimes wonder if my most dramatic and virtuoso performances didn't happen at home rather than abroad. Perhaps I could blame the fact that I was Canadian, skating in a country that always produced top skaters, for the fact that I blew my load at Canadians and then had little left to dish out at Worlds.

A Slap in the Face

I won the school figures. Ronnie was second. It would all come down to the free skating.

I won the short program every single time I skated it. The record is nine out of nine (in Canadians, Worlds, and Olympics).* Again, I had to shoulder the reputation of being the *artiste* when, in fact, I won the bloody short program nine times out of nine, and isn't that a measure of technical skating?

So the night came. I walked into the arena, and everything was right. I felt good. The atmosphere was warm – no, hot. The ice was that wonderful ice that only figure skaters can appreciate. A bit sweaty, a bit on the soft side. Glistening. Inviting. Exactly my cup of tea.

I had arrived rather early. The evening went on and on and on, and by the time the men took the ice (the very earliest of the men), it was eleven o'clock. It must have been close to midnight before I skated. By then, the atmosphere had chilled considerably. The ice

---

* In point of fact, Toller won the short program, introduced for the 1972-73 season, at four Canadian championships, three world championships, and the 1976 Olympics, for a total of eight times out of nine. He was third at the 1975 Worlds.

had turned to a glacial frost, the kind that I hate more than any-thing. If there had been a glow, a warmth, in the arena, it had faded, and we seemed to be skating in a deep freezer. The audience was frozen, too. It was exactly the kind of scene that would have been perfect for an execution.

Unlike any other skaters I have known in the last thirty years, instead of arriving with *the* costume that I had chosen to wear for the competition, I always brought an armful of costumes, usually jewel-studded variations on the theme of black. For some reason, on this occasion I chose an electric-pumpkin beaded shirt and black pants, very shades of Halloween. Orange and black, by any stan-dard, is an unusual colour combination for any skater in any com-petition. I'm not sure that I've seen it since.

The warm-up started. I stepped onto the frosty, uninviting ice and entered what can only be described as a conscious som-nambulistic state. My body simply wouldn't move. I was dazed. (People who smoke pot could relate to it as being stoned, but I was sort of naturally stoned.) All the other skaters whizzed around like water bugs.

Ronnie Shaver seemed to have sold out the building. There were virtually no Cranston fans that I could detect. Every time I skated by, the audience erupted in cries of "Yay, Ronnie! Yay, Ronnie!" like a huge swell in the ocean, countered by slightly softer but no less significant applause for one of Canada's great unknowns, Stan Bohonek. Stan, of Czechoslovakian extraction, skated at the Granite Club in Toronto.[*] Busloads of university students arrived to support him. He passed out pamphlets explaining why he was so great and why we weren't. Between "Yay, Ronnie!" and "Go, Stan!" I basically didn't exist.

---

[*] Bohonek was junior champion of Czechoslovakia before becoming a Canadian citizen.

The warm-up was so dreadful that I can't imagine ever feeling more solitary or abandoned by the powers that be. I was isolated, cold, and alone, skating on an evil pond of molasses. I had virtually forgotten how to skate. I think that I gave birth to a waltz jump, but that was about all I could muster. Every time I tried to jump, I was either cut off by one of the zippy competitors or I froze (the curse of any skater – to freeze on a jump). Better to crash and burn than to paralyse in mid-air.

As if marching consciously to my own doom, I immediately started to size up the scene of the crime. I thought, "This is the end of Toller Cranston. This is the environment where it will play out. These are the people who will be privy to it." I was a director in a play, understanding, in an historical context, the out-of-body experience that was to be my demise, my final chapter.

I had drawn to skate last. I stepped off the ice after the warm-up only to be greeted by a slap in the face from Ellen (who called me, if I may be precise, a "fucking fool").* What was I doing? How could I be so weak and pathetic? (I heartily agreed.) I remember whimpering in a tiny voice, "I don't know what the matter is. I can't skate. I've forgotten how."

Ronnie Shaver skated. I had gone, quivering and quaking, back to a tiny dressing room under the stairs – the hockey players' dressing room, judging by the smell – and I thought, in the way that somebody on the *Titanic* would have thought, knowing that the ship was going down, "What can I do to save myself?"

What I did was change into an all-black costume.

When I took the ice again, the audience didn't recognize me. Who was this new competitor in black? Toller Cranston was wearing electric pumpkin. Then the announcer did something so historical, so extraordinary, and so forbidden that, to this day, I feel as though

---

* Ellen recalls only the slap, not the verbal assault.

I have to mention him in my will. It was the final tipping of the scales in my favour. His name is Wilf Langevin. He still announces today. Every time I meet him, I remind him of that night and thank him profusely for what he did. When I came out to compete for the national title, he brazenly announced, "And the last skater of the evening will be – the one and only Toller Cranston."

You're not allowed to do that, of course. You can't say "the one and only" in a competition. At that moment, I slammed back into my skin and became my good old pompous, egocentric self. I stood ready to start the program, knowing that if I were going to crash and burn, I would do it spectacularly.

I tore around the ice with my skates barely touching the surface. I did jumps that should have been singles, but they were so huge that they turned into doubles and triples. I skated a desperate, flamboyant, and perfect program.

That experience taught me something. Even in the last second, even when everything around you spells disaster, the human spirit can triumph over almost anything. The only problem is that we don't know how to tap into it with any consistency. I could not have done what I did without spiritual help. Brian Boitano said in 1988 that while he skated the winning Olympic performance, he had a sense that the angels were helping him. My performance, of course, was not to be compared, but I also had help. As a human being, I was too weak to do it myself.

As I finished to a tremendous ovation – standing and screeching – suddenly life became quite sweet. There was an avalanche of 6.0s.

Ronnie was hanging over the boards. He had tasted the medal that he was going to win because a block of 5.9s is next to impossible to beat. He said to me, "I don't believe what you just did!" And I, sort of bowing off the ice, back to my old self, said, "Ronnie, sometimes I even surprise myself."

So I won the short program. The long program just followed suit. I had won yet again, in Ronnie Shaver territory, and he had come second again (a brilliant second, mind you). Ronnie went on the next year, for the one and only time, to win an unimpressive Canadian men's title. He didn't have me to push against. When he was out there on his own, he lacked his usual spark. He skated his greatest performances in losing to me.

Of Hircine Odours and Ronnie Shaver's Clothes

A funny thing happened that night after the Olympic team had been announced.[*] The trophy was a rather smallish, well-worn cup engraved with many famous old Canadian skating names. With my name going on the cup for the sixth time, there was no more room. That competition ended the cup, it ended an era, and, as it turned out, it ended my Canadian amateur career.

My sister was living in London at the time. Phillippa was always my greatest fan. She is extremely pit-bullish in certain ways, aggressive like me, tough, opinionated, and impervious to suggestion. To say that she was convinced of my abilities as a skater is to make light of the truth. She was intense about it all.

Phillippa, then a theatre arts professor at Western University, is the true eccentric of our family – far more so than I and second only to *Maman*. I come third in that competition. In those days, as an international goat judge, Phillippa always had a somewhat *hircine* odour about her (which is "evil-smelling, as in goat" – you can look it up). So did her boyfriend, Dan, with whom she lived. She was not only hircine in the smell department but fond of flea-bitten raccoon coats. She generally looked very Davy Crockettesque.

---

[*] Shaver and Bohonek went on to the Olympics with Toller. Shaver placed sixth in figures and third for the short program before withdrawing with a torn adductor tendon. Bohonek went 17-15-13, for a fourteenth placement overall.

That night, after my grand moment of glory, after I made the Olympic team, won my sixth title, and became the toast of the town, Phillippa and Dan offered to take me back to the hotel in a pickup truck that also smelled of goat. There was no room for the trophy, so we threw it in the open truck bed. They dropped me off and I went up to my room to review what had happened.

A few friends from Montreal who had come to see the performance joined me afterwards in my room. Marijuana was then very much in vogue. They pulled out a joint, and we had a good old puff.

There was a loud knock on the door. I jumped, being more than slightly paranoid.

"Who is it?" I asked, quivering.

"It's the police."

I paralysed. I thought, "Oh my God, after my big moment, now I'm going to be thrown into the slammer. *La presse! La publicité!* It's all over, and I won't be allowed to compete in the Olympics."

The smouldering marijuana was hastily flushed down the toilet, and puddles of Old Spice hit the bathroom floor. I opened the door. Indeed, it was the police – holding my trophy in its box. It had plopped off the truck, and someone had found it in the parking lot. I thanked the officers, took the trophy, and slammed the door. Then we pulled out several more lovely joints and resumed puffing.

There was one other tiny little thing that I rather enjoyed, although it fuelled the fires of my insecurity. I was about to put on my Olympic clothes, all those free clothes that you get, when I noticed that Ronnie Shaver's name was handwritten on the labels. I ended the episode by informing the Olympic officials that Ronnie Shaver's clothes were just too small for me.[*]

------

[*] Shaver was not aware of the mix-up. What he does remember about the Canadian Olympic clothing is that it was basically mass-produced in one size: large. All the items he received would have fit the average luger.

The Balloon Deflates

Whatever I was or whatever I wasn't, I was the last of a certain breed. Regardless of my behaviour, my temperament, or my personality, I adhered to discipline in a way that few have ever done. I did what I was told. I believed implicitly in Ellen Burka. When she pulled my cord, I jumped.

The day before I was to leave for the Olympics, for some reason, Ellen decided not to go to the rink. I was left on my own. Dutifully, in my most disciplined way, I executed yet another long program run-through. What happened then was a terrible thing that has happened to many other skaters. As it was happening, there was a certain thrill to it, a certain rush, a certain euphoria, and a certain horror – all at the same time. *I was skating the performance of my life.* I could do no wrong. In an era when three triples were quite a lot, I think I did seven.

There were two camps within the Toronto Cricket Skating and Curling Club. Ellen and I had waged many a battle with Sheldon Galbraith, the former teacher of Donald Jackson and Barbara Ann Scott. For years we didn't speak to each other. On that particular day, he came up to me and gave me a tremendous hug. He wished me luck and told me that I was truly great. It completely upset my equilibrium.

I was never quite the same after that. Somehow that remark had taken the wind out of my sails. It's easy to hate, to push against something. It's far more difficult if your enemy hugs you and tells you that you're great. It is extremely disarming and saps every ounce of your strength. Incidentally, it is a devastating technique when applied to one's most feared competitors.

I went home, only to face another strange occurrence. My mother, who had been silent for weeks – maybe years – phoned me and, in an agitated, slightly hysterical, aggressive, and frightening

way, told me that I'd better not screw up, that this was my big
chance, and that I'd better not blow it. Perhaps it was all said with
the best of intentions, yet at that moment it affected me negatively.
If the Galbraith thing had cut me in half, that cut me in quarters.

I went to Innsbruck. Being the self-invented renegade *artiste*
that I always was, instead of wearing the Olympic coat and uniform
(Ronnie Shaver's, to be precise), I arrived in a floor-length sheared
muskrat coat and took my accreditation.

My first practice was an indication of what was to come. The
hothouse plant in the fur coat had to go out onto a totally freezing,
windy, open-air rink in the centre of the speed skating track. I didn't
make the impression that I wanted to make. I was more concerned
with attempting to jump downwind. I couldn't weave my mystical
star magic, because there were too many distractions. Several skaters
ended up in snowbanks.

I instantly forgot, from one day to the next, how to do a triple
toe loop. There were several in my program, but launching them
was like writing with one of my feet. This was the era of a terrifying
new kind of ammunition that skaters such as Terry Kubicka and Jan
Hoffmann were armed with and others were starting to acquire –
triple Lutzes and triple flips. The underlings were doing those pet-
rifyingly difficult jumps, so the great dial of progress had turned
before the competition even dawned.

When the figures commenced, I felt quite calm. My figures
looked pretty good on the practice patch, and I thought, "God,
maybe I really *am* going to win, because look! My figures are better
than everyone else's." (I actually had, at that point, learned how to
do them.) I went out to do my first figure, a favourite of mine, a
rocker. I pushed off, and then I don't know what happened –
whether it was the result of nerves or something else – but my eyes
filled with tears, and I became blind. The tracing was so horren-
dously dreadful that the die had been cast from the very first figure.

I think that I got marks in the 2s, but the dear, sweet, wonderful Canadian judge held me in the 4s. Her name is Suzanne Francis. I attribute my bronze medal to her and her alone. My next figure was slightly less bad. The last was a smidge better – but the damage had been done. John Curry won all the figures.[*] I found myself in seventh place. The Olympic gold medal had just evaporated.

The short program took place in the Olympic stadium, in an environment that was not at all to my liking. There had been a hockey game before the men's event, and the hockey players, who demand hard ice, had won out. The ice was like granite, most unappetizing, encouraging mistakes and falls like no ice surface that I'd ever been on before. I wore black, the colour that I always wore for the short program. I skated with such veracity (or ferocity, or velocity) that I destroyed everyone, and I won (with a 6.0 from almost every judge). I then pulled from seventh to fourth, which put me in medal range – although I still felt like a failure.

The long program came around, and something terrible happened. Funny how the winds of destiny blow, and one cannot deflect them. Either because I was on the decline (having hit the heights during the last Cricket Club practice) or because of the figures, I no longer had any interest in the Olympics. I didn't want to be there. Every time I looked at the judges, they metamorphosed into grimacing Tolkienesque characters. I did not wish to be judged by them. I did not wish to have my destiny determined by such silly and superficial people.

Incidentally, many of those silly people are still around, because the judging world is an eternal Jurassic Park. There are always the same dinosaurs out there. They're immune to the aging process. As

---

[*] Curry was the top point scorer, but he was first on the cards of only four judges. Without the requisite five, he was overtaken for first place by Sergei Volkov with a majority of seconds or higher.

old as they appeared to be in 1976, they're identical (in my mind) twenty years later. They simply refuse to die.

I'm uncertain why I did it, but I chose to skate my long program in sky blue. Now that I know so much more about the importance of colour, I realize that that was a fatal mistake. The costume was quite elaborate, with heavily embroidered net leaves and beaded flower designs on the front. I was an exotic tropical bird that had flown too far north. That approach was countered by John Curry's. He wore an extremely conservative, meat and potatoes, understated black jumpsuit with a beige shirt and a little leather belt. Even while I waited to skate, I felt that I had lost. I sensed that I was a bit over the top – and probably was.

My costume had been stupendously well fitting, but with all the free meals that one has at the Olympics, I was starting to gain weight, so it didn't really fit me. I had to perform with my stomach sucked in.

I didn't see John Curry's performance until years afterwards. I knew that he had skated well, but, in truth, he skated brilliantly. I didn't really have to skate, because it was clear that he had won. The passageway to the ice surface was filled with members of the British contingent wearing British team uniforms and waving British flags. They were squealing and wailing, "He's won! He's won!" even as the announcer was calling my name.

I couldn't get past those people. I remember saying – it actually became quite funny – "Excuse me. Hello. I still have to skate. Hello. Could you let me get on the ice, please?"

The announcer was saying, "Toller Cranston, report. You have only two minutes to report."

I saw the absurdity, the surreal twist. I thought, "Oh my God! Here I am, standing in my sky-blue costume, ready to skate, and I'm going to be disqualified because I can't walk the last five feet to the ice." That idea registered loud and clear. Indeed, it lightened my mood. I think I even chuckled.

Nasty Political Realities

God knows I tried my best, but I was on the down, and John Curry was on the up. I did come second in the free skating. I know that I shouldn't have *won* – but I came third overall.[*]

I was always trying to make cheap deals with God. I would have been deliriously happy with second. Second is such a nice position. You did well, but you just missed. There's a certain comfort in it. I came third – to the disappointment of the East Germans, who really had counted on a medal from Jan Hoffmann. Frau Jutta Müller, Jan's coach, never quite forgave me.

However, I had been given no political help whatsoever, while John Curry had been helped in every conceivable way. Carlo Fassi, John's coach, was flying about as high as he ever had. He was in fine form in the political arena at a time when that counted a lot. There is absolutely no doubt in my mind that he pulled strings. At the time – and I do go on record – the attractive, leopard-skin-swathed International Skating Union (ISU) referee Sonia Bianchetti was also flying high and seemed to me to be sympathetic to Fassi, a fellow Italian.

Vladimir Kovalev, one of skating's lesser-known characters, came third in the free skating and won the silver medal. He was little more than an engineered political buffer zone between John and me. Like the battle of the Brians, it should have been the battle of the Cs, Curry and Cranston. I got a nice little tap on the wrist and came third instead of second. So there I was.

I was totally disenchanted with the whole thing and really rather hated skating. Many Olympians (Debi Thomas, for one) feel

---

[*] The Canadian judge placed Toller first overall, as the Soviet judge did Vladimir Kovalev, but neither had a majority of second placements. Each had five thirds or better. The decision for second place was then based on the tie-breaker, the lowest sum of total placements. Thus, under the arcane system by which results were then determined, Kovalev's 28 beat Toller's 30.

the same way. What should be your greatest moment becomes a
tragedy, a complete letdown. Everything goes wrong. Some people
rally and rise to the occasion. Others do the opposite. I did the
opposite – but not for lack of trying. It was not my destiny to be the
1976 Olympic champion.

The next thing I remember, I was standing on the podium. They
turn the lights down, and you see all those players who have
somehow influenced your life and your career standing around you:
the Sonia Bianchettis and the Donald Gilchrists (a perennial ISU
assistant referee, who, although a Canadian, seemed to me to be
very much in the Fassi camp and philosophically allied with
Bianchetti. I sensed that he favoured Curry at my expense).

Although John Curry was little more than six inches higher than
I on the podium, he was on Mount Everest, and I was in the gutters
of Calcutta. He had won; I had lost. He had graduated; I had failed.
I knew that I would have to spend the rest of my life trying to prove
that I was a great skater and that it had all been a terrible mistake.
If there was a press conference after that, if there was *anything* after
that, I do not recall.

I only remember that frozen moment on the podium (a moment
that, by certain standards, represented some sort of accomplish-
ment). It was, and remains, nothing less than having my nose
rubbed in my personal failure. I had not seized the moment. I tried,
but part of me was afraid of winning.

That kind of failure is the one thing (unlike, I suspect, disastrous love affairs) that time does not cure. If anything, it becomes
more monumental as time goes on. I can never change the colour
of my unhappy bronze medal.

The Birth of the Peacock

The evening after the Olympics ended, there was a big shindig for
all the competitors. In those days (and even today), you traded your

uniform with foreign athletes. I had been vaguely lusting after the gold lamé ski suit worn by the Austrian team. I arrived at the party in a black velvet fedora, several black scarves that entwined my neck, and my newly acquired golden ski suit. As I wandered around the party, I could have been Jesus Christ wandering in the desert. Never have I felt so alone, so much a failure, so heavy of heart.

At that moment, I began an odyssey that spanned twenty years: twenty years of performing non-stop; twenty years of painting non-stop; twenty years of surviving constant flux. I saw the skating world and the players within it change. I saw gods crowned on Mount Olympus, only to disintegrate into the dust of anonymity.

Above and beyond skating, I saw the world in a way that few people have had the privilege of seeing it. I had moments of glory that far exceeded anything that I achieved as a competitor, and I had moments of abject failure. I spent twenty years looking for love (any kind of love) without finding it. The subset of that, ironically, is that at the end of twenty years, I'm not sure that I would have recognized it if I had found it. It might have been right under my nose, but I didn't have the sensibilities to discern it.

My last evening in Innsbruck saw the creation of a professional image that lasted almost until today. It was an illusion, a persona created for the benefit and amusement of others; a personal style designed purely for effect. Look at me. I'm somebody. I've *got* to be somebody, because look at how I'm dressed and how I act and how I skate.

It was not an entirely false image. It reflected a certain side of me that was to flabbergast, intimidate, and horrify many people over the next twenty years, but it had an effect that was memorable, and that, in the final analysis, was exactly what I craved.

I can think of that person without malice or embarrassment. I'm not that person any more, but I *was* that person, and isn't it funny? Maybe it's all part of the texture of one's life. At the time, I was ready to catch fire. The gold lamé ski suit and black fedora were the beginning of something that would be far more extreme in the future.

Now I have to undo all of that.

Curry Tells His Secret

If I had lost interest in competing and being judged, I hit an all-time low when the Canadian team trotted off to Göteborg, Sweden, for the 1976 world championship.

I had not laid eyes on John Curry since the Olympic medal ceremony. During his press conference, he had confirmed to the world that he was gay. He had not exactly proclaimed, "Now that I'm the Olympic champion, I wish to tell you . . ." Someone asked him the question, and in that incredible way that John had of locking antlers with any problem and doing it nobly, he simply said, in effect, "Yes, it's true."

I didn't see the British press, but I saw the European press (particularly *Bild-Zeitung*, the German answer to the *National Enquirer*). John's acknowledgement had caused a huge scandal. He had made the disclosure as an Olympic athlete, as a gold-medal winner. He wasn't the first, and he won't be the last, but he nailed it right between the eyes. He wasn't evasive. Then he retired from skating and went home.

I, too, had done something that I suspected I was going to be punished for in Göteborg (but at that point I didn't care any more). In my press conference, I had posed the questions, "Why? What is the Russian mystique? Why is everyone so afraid of Russians? If a Russian makes a mistake, why is that okay, but if someone else makes a mistake, it isn't?" My punishment lurked like a wild beast, ready to pounce in Sweden.

The Demise of the Warrior Queen

I limped to Göteborg, a wounded animal. I had to get up and do those disgusting school figures every morning in the freezing rain. What I should have done was take a short Caribbean vacation – but no, I had to be trained to the max.

My spirit was broken. My body was broken. Many times, I said, "Phone the alternate!" I was beginning to have an uneasy relationship with Ellen Burka (who was at her wits' end, equally frustrated). She took it out on me, and I took it out on her.

The highlight of the training period was a ravenous slot machine in the lobby of the Europa Hotel in Göteborg. I'd get up early just to throw a few more kroner into that machine. When I came back from my days of doing double three change double threes, loop change loops, and bracket change brackets, even more than I needed food, I needed to hit the slot machine one more time. Perhaps this was an omen: I never won a dime from it. [*]

The competition started. Lo and behold, John Curry, who had retired, made a comeback. I thought, "Wow! That's pretty gutsy. After you've admitted to the world press that you're gay, there could be a backlash."

He hadn't done figures for weeks, and I had been doing them relentlessly. Then, on the night before the figures competition, Ellen's back flipped out (from the stress of it all, I believe). While I was standing on the practice ice over my loop change loops, I glimpsed a great horizontal warrior queen being carried off on a stretcher, not to be seen at the rink again. I was abandoned. That was something that I had never imagined – competing in the Worlds without a teacher – yet my spirit was gone and good old Murphy's Law had set in, so what did it really matter?

---

[*] According to published reports, Toller's persistence in fact yielded roughly 200 kroner.

I was even less than the declining Canadian champion in the eyes of the CFSA, so I went out and, for the first time ever, experienced neither pressure nor nervousness in figures. If ever there were a chance for me to win, that was it. I did figures that were superior to both Jan Hoffmann's and John Curry's. Yet as my figures got better, my marks sank lower, and as their figures got worse, their marks climbed. John Curry did – to this day, I remember – a back left bracket change bracket that any neophyte could have done better. In a day when flats and changes were the sweet kiss of death, I don't think that he had a running edge in the whole thing. He was shaking with nerves. It was the most terrible school figure ever traced in the history of figure skating.

He barely made it to the centre, and I said to Donald Gilchrist, "Now, what are they going to give *that*?" (In other words: 1.1 or 1.2?) Instead of being a man about it – an official who was not on the panel – he said, "Oh, I don't really know. Let's see." He wouldn't acknowledge that the figure had been a disaster. When the marks came up, Curry was second behind Vladimir Kovalev. I came a shabby fifth.

The rationale seemed to be, "Out with the old and in with the new, but we might as well let the champion stick." I think that many people knew that Curry didn't deserve his placement, but he *was* the Olympic champion and, well, they gave it to him.

I walked back to the hotel with Nancy Streeter, John's New York sponsor. I just had to speak to *somebody*. I wanted someone to tell me that I was right, that the figure really had been awful, and it was too bad for me – but no one would do that.

Murphy's Law Ascendant

I didn't go to the short program draw, so the president of the CFSA, the man who had dubbed me "the declining champion," drew for me. Just my luck. He drew first to skate in the last group – a misfortune for almost any skater. Murphy's Law had prevailed again. It didn't matter any more what happened. I just had to get through it. Some skaters have walked out in the middle of a competition and regretted it for the rest of their lives.

Once again, I hauled out my basic black, jewelled costume for the short program. I planned to warm up aggressively, but immediately I felt like a bug in an entomologist's lab. I had one too many pins stuck in me, and my legs refused to wiggle. I couldn't move. I was numb.

So what I did – unprecedented in the world – was skate around the ice once, then sit on the boards and have a chat with some friendly Canadian strangers in the audience. Then I took the ice, skated a perfect program, and won.

"Okay," I thought. "This is my chance at last." John Curry fell on his ass in his combination. Vladimir Kovalev, running second, slid on his stomach.[*] (This is in the short program, where deductions are mandatory.) The long and the short is that yes, I did win the short program – but the Canadian judge awarded us *all* 5.8s and tied us like three little birds on a telephone wire. Later I confronted her. In a voice that could have split an iceberg, I said, "Here you had the chance, the one chance, to help me. You were justified in dropping them, and you gave us all 5.8s. Tell me, exactly why am I skating? Am I skating so that next year Canada can have three men at Worlds? I should just turn around and go home."

She replied, "Oh, dear. I'll make it up to you."

In a whisper that could have levelled an army, I said, "It's too late! It's too late! The damage has been done, so what the fuck!"

It was unprecedented to talk to an international judge that way in the middle of competition, but my situation was like that of Surya

---

[*] Both Curry and Kovalev made errors in compulsory elements, but there is no written corroboration that either of them fell.

Bonaly when she took off her medal on the podium in Chiba, Japan, in 1994. I felt a certain empathy for her. Whether I agreed with her opinion of her second placement or not is unimportant. When you have been broken by the system, when you can't even think straight any more, your action may be wrong diplomatically or in the context of skating etiquette, but it is what your human spirit tells you to do.

So I told her that. I was informed that afterwards she cried.

I left the building and went to apprise the slumbering warrior queen of my results.

There was darkness all around me. I didn't see a way out. I thought, like Christopher Columbus, that I might fall off the end of the world, which didn't seem an unappetizing prospect. I foresaw no career whatsoever – only a loss of face, a loss of persona, a fall from grace. That was what I was up against going into the long program.

In a twenty-six-year-old sort of way, I couldn't understand why the judges had held up the guys who had fallen and had given me only a smidge of a lead. So I had pulled up to fourth. Big deal.

The man who had proclaimed me the prince of decline drew my skating position for the long program – and drew first again. At least my bad luck was consistent. I wore black. When I skated around the ice, the same nausea and apathy hit me. All the judges sat there, waiting to judge me, waiting for a mistake. They looked to me like hungry vultures, nine in a row, ready to pick my bones clean.

Sonia Bianchetti Loses a Round

Once again I sat out the warm-up. I was second in the free skating, but in some perverse way, they put Jan Hoffmann over me. Poor thing, he hadn't won an Olympic medal, so it's okay. Why don't you just trade positions with Cranston? And that ridiculous Vladimir

Kovalev (who was a dear friend of mine but a "hammer-thrower" in skating vernacular) skated, in the artistic department, like a meat chopper. They pushed him over me.* And John Curry? Well, after all, he is the Olympic champion – but he did skate well in the long program, I must admit. So I came fourth again.

As the fourth placer, I skated an exhibition on Sunday and caused minor sensations and had four encores. I remember hearing that when I skated (I think it was *Pagliacci*), Ludmila Pakhomova, the Olympic and world ice dance champion, came running out of her dressing room, half naked, to watch me. That was a nice little compliment. I shared a great rapport with her. We understood each other.

I went to the banquet. In those days, you got presents. I think someone won a bicycle. I got a box of chocolates for coming fourth. Then something happened that I shall remember to the bitter end.

I was sitting at the table when Peter Krick, head of the German federation, Sonia Bianchetti, and I don't remember exactly who else came up to me and said, "We hear you're not going on the ISU tour."

"No, I'm not."

"But you have to. All the buildings in Europe have been sold out with your name. You're headlining the Olympiahalle."

In essence, I replied, "You people don't seem to understand. I have always given myself, body and soul, to skating. I have never refused an exhibition. [In those days, you skated – maybe for twenty dollars – and sold out buildings and did countless encores, because it was all in the name of Art.] Considering how I have given myself to skating, why was I never helped like the others? Why the Russians? What was wrong? Why not me?"

---

* Curry (2-3-1) won the free skating and the event. Kovalev, who fell during the long program, placed 1-5-4 (second overall). Hoffmann placed 3-2-3 (third overall). Toller placed 5-1-2 and finished fourth.

Out of Sonia Bianchetti's mouth, or from the mouths of all three at the same time, came, "Well, well, well. Don't worry about it. I'll tell you what. How would it be if you skated last in the tour?"

"Last? You mean after the Olympic and world champions? What are you trying to tell me? Fourth is a very replaceable spot. You're saying that I should skate last, after the Olympic champions, yet, in the record book, I'm only fourth? Well, I will tell *you* what. I have always tried so hard [I was crying, too], and I've given everything I could, but now I'm thinking about *me* for a change, and *my* career, and *my* future, and no, I'm not going on your tour!"

The Norbert Schramm Connection

I feel a great camaraderie with the West German champion Norbert Schramm. He was ranked second in the world when he changed coaches, to Carlo Fassi, early in 1984. Rudi Cerne, second to Norbert in Germany, then switched to Norbert's former teacher, the *Bundestrainer* Erich Zeller. Rudi became the favourite son, and Norbert became *persona non grata*.

At the Olympics in Sarajevo, Yugoslavia, Norbert was suddenly ninth in figures, seventh in the short program, and eighth in the long, for ninth place overall. Rudi was third in figures and finished fourth.

A month later, when Norbert went to skate his last figure at the world championship in Ottawa (after marks in the 2s and 3s), he could not even push off. He stood there quivering and quaking, and he thought, "Why? Why am I, a man, shaking like a little leaf in front of these horrible people?" He couldn't do it, and he didn't. He just went over to Sonia Bianchetti, the ISU referee of the men's event, and said, "Thank you very much, but I can't."

She said, "Oh, come on. You can do it."

He didn't. Those people do not understand how the unfairness can break you – even if you're a big, strapping man who can do triple Lutzes. After he walked off the ice, Norbert went straight to a telephone booth (still wearing his skates) and phoned me. He reached out to me because he thought that I would understand, and I did.

His actions led to a gigantic fall from grace. He could have made millions in Germany if he had continued, but the Germans didn't approve of his withdrawal. He had to do what I did: fight back with years of hard-nosed skating in Holiday on Ice.

Skates Overboard

Many things that I have done in my life have been done for effect. The skate-throwing incident is a good example, although there was more to it than met the eye.

School figures had always been my Achilles' heel. Originally, I wasn't terribly proficient, but with help from Ellen Burka and with the kind of discipline to which I adhered, I did learn to do them respectably.

My figure boots and blades were like the Dead Sea scrolls. They were so precious that if anything happened to them, if the sharpening wasn't exactly right, I didn't feel that I could do my best work, which would prevent me from winning medals. When I realized, in Göteborg, that I no longer needed those horrid skates that had been so carefully coddled, I decided that their only fitting resting place was a Swedish sewer.

A good friend of mine, a German journalist and photographer, Sepp Schönmetzler, said, "When you throw them, let's photograph it for posterity."[*]

To be absolutely truthful, I practised throwing them several times before they went into the sewer – or, more exactly, a rather filthy canal.

There is a perfect shot of me with the skates flying over my head. They hit the surface, floated momentarily on the sludge, then

---

[*] Schönmetzler, a German men's champion, seventh in the world in 1963, edits *Eissport* magazine.

disappeared from view. It was very similar, I thought at the time, to the scene in the movie *Oliver Twist* in which Fagin loses his jewels in the muddy Thames.

The picture was sent all around the world and, I believe, misinterpreted. Many people thought I had thrown my skates into the canal because I was angry that I hadn't done well in the competition. That was not true. It was just that I was so tired of carrying those bloody things around and treating them with such deference that the only real way to rid myself of the emotional burden was to dump them. I did it with a great deal of humour.

The dénouement of the story is that no sooner had they hit the water than a skindiver went down into the poisonous filth, which turned out to be only three feet deep. The skates were retrieved and laid to rest in a Swedish sports museum.

Elva Oglanby Enters, Stage Left

My guest at the final banquet was Mrs. Elva Oglanby. She came over to Sweden for the exhibitions, and we flew back to North America together.

Elva had estranged me from Ellen Burka because, at the time, I was vulnerable. I wanted to hear good things, not bad. Elva whispered sweet words in my ear.

I arrived on my home soil as the Canadian tragedy. When I went through customs in Toronto, the officer said, "Gee, Cranston, you really blew it, didn't you?"

Elva had bought a fire-engine-red leather wrap-around coat in Göteborg. She no longer had it after passing through customs. I, with my broken ego, slipped into a waiting limousine, somewhat crushed. Elva slipped into the limousine beside me, somewhat crushed and somewhat chilly, because she had no coat in the subzero Canadian winter.

That was a forecast of what was to come.

· 2 ·

The Descent into Fantasy

*I*f you poison yourself, you vomit. The human mind has a similar ability. It can expunge pain, whether physical or emotional. In the longest stretches of memory, one tends to bury the bad things.

For me, writing about this episode means retrieving ancient memories that are perhaps best left undisturbed. Yet, if I'm truly going to confess the last twenty years of my life, this is singularly the most dramatic and important part of my theatrical experience. It is also the most painful and bitter. Unlike other tales that I've woven (that I've thought of over the years with a certain pleasure), for this one I have to reach deep. I'm not at all sure that I'm going to enjoy it.

I cannot remember precisely when it was that I first met Elva Oglanby. I suppose it would have been 1974. Nor do I know exactly who she was. In those lonely, desperate days when I was worried

about competing and winning titles, the thought of checking someone's past (the way one does now as a jaded professional) would
never have entered my head. I believed every word, and I took
everybody at face value.

There was a kind of documentary of which she was the orga-
nizer, director, or whatever. I might add that I was nothing less than
a folk hero in Canada. I was flying high, having just come off a
rather triumphant failure at the Worlds in Munich, West Germany,
where I had won the free skating and the bronze medal and had
devastated the world – or at least a few people – with a revolutionary approach to skating.[*]

Elva was a housewife from Vancouver, the mother of two sons.
She was of British extraction. At the time, she had an accountant-
type husband who wore horn-rimmed glasses. His name was Bill.
(They divorced not long afterwards.)

She came to Toronto when I was extremely vulnerable. I was in
the last years of my amateur career, when there actually was a
chance that I could become an Olympic gold medallist or world
champion. I was lonely and sensitive and rather tired of being told
what to do (and could I please go through my long program just one
more time?)

I wanted somebody to be nice to me. I wanted a certain kind
of affection. And, more than that, I wanted someone to tell me the
things that I wanted to hear. Elva obliged.

During the filming of whatever-it-was in Toronto, Ellen Burka
got bad vibrations from Elva. Ellen explained her feelings by asking
rhetorically, "What kind of person, on the very first meeting, kisses
you, declares you her long-lost best friend, and, as a thank you,
sends you three dozen long-stemmed red roses?"

Elva was charming, literate, immensely articulate, and wickedly
funny (countered by me being even more wickedly funny, or so I

---

[*] It was in Munich that Toller débuted his exhibition to Leoncavallo's *Pagliacci*.

thought). She appealed to one thing I'm not proud of: my snobbery. She fed me dreams of unimaginable love and hopes of becoming a movie star, a sex symbol, a god, something slightly beyond Michelangelo in the art department and just a smidge better than Shakespeare in the literary department – all music to my ears.

The relationship continued through long-distance phone calls, to Ellen's chagrin. Elva gradually became my quasi-manager. She arranged to have me skate exhibitions in Colorado Springs during the summer of 1974.

Colorado Springs at the time of the Broadmoor rink was one of the meccas of skating. Although I can't be sure, I suspect that Elva wanted to get me away from Ellen so that she could have me to herself. We talked. We laughed. I performed. I took lessons from a very nice man named Jack Raffloer. Elva did her best to get me to leave Ellen and continue that lovely life in Colorado Springs: living at the hotel, taking lessons from Jack Raffloer, and having everything paid for by the Broadmoor.

It was a seductive suggestion, yet old friendships run deep with me. I believed strongly in Ellen. I could not imagine ditching her at that important time in my amateur career, so I declined.

As I left the Broadmoor, I felt the stirrings of an unfamiliar restlessness. I remember flying home in first class, something novel to me at the time, and having a good old cry. I'm not exactly certain why. Perhaps it was because I had savoured something new and different, yet I was returning to the salt mines. The amateur world had become arduous and intense.

At that point, I committed a sin. Elva persuaded me to go against the CFSA's wishes for the first time. I did not attend the national seminar that was held a week after the exhibitions. Perhaps, in retrospect, that was not the right choice. It broadened the abyss between the association and me.

It seems to me now, more than twenty years after the fact, that Ellen had also committed a sin with respect to our teacher-pupil relationship: her emotions had become involved in my career. She reacted more aggressively to bad things, became more nervous in competition, and was more intense than she should have been.

Several events tugged away at me and pried me from Ellen. Elva arranged for a documentary film to be made during my preparations for the 1975 world championship. That sounded pretty good, except that it diverted my attention from training, a result that Ellen was not at all pleased with. Without going into all the sordid details of Worlds in Colorado Springs – although I did well in figures and I did win the free skating, I came fourth overall – shall we conclude that it was yet another disaster?[*] I did not do what I was supposed to have done.

Elva, the quasi-manager, good friend, confidante, and career-builder, persuaded me to write an autobiographical picture book.[†] I was convinced that the book was cool because it was about me the personality, me the artist, me the renegade, me the anything-but-skater. Ellen, however, was not at all pleased about the book. It was published shortly before the 1976 Canadian championship, concurrent with a televised benefit Ellen had arranged: The Real Thing on Ice, a standing-room-only exhibition in Maple Leaf Gardens.

I had major signing sessions with various booksellers, notably the Hudson's Bay Company in Toronto, where queues went on for miles. Hundreds and hundreds of books were sold. I had a painting exhibition to coincide with that signing. The world was looking rather rosy.

---

[*] Toller was fourth in figures, third in the short program, and second in the long, for fourth overall. Other placements were: Volkov, 1-6-4-1; Kovalev, 3-4-3-2; and Curry, 2-2-5-3. Yuri Ovchinnikov won the short program.

[†] *Toller* by Elva Oglanby, with illustrations by Toller Cranston and photographs by David Street, was published in 1975 by Gage Publishing Limited.

Then Elva told me that the CFSA had delivered an ultimatum: unless I signed over all rights to the book (which meant every cent), they would proclaim me professional on the spot. I would not be able to compete in the Canadian championships, nor would I be eligible for the Olympics. I was extremely upset and insisted that we succumb to the association's wishes.

Elva was not at all thrilled. She almost went to war with the CFSA. I have no idea how much money was sent to the association. The book was number one for many weeks and among the top ten in Canada for months. It retailed for $9.95. At a modest guess, about 75,000 copies were sold. You can figure out the arithmetic.

I received not a penny. What I did receive was a great deal of flak from the CFSA.

Christmas Dinner with the Happy Hooker

At the time, Xaviera Hollander, the famous Dutch madam who had written the book *The Happy Hooker*, was living in Toronto and fighting extradition by the Canadian government. Some of the wildest parties on earth, the kind you read about in the *National Enquirer*, were happening almost nightly. I attended a number of them. They were quite the most exciting events that I had ever witnessed. Curiously, they were non-sexual. The guests were interesting people who danced and smoked grass. In many ways, they were the groovy who's who of Toronto.

Ellen, a former Dutch skating champion, felt sorry for the poor little Dutch girl in a foreign country. Well, the poor little Dutch girl was pushing fifty, I think, although she claimed to be thirty-seven. Ellen invited Xaviera and her mother to a Christmas turkey dinner. That was all rather titillating for me. I began to compile a list of sordid questions that I wanted to ask our guest, particularly about the German shepherd that she claimed, in *The Happy Hooker*, to have seduced in South Africa.

It was not to be. Xaviera was more interested in Santa Claus and the candy at the bottom of her stocking than she was in furthering my sexual education. Sex never entered the dinner conversation. She left thrilled, and I went to bed bored and disappointed.

Xaviera made a surprise appearance at my book signing at the Hudson's Bay Company on Bloor Street. She was wrapped in a leopard-skin coat, and I knew exactly why she was there – to promote herself. I blanched when I saw her in the queue, because I suspected that she wasn't quite in the image that was appropriate to a future Olympic champion. Although I knew her well, I greeted her with a somewhat chilly hello, and there was no incident.

Shortly before Worlds, Xaviera, like a kind of camp mother, threw me a party in Ellen's house. The most exotic specimens in the land attended – interesting people that I normally would not have had access to. Many of the neighbours must have been glued to the windows. I'm not sure whether Xaviera's species had ever before hit the North York suburbs.

At exactly twelve midnight, when Ellen and I thought that maybe things were getting slightly out of hand, Xaviera sized up the situation and announced, "The party's over. Toller has to get some sleep." The party and the guests vanished within two seconds.

Cranston Defeats, Decimates, and Destroys Curry

That winter, John Curry and I were in flaming competition over who was getting what telegrams from which famous people. I began the race by informing him that I had received a telegram from Pierre Elliott Trudeau. He topped that by swearing that Elton John had sent him one. I rallied to my own defence by waving one from Johnny Mathis under his nose. He topped the Mathis telegram with one from George Harrison. In the final analysis, I think I won. When Bette Davis sent me a telegram, I felt that there really was no contest.

Ready to Dance

The Olympics came and went, Göteborg came and went, and let us pick up the tale after our arrival back in Canada. So many things happened during that period that it's hard to reconstruct them, but one event that I shall never forget was my twenty-seventh birthday party in Toronto.

If you're an athlete, an Olympic competitor, you don't really have to be told that, in order to succeed, you must be abstinent in every conceivable way. You must have tunnel vision. You must do what you are told to do. You must train. You must sleep. You must give everything, body and soul, to the sport. I did that with spiritual fervour.

But my amateur career was over, and I was ready to dance.

The morning of my twenty-seventh birthday dawned without incident. In the late afternoon, Elva phoned to suggest that we have a party. Within perhaps an hour and a half, many more phone calls were made.

Elva had rented what subsequently became a notorious house, following her tenure there, at 91 Hazelton Avenue. One day, the mistress of a well-known businessman flew mysteriously out a third-storey window, the very floor that had held my party, and landed, ever so dead, in the front garden. Nothing quite *that* dramatic occurred at my party.

Guests poured in. There was a dollop of the dance world with Karen Kain, a famous Canadian ballerina, and Ann Ditchburn, the National Ballet dancer and choreographer who had just made a movie in Hollywood, *Slow Dancing in the Big City*.

There were a number of groovy, trendy, artistic types (similar to the Xaviera Hollander clique), a handful of lawyers, a token group of street people, quite a number of spinsters from the Cricket Club, and good friends of mine who would have included: Louis de Niverville, a renowned Canadian artist; art dealer Ruby Bronstein;

and a dear friend, an aristocratic British lady, the "Countess" Caldwell. There were one or two unknown transvestites; a blonde prostitute I'll call E who, since that party, has become a devout skating fan and, from that very day, has never missed a world championship; Roberto Carboni, a hip Yorkvillian type who was the featured design artist at Fiorucci before it went bankrupt; and a smattering of skating notables whose names I don't remember.

The party started. The party started to boil. Mescaline was a drug, new for many, that was passed around liberally by a guest who had flown in from Montreal. (I might add that the guest who flew in from Montreal also invited his taxi driver to join the party.) Realizing that it was about to become the party of the decade, I started to make slightly intoxicated phone calls (I was flying high on mescaline) to friends in Ottawa, Cambridge, Hamilton, and London – and anyone else I thought might dig the scene.

There was virtually no furniture in Elva's house, which made it ideal for a dancing party. Donna Summer was riding high in those days, not to mention the real queen of dance music, Gloria Gaynor. Disco reigned supreme. More and more people poured in, and more and more foreign guests arrived. By then, it was past midnight. I'm not sure if the house actually rocked in its foundations. I suspect that it did. I can only liken that party to a race car zooming down the track completely out of control. By some fluke, it stayed on course – but just.

I suppose we all should have been arrested and thrown into the slammer. The people who attended that party, as well as the neighbours, still talk of it with nervous elation. At the absolute height of the frenzy, we all joined together in a huge circle, grasping and clutching at each other's waists, gyrating and moving in and out to the music. Half the circle was out of its gourd on mescaline.

The music was roaring. The party was bubbling – although, as far as I know, there wasn't much to drink, and certainly nothing more to eat than potato chips. It was a rather exhilarating celebration of an end to something – and whatever the end was, it was different for each person. Maybe it was merely the end of winter and the beginning of spring. Each guest, in his or her own way, exploded in a kind of catharsis, and by the next day, all of our lives had changed to one degree or another.

An enormous transvestite who frequented such parties seemed to repel a Bay Street lawyer. There was a minor incident, and the lawyer threatened to leave – but at the end of the evening, they were necking furiously in the corner.

The Countess Caldwell, I suspect, had had a good old snort of mescaline. (To this day, I don't think she knew what she was doing.) The next day, she phoned and thanked me profusely for the lovely party, and when would we be having another one?

The hour got later and the party got wilder. I remember a female skating teacher – this is truly telling tales out of school – having a violent smooching session with E, the prostitute. Finally, guests began to leave. At six o'clock in the morning, a few of us were left lying on our backs, vaguely gyrating to the music. I crept out of the house at dawn, took a taxi back to Ellen's, and spent the day licking my wounds and answering congratulatory phone calls.

Some weeks later, I ran into Ann Ditchburn. In her squeaky little voice, she meekly thanked me for the party but suggested that maybe she could only attend *that* kind of party once a decade.

In that one night, at that one party, all the pent-up anxiety over what I thought I had missed out on during my disciplined youth had peaked and climaxed. I felt ready to take on my professional obligations.

Miss Marple from Montreal

There was another party guest I haven't mentioned: an older woman, a dear supporter of mine, who had helped sponsor me over the years. She had been around the world twenty-seven times and had an international gift shop in Montreal.

The dear lady, a clone of Miss Marple from the Agatha Christie mysteries, became quite thrilled with that divine white powder called mescaline. In fact, she couldn't really get enough of it. When she returned to Montreal, she phoned me, thanked me for the party, and said that she had gone straight to the pharmacy and demanded mescaline for her head cold.

"Madame," the pharmacist had told her, "I am sorry, but that drug is highly illegal."

"But," she said, "when I snorted it last night, it did wonders for my sinuses."

Changing Tax Brackets

My final amateur performance was a televised exhibition that benefited the Bursary Fund. Perhaps in a somewhat non-purist, slightly corny way (as I was always to approach skating in the years to come), I chose to skate to rather maudlin lyrics sung by Tony Bennett. They suggested that maybe this time I'd be lucky; maybe this time I'd win.

Many people cried, but many others howled with laughter. I know that Johnny Esaw, the commentator for CTV, managed to boo-hoo on cue into the camera, so I guess that somebody bought my act.

I began to skate exhibitions in different parts of Canada – for money. One engagement included three shows at the Winnipeg arena. The year before, I had skated the shows free of charge and had received a lovely sweater. In 1976, I demanded and got $10,000 in cash.

Lawyers and accountants and people who really "knew what they were talking about" (God!) told me that I had to change my domicile and find a tax haven for the millions of dollars I was going to earn. I didn't question their wisdom, although, deep down inside, all I really wanted to do was stay in Canada and have a home of my own. I had never had one, because I had lived with Ellen for almost seven years.

It was decided that Bermuda would be just the place to shelter my millions. Elva and I flew off the next day – in first class. Kitty Carlisle of "To Tell the Truth" fame was in economy.

We arrived in Bermuda and went scouting for real estate to rent. I don't remember how it all happened, but we agreed that a gorgeous strawberry-pink mansion opposite the Elbow Beach Hotel would serve our needs to perfection. That particular property, known as the Frith Home, included a guest house with a swimming pool – but not one stick of furniture.

With the paltry amount of money that I had saved (I think it came to a total of $2,000), we furnished the twenty-five-room house. We went to a thrift shop in Hamilton, where I bought a dilapidated, psychedelic purple couch and a pair of violent tangerine-orange corduroy chairs. I bought a mattress, and Elva bought a mattress. These items and a few sheets and towels were the extent of our furnishings. Then I decided that I preferred to sleep on the cot in the guest house. I don't think that I ever spent a night in my lovely strawberry palace – only no one ever knew that. My new financial advisers assured me that I only needed to prove that I really lived there: then I would be able to keep the fortune that I was destined to make.

Since the Olympics, almost without exception, all my good friends had become (in my view) boring, uninteresting, and my enemies. I was on the way to making a whole pile of new friends who were infinitely more interesting, more international, and more my *tasse de thé*. It seems to me, as I sift through the ashes of what was to become a bigger disaster than the *Titanic*, that my good, dear friends in Toronto didn't like me – or like what I had become.

I made frequent trips to New York and spent less and less time with Ellen. A pattern emerged that was to repeat itself over and over again. Elva and I would fly to New York, always elaborately dressed and ensconced in first class. We would reside at grand hotels: the Regency on Park Avenue, perhaps. On a bad day, if we couldn't find rooms there, we succumbed to the St. Moritz on Fifty-ninth Street.

Many times, as we were checking out of our suite overlooking Central Park, I would ask Elva, "Have you straightened out the bill?"

"No problem," she would say. "They're sending it to me in the mail."

Then we would speed off in our limousine.

The Birth of The Ice Show

Through Elva, I was developing New York connections. I was going to be under contract and build my own show, produced by the Sol Hurok company. Sol Hurok was a world-famous impresario who had imported the Russian ballet, the Moiseev company, a Polish folk company, and many European musicians who devastated America. To be produced by his company was supposed to be a gigantic coup.

In some ways, it probably was. However, I found out when I got to New York that, although his company still existed, Sol Hurok had been dead for a number of years. The Hurok company now had two presidents: Maynard Goldman, a Boston lawyer, and Paul Del Rossi, an Adonis type who could have rivalled Rock Hudson in the tall, dark, and handsome department.

I have remained friendly to this day with Alex Dubé, a tall, extremely charming, slightly balding young man with a devastating smile and a great laugh. He left the Hurok company after its demise and opened his own dance agency along with Isabelle Zakin. They managed such stars as Cynthia Gregory and Gelsey Kirkland.

I had spewed for quite a long time about the vulgarity and cheapness of such shows as Ice Capades and Ice Follies, not to mention Holiday on Ice. The ice shows would exact their revenge on me a year or two later.

Now, a revolutionary new ice show was about to be launched. By design, it had no sets. It did have lovely costumes, diverse music, excellent lights, and a little black tunnel that served as entrance and exit. Toller Cranston's The Ice Show was to be the first of its kind, the way of the future. I was the first skater of that era to have my

own show. International Management Group's (IMG) multimillion-dollar success Stars on Ice, of which I was a charter member, is an exact clone of The Ice Show.

The cast was chosen for talent and crowd appeal alone. Gordie McKellen, a competitor of mine, an American champion, was first and foremost on the list, followed by Americans Colleen O'Connor and Jim Millns, 1976 Olympic bronze medallists in ice dance. Then came Canadian Bob Rubens, an attractive sex symbol when he skated, an old adversary and slightly bitter love/hate competitor of mine. Barbara Berezowski and David Porter were Canadian dance champions. Barbara was among the most attractive women in Canada.* David was right up there with the most miscast figure skaters of the century – infinitely more comfortable driving a tractor in a muddy field than encasing himself in a sequined suit to perform a fox trot.

---

* Berezowski won the Miss Toronto title in 1975. In 1976, she was crowned Miss Winter Olympics.

The greatest unknown pair in figure skating history also starred in my show: Canadian and many-time professional champions Don Fraser and Candy Jones. There were two female solo skaters: Kath Malmberg, a rather cool, statuesque blonde who was not a great skater; and feisty, peppery, passionate Elizabeth Freeman. With the American pair Emily Benenson and Jack Courtney, that was our cast.

Each skater was to be paid by the show, and Elva felt that they should be well compensated. Let's say that Colleen O'Connor and Jim Millns were to receive $600 apiece. If they skated ten shows a week, that was rather good money. I, on the other hand, was to receive $2,000 per show. There was a point when I realized that it had been a good week: I had just made (on paper, at least) nearly $25,000. For a non-Olympic champion in the late 1970s, that was not bad pay.

Strangely enough, although it was my show, I had almost no creative input. Nobody listened, or wanted to listen, to what I said. I was a figurehead only. That was peculiar considering that my fame did not rest upon medals but rather upon creative innovation. Conspicuous by her absence was Ellen Burka (but perhaps not so conspicuous, because Elva had not encouraged our continued association).

Elva knew a fellow, Ronald Clairmont, a New York voice teacher with capped teeth and the kind of body that taxi drivers get from sitting in the car too long – a slushy body. She appointed him musical director. He lived in a strange apartment on Fifty-fifth Street. It contained one large, twinkling Moroccan lamp and a quantity of rare Chinese porcelain – but not a single window. Ronald Clairmont eventually became Elva's husband (in name only, I believe), so Elva Oglanby became Elva Clairmont, a legal American resident.[*]

---

[*] Although her name would then logically have been Elva Oglanby Clairmont, Elva co-wrote the 1990 Elizabeth Manley book, *Thumbs Up!*, under the name Elva Clairmont Oglanby. She wrote the 1995 John Curry biography, *Black Ice* (enjoined from publication by Curry's family), as Elva Oglanby.

While we were building The Ice Show, in the late spring and summer of 1976, Elva and I resided in a two-bedroom apartment/hotel off Third Avenue in the upper forties. We started to meet a plenitude of unusual specimens. I was the bird that had flown from the cage. I was in New York. I was onto something. I was shedding my skin, and, in many ways, I had absolutely no idea what I was doing.

I continued to paint and draw (as I always did) in that large, spacious, somewhat seedy apartment, and I gave birth to my second book, *A Ram on the Rampage*. All the illustrations and text were done in that apartment – an antidote for my unsettled lifestyle.

The lawyer retained by Toller Cranston's The Ice Show was a jowly, red-faced, yellow-toothed, slightly balding expert in tax law. Elva and I fed each other's fantasies. The players in our lives acquired nicknames. We called the lawyer ChanChan.

There was another absolutely strange creature whom Elva appointed as my private secretary. His name was Bill, and he was decidedly down on his luck. I demanded, at a certain point well into the show, that he be fired because of the length of his long and hairy toes. One can see how far out of line I was getting. I had no idea how insensitive I had become.

The Predatory Wolf

The Baroness von Wolf wasn't a real baroness, but she was a Munich aristocrat – way over six feet tall, attractive in a Teutonic, rather severe sort of way, chic, international, cultured, insecure, and very hot for me.

I met the Baroness von Wolf not exactly by accident. She preordained our meeting. Having seen me on television, she flew from Munich to Worlds in Göteborg and somehow entrapped me in the voluminous folds of her Valentino cape. From that day on and for many years after, she pursued me all over the world.

I was naïve. I didn't have much experience with people. These groupies, these possessive women, these man-eaters, chased me all

over the place, as they do many of the top skaters today. I didn't
know how to say no. I didn't know how to get rid of them.

I evaded their attempts at contact and their phone calls and
their letters, but often they simply wore me down. I would end up
having dinner with them – which only added nitroglycerine to their
fire. There were times when I thought that I would go insane,
because what I said and what I wanted had no effect.

Many times the baroness chased me down the streets of New
York. I would be trying to leave the scene of the crime – an incident
in a restaurant or a fracas in some hotel lobby. As I flew down the
street, she went chasing after me, towering above me in flat shoes,
with her dramatic capes, shawls, and long trench coats trailing in
her wake. Several times police had to be summoned.

Part of me liked her. Part of me enjoyed our conversation. She
was cosmopolitan, she was an heiress, and she was determined to
have my baby, no matter what. The subject was discussed. My price
was $3 million U.S. Although we negotiated for three months, no
deal was struck.

The War Machine

I was a speedboat out of control, going faster than I had ever gone
in my life. Sometimes, like Dorian Gray, I'd look in the mirror and
hate the reflection I saw. I was the merest shadow of what I'd been
before: a sincere competitive skater who performed and painted. I
tried not to look at the reflection too often or too closely.

How wonderful, how amazing, that one can block out memories.

There was a time when we left the apartment in the upper
forties and Elva took me to a brownstone on the East Side, with steel
gates across the front door – a touch of Sing Sing. We walked in and,
with an imperious wave of a hand, said, "This will be just fine." We
paid something like $3,000 down. The large living room, bedroom,
bathroom, and kitchenette occupied an entire floor. The interior was
decked from one end to the other in swamp green and acid-pink

chintz. I never did stay in that apartment. Something makes me think that I might have gone back to Toronto.

This is where fantasy started to creep in, where truth and fiction became interchangeable. Lying about all things, exaggerating all things, was entirely normal for me. Together Elva and I were a team – a pair of stalking, carnivorous beasts. Elva fondly referred to our partnership as the War Machine. If we scored a hit, destroyed someone, pulled the rug out from under somebody's feet, it was just the good old War Machine doing its clever tricks.

Elva told me that she had been attacked and robbed at gunpoint at the Green and Pink and couldn't possibly stay there any more.

"Let's not make any attempt to get that $3,000 back. Let's just let it go. I could never stay in that dreadful place – not for a second."

"Of course, my dear, you couldn't," said I, posing as some twisted character from *Alice in Wonderland*. "How absolutely terrible. Let's move immediately."

After that we began to reside in splendid suites at the Drake Hotel on Park Avenue. There were a number of other people living at the Drake who subsequently became famous. Jane Seymour, the actress, for example, had just come from England, was a complete unknown in the States, and was trying to ply her wares to the New York and L.A. acting industry – without an agent, I might add, which was unprecedented. We talked about our ambitions. Robin Cousins had met her a number of times at the Richmond ice rink. She loved skating, had star quality, was stupendously beautiful, but hated her short legs.

I also became friendly with the manager of the Drake, a roly-poly, Santa Clausish, smart British man who was decidedly mad and decidedly wonderful. He was well known to everyone in the hotel business. Elva and I called him RahRah.

RahRah was extremely kind and helpful. It was through him that we were able to rub shoulders with people like Sir Laurence

Olivier and Emil Gilels, a famous Russian pianist whose daughter
had just débuted at Carnegie Hall.

At about that time, as I remember, I went across the street to an
Irish pub (Wilde's Pub, as in Oscar Wilde). There was a quote on the
blackboard. If you could fill in the remaining lines of the quote, you
got free beer and dinner on the house. For some strange reason, I
was able to complete the quote. It might have been the only Oscar
Wilde quote that I knew. At the time, it was prophetic.

"To get back to one's youth . . ."

I summoned the waiter and said, "'To get back to one's youth,
one has merely to repeat one's follies.'"

The way things were going, I was assured of getting back to my
youth.

Flying High

The cast was short one girl, so I flew off to L.A. to audition someone
named Roberta. Several people told me that she'd be just the thing.
Gordie McKellen reported that she had caused a minor sensation at
U.S. nationals.

She was an extremely young, defensive girl who skated at the
Paramount rink – but she hadn't skated for months, so all that I
could audition were hints of an outside edge and a spiral. I assured
her that she would be splendid. Then we went to meet her fiancé's
father, an aggressive, bulldog kind of guy who was there to negoti-
ate her contract – the contract of a girl who hadn't skated for
months. I tried to be encouraging.

The father of the fiancé took me to a private airport where he
serviced planes. Would I like to return to New York in Elton John's
private jet? I said that I would. When we got there, however, Elton
was not at all pleased – even though, of course, I was a great star. I
think that he had designs on certain members of his entourage, so
I was not at all welcome. I caught the drift.

The person who escorted me around L.A. was Robin Cranston, the son of U.S. Senator Alan Cranston. Robin had tracked me down in Toronto before the 1976 Olympics and claimed a remote family relationship with me. He was some sort of cousin. He was very supportive and wanted to be part of my blossoming career. He had big contacts in L.A. After all, he *was* the son of Senator Cranston.

Since I couldn't fly in Elton John's jet, Robin offered to take me to his house to await my regularly scheduled flight. That was fine with me. We could have a little drink, and then I would take the 6:00 P.M. from L.A. to New York. Well, that was not to be.

I really didn't know much about drugs. If I had a joint here and a snort of mescaline there, they were truly not part of my repertoire. Robin Cranston took me to a tiny cottage somewhere in L.A. I have never seen anything quite like what I saw when we entered the rather shabby living room. A veritable mountain of cocaine, probably as high as a pop bottle, lay on the coffee table. A pile *that big*. A cone of it. A pyramid. Would I like a snort?

"Why not?" said I.

Around midnight, in a stoned state the likes of which I don't think, to this day, I've known again, I felt a strange sensation come upon me. I lost all body control.

I could not move a finger. I could not move an eyelash. I could not move a toe. I was rooted to the spot. Robin Cranston had passed out some hours earlier. I was not at all sure that he wasn't dead.

I sat glued to my seat for the entire night. The only thing that I could think about was whether, when the police arrived, I would be able to raise my arms for the handcuffs.

At about 7:30 in the morning, I managed to wriggle out of my paralysis. Robin was still unconscious on the floor, and there was still a mountain of cocaine on the table.

I'm an instinctive survivor. When my brain cleared, I knew that I had to get out as fast as I could. I grabbed my little suitcase and ran out onto the street. I had no idea where I was or what I should do. I was stymied, disoriented, and baffled. I don't know where it came from in that residential neighbourhood at such an early hour, but a taxi materialized on the street like a camel in the desert. I ran in front of it and dove onto the hood. Very carefully, half in words and half in semaphore, I indicated to the driver that I needed to go to the L.A. airport.

I threw myself at American Airlines and, wouldn't you know it, a flight was leaving for New York in fifteen minutes. I don't remember the flight.

I got back to New York and took a taxi home, only to be greeted by my parents – but L.A. was three thousand miles away, and *that* part of my nightmare was over.

A Brush with Colgate

Somehow, some way, Toller Cranston's The Ice Show went into rehearsal at Colgate University in Hamilton, New York. Hamilton again. Hamilton, Ontario (where I was born). Hamilton, Bermuda. Now this. The Hamiltons in my life were piling up.

There had been no preproduction. It was, "Gee, why don't we go out and buy some cassettes and see if we like any music?" and "Gee, what do you think I should skate to?" and "Gee, I don't know. What do *you* think I should skate to?" That was about the extent of the artistic direction.

Brian Foley was a choreographer/tap dancer/modern jazz sort of guy from Toronto.* He was appointed artistic director of my show.

---

* At age eighteen, Foley was the youngest Fellow of the British Dance Teachers Association. He went on to own and operate the largest dance complex in Canada and to choreograph and direct in the areas of theatre, television, gymnastics, roller skating, casino entertainment, and ice. He directed Robin Cousins's theatrical ice show Electric Ice.

Had he been appointed artistic director of a Las Vegas show, that might have been more up his alley. Brian and I were certainly at loggerheads with regard to the artistic direction that the show should take. He was a tits-and-ass kind of guy. I was more inclined to emulate Rudolf Nureyev in *Swan Lake*. I'm not at all sure that Brian ever choreographed for me personally, but I suspect that he did not.

Meanwhile, my skating technique had hit an all-time low, and I didn't know what to do, because the person with whom I had worked for so many years, the person who had invented me (if I hadn't invented her), was Ellen Burka – and she had been banned by the powers that be from any artistic input in the show.

Finally, after a tremendous scene in which I threatened to quit and leave, Ellen was summoned to save the day. She brought five numbers, each one more perfect than the last, and, in probably one and a half days, she choreographed my numbers with me. All of a sudden, I was feeling a smidge better.

While the show was being put together, Elva and I decided that we would go to New York and pick up Dick Button in a private plane flown by the show's manager, Michael Crowley, so that Dick could come to see the incredible new show that was in production. It's a miracle that we are all still alive. Before we touched down at Colgate, the plane's nose suddenly pointed straight down. We thought a crash was imminent. My feet were on the windshield, if that tells you anything. By a fluke, Michael pulled out of the dive, and we landed. Dick had turned a bilious shade of green and continued to be green for the duration of his stay at Colgate.

It was at about that time that I met Miles White, a charming, artistic man who had designed costumes for many megastars including Marlene Dietrich in *Around the World in Eighty Days*. He had further distinguished himself by decorating P. T. Barnum's elephants in upscale pachyderm *haute couture*. Miles was given the contract to design our costumes.

We adored each other on sight. He was a refined, diplomatic, magnificently attired gentleman of an indeterminate age who had a wry sense of humour, a feel for style, and a keen intelligence. Anyone in New York knew the name Miles White.[*]

He conceived of costumes for The Ice Show that were elegant and original. Because he liked me as much as he did, my costumes were the top of the line. The peacock costume that was by far the best I ever had – a costume that simply refused to fall down and refused to make one look fat – lasted for almost fifteen years. To this day, it is still my favourite. There was never anything in the entire world to compare to it. Almost anyone on the planet who dared to put on that costume would have been laughed out of the arena and tarred and feathered, but it was made for me, and I was made for it.

Well, the costumes were happening, and despite the tremendous dramas that were occurring either in front of me or behind closed doors, somehow, some way, a sort-of-a-kind-of-a-show was put together, and somehow, some way, we were going to open in Buffalo, New York. That was just fine because, with one twenty-minute hop across Lake Ontario the next week, we would make our Canadian début at Maple Leaf Gardens.

The War of the Rhinestones

The show sort of happened. Perhaps it even got good reviews. I don't really remember any of it.

The only thing I do remember from the opening in Buffalo is that when I arrived encased in my Barbara Matera costume (the only one that hadn't been made by Michael-Jon Costumes, Inc. in Greenwich Village), Colleen O'Connor blanched and almost fainted.

---

[*] At the time, White had already won two Tonys and three Academy Awards. His résumé included *Oklahoma*, *Carousel*, Ice Capades, and Sonja Henie's *It Happened on Ice*.

She realized that it was quite possible that I had at least 3.5 million more rhinestones than she did, and it wasn't fair. From that day to the end of the first Canadian tour, at every single performance, Colleen's costume had just a few more rhinestones.

Playing the Provinces

During the Buffalo run, a friend of mine, Sid Adilman, wrote a splendid article about me for the *Toronto Star*. Its headline was CRANSTON SIGNS CONTRACT FOR $3 MILLION. When the article came out, I summoned a number of my friends (Ruby Bronstein, Louis de Niverville, and Ellen Burka, perhaps; Elva was also there), and we went to the swanky Courtyard Café in Toronto where the beautiful people met. We toasted and drank, but none of us – including me – really believed any of it. There was an artificial joviality to the luncheon. I knew, and they knew, that it was all bullshit (but we pretended that it wasn't).

There was a great deal of publicity attending the Toronto opening. There were whisperings of "Gee, I think it's sold out!" and "Gee, I think it's going to do well!" It was all so phony. Well, when the show opened, it was more than sold out. To this day, in the annals of Maple Leaf Gardens, they cite *that* night and *that* show as having the largest audience the Gardens ever held.* Regardless of what other ice shows may claim, my show was theatre in the round, and at my show they were hanging like bats from the ceiling. I have seen a lot of enthusiastic audiences over the years, but I doubt that many have eclipsed the roar of that audience when the show started.

My entrance was never an opening solo. It was just "Here I come in my peacock costume. Adore me." Then I did a huge back spiral around the ice. As my back leg went higher, my skating leg started to tremble with nervousness, which made the top of my free leg

---

* Staff at the Gardens did not respond to an inquiry.

bobble out of control – but at least half the audience would have thought that it was my latest innovation. A warbling spiral. How original!

The show was a major hit. It seems to me that I made absolutely no mistakes during that run in Toronto. There were many triple loops, triple toe loops, triple Salchows, dozens of double Axels, and a heavy helping of *Weltschmerz* – which was basically my entire repertoire to date.[*]

Business at the Olympic velodrome in Montreal was incalculably incredible. We were sold out every night. I became the sensation of the city. My local friends occasionally took me out to wild dance clubs. At the height of my success, I limousined my way to a discothèque wearing quite an extraordinary costume. To this day, if I saw it, I suspect that I would gasp, and even though I might think that it was absurd, I would admire anyone who had the nerve to wear it.

I wore a white satin blousey shirt in the Russian Cossack style: pleats on the sleeves and down the front, rows of pearl buttons, a Russian collar, and a hemline that dropped past mid-thigh. There were matching white crepe pantaloons that came in at the knee, high black riding boots, and – an inspired touch – an eight-foot-long, electric-fuchsia silk scarf with tassels. I was able to wind it around my neck, cross it in front, and wrap it ten times around my waist with the tassels hanging down the side. I must have looked like a somebody, but I won't say who – perhaps Genghis Khan in *La Cage aux Folles* would come close.

I marched into the discothèque, full of all of the trendiest people in town, and danced the night away. At least for that moment, I believed that I had arrived. I enjoyed the dancing, but I enjoyed descending the staircase and vanishing into the limousine even more. It seems to me that, right or wrong (and who is to say?), I was

---

[*] *Weltschmerz*, world-weariness, is extreme German melodrama.

performing a fantasy that I might have dreamt about or imagined years before. I was living the star trip. I can't help but think that nine people out of ten totally went for it, because if you do anything with complete conviction, most people will believe it.

My clothes at the time were so positively out of this world that each dawn and dusk brought new sensations. The 1970s was the era of "Do your own thing. Express yourself." I was doing far more than my own thing.

I wrote newspaper articles about clothes and fashion, and I hit the covers of magazines in wild get-ups. It seems to me that I had an entirely original way of putting myself together. It was all part of being the mad, eccentric *artiste*. I might add that Rudolf Nureyev's androgynous (but never feminine) glitter suits were gas to my fire. I wanted to be just like him. Sometimes I may even have eclipsed him.

It was in Montreal that fur coats hit the scene. We went to a wholesale furrier named Gilles Allard. I think that David Porter, the guy who was more comfortable driving a tractor than wearing sequined suits, was the only one who didn't succumb to a fur. Colleen O'Connor acquired a full-length white mink that topped her partner's rather boring badger, only to be topped in turn by Elizabeth Freeman's sleek black mink.

However, mine was so incredible that it could not be purchased from the rack. Mine had to be custom-made. It was a floor-length arctic wolf, and it came with two hats. The Davy Crockett hat featured a stuffed fox head with penetrating jade eyes and a few tails cascading down the back. The much more spectacular hat rose almost three feet in the air and had flaps that could be buttoned up or down. If I wore the coat with that hat, only slivers of flesh could be detected. The rest was fur.

The coat made its début on a rainy day in Vancouver, when fur was not exactly the thing to wear. Later I was chased down the streets of New York, executing jetés over snowbanks, with anti-fur people in hot pursuit. I escaped with my life only because the anti-fur people couldn't be absolutely certain that I wasn't a fugitive from the Central Park Zoo.

The Ice Show started to cross Canada. Not all the nights were as splendid as those in Maple Leaf Gardens. We might have gone to North Bay; we probably went to Peterborough; we would have gone to Winnipeg; I know that we went to Vancouver; we definitely would have gone to Victoria; and I remember falling asleep in the middle of a double Axel in Nanaimo, so I think that we went there as well.

One fact became increasingly obvious. I'm quite sure that Robin Cousins, John Curry, Jayne Torvill and Christopher Dean, or anyone else who is stupid enough to start his own show soon realizes that not only do you have to perform in the show, but the publicity and promotion are also squarely on your shoulders. If you don't give twenty-seven interviews a day, there won't be any people in the building. I acknowledged that and fulfilled my obligation.

We really did rather well. After all, there were only about twelve people in the cast, and a certain amount of money was being made. Shall we say that Elva and I and the Hurok company were ready to take Broadway by storm?

There was a performance at the Boston Gardens, where ticket sales were rather disastrous. Paul Del Rossi met us at the airport. I heard afterwards that he had been on the street corners of the seediest parts of downtown Boston passing out tickets to paper the house. Maybe that was a little unusual for the president of Hurok Concerts Inc., but we tried in every way that we could.

The Phantom Blizzard

We trained for our incredible Broadway opening in the small rink in the Olympic Center at Lake Placid. Things became exciting. People visited from New York City. There was a great deal of buzz.

Then something happened that signalled the beginning of the end. The day before we were to leave for New York to play the Uris Theatre, I was summoned to a meeting of the top brass, and I was told that the Hurok company had just declared bankruptcy.

All the funds from Toller Cranston's The Ice Show had been frittered away on doomed projects. The Ice Show had been keeping ballet companies and Polish dancers and various other bombing Hurok productions afloat. I don't know exactly how much money had been made, but although the other skaters had been paid, I think that I had no money at all. Of course, I did have my strawberry mansion in Bermuda that I rented but never stayed at – because, you see, I had to save on taxes. I write that with sarcasm.

This is the beginning of what I remember with crystal clarity. I was told that there would be no Broadway show but that the cast must, at all costs, be kept in the dark. It was officially decreed that the announcement would be made in New York.* That period was emotionally draining. I think that, more than anything, I feared the vitriol of the other skaters – and their disappointment.

That night, the cast was terribly excited. We were going to Broadway. We were going to become great stars. I knew that we were not, but I was sworn to secrecy. At three or four o'clock in the morning, we were summoned. There were knocks on our doors at the Holiday Inn, and we were told, "Get up. We're leaving immediately. There's a tremendous blizzard in New York, and we have to start early." That was one of our more spectacular exits from hotels without paying.

Years later, when all of it was over, I was asked to skate in Lake Placid. I was paid $10,000 for the performance, but I never saw a cent. I had been sued by the hotel, and every dime went to pay the

---

* Hurok Concerts Inc. announced the cancellation on January 20, 1977. The show had been slated to run from January 24 through February 27.

bill. That was okay by me, but it really wasn't my responsibility to pay for everybody's accommodations and room service. Hurok Concerts Inc. had been the producer, yet that was one more bill that I had to pay personally. It hurt my bank account but assuaged my conscience.

We jumped onto the bus and left. I thought that by taking Bufferins and 222s, I might pass out on the bus ride. I didn't want to be privy to all the excitement. No matter how many pills I consumed, the strategy didn't work. I ended up feeling decidedly awful.

The closer we got to New York, the more tropical the weather became. When we arrived in Manhattan, there were daffodils in the park – but the skaters were too excited to acknowledge that there was no blizzard, that the story had been a lie.

We arrived at the Mayfair Hotel and were summoned to the grand ballroom. Paul Del Rossi and Maynard Goldman entered to a tremendous ovation and walked onto the stage. The skaters assumed we were going to be welcomed to New York and given our marching orders. Maybe there would be champagne and strawberries. Instead, Del Rossi and Goldman announced that the company was bankrupt.

"There will be no show on Broadway. It was really nice working with you. Good luck."

The two men left.

I'm not absolutely certain that the reality of what had happened sank in. The skaters went into shock. The Ice Show had just blown up in their faces; their careers had just evaporated; and no, they weren't going to Broadway. It was too much to adjust to in an instant.

That evening, I strolled down the street with two other cast members. We wafted past the Uris Theatre, slightly under the influence of cannabis, just to see what might have been: Toller Cranston's The Ice Show. Strangely enough, if a show doesn't fly or the producers go bankrupt, the marquee doesn't change until another show comes in. For quite some time, I was able to walk by and see my name in lights.

Many of the skaters, including Gordie McKellen and Colleen O'Connor, offered to donate enough of the large amounts of money that they (unlike me) had saved, to open the show. They felt that it would then kick in, and all would be well. That was not to be.

Hooked by the Basses

The War Machine couldn't take no for an answer. How it happened, I don't know, but there must have been calls between Elva and Robin Cranston (last seen passed out on the floor in front of a pyramid of cocaine).

Robin advised Elva, "Come out to L.A. I have an immensely wealthy friend who's looking for a new creative project. He might be interested in putting your show on Broadway."

"Wonderful, splendid, great," Elva chirped.

She told me, "Let's fly out to L.A. tomorrow."

So of course we did, and of course we flew first class, because what else could one do? How that was paid for, I have no idea.

When we arrived at the L.A. airport, Robin was not in evidence. King Hussein's burgundy Rolls-Royce, however, was there to pick us up. It had his insignia on the doors. How very kind. Exactly what we expected.

Even in L.A., King Hussein's Rolls-Royce caused a flurry. The chauffeur drove us to a remote part of Bel Air, up a raised street to a pair of enormous white iron gates that opened on command as the Rolls-Royce cruised in. The driveway swooped downward in a graceful arc, and we found ourselves at the entrance of what I can only describe as a cross between the White House and Tara, but it was bigger than both. Many columns, very ante-bellum. There were two stone lions out in front and a veritable cluster of Rolls-Royces

(three pastel Corniches) in the parking lot. We also spied a few
BMWs and maybe a Mercedes in one of the garages – for the servants,
presumably. Things were looking good.

The maid showed us in. We wandered through a number of the
rooms, which, to be fair, were not sumptuously furnished, but it was
still impressive. I particularly remember the size of the rooms, the
number of chandeliers, and the enormous and valuable oriental
carpets. The owner of the *palazzo*, Dennis Bass, was sitting, barefoot,
in a chair with Robin Cranston beside him.

Dennis was a tallish man, fairly well built, with salt-and-pepper
hair. He looked something like an Italian golliwog. He had bad skin,
a conspicuous nose job, and a nice set of L.A. capped teeth. He was
dressed in a white shirt and tattered jeans.

At that point, a strange, beautiful nymph appeared. She had the
body of Raquel Welch, a rather lovely American face with deep,
wide-set brown eyes, and stunning hair of a chestnut hue that went
well down the middle of her back. Bobbie Bass, the wife of Dennis,
made an entrance with few words, then floated up one of the circular staircases.

Dennis took me into the bowels of the mansion, to the wine
cellar, and pulled out a variety dating back to 1920. Did I like
vintage whatever? "Yes," I said, although I knew nothing about wine.
"That's my favourite." He brought me back up to the living room.
We clinked our crystal goblets and started to talk biz.

Elva and I were under a certain amount of stress, rather expec-
tant, and on our very best behaviour. Because of nervousness,
fatigue, and anxiety, I hadn't eaten anything on the plane. I took one
sip from my crystal goblet, fell onto the oriental rug, and passed out.

When I revived, things were definitely looking rather good.
Dennis was quite interested in our show.

Bobbie Bass was nice but a bit spacey. She asked if I would
like to see her clothes. I remember going up the staircase carpeted
in white broadloom. One of their Great Danes had defecated

prodigiously upon the carpet. Bobbie stepped over it and continued up the stairs, pursuing her *idée fixe*. We went into a series of rooms with neither furniture nor curtains.

"This is my wardrobe," she announced with a flourish.

I subsequently learned from Dennis that his wife had spent a cool $2 million on clothes. Every article was in a plastic bag. I had never seen such clothes in my life. There were many evening dresses. Every designer label was represented in profusion. It was an art collection, to say the least. Bobbie asked if I liked the black cashmere cape edged with dozens of little sable tails. I confessed that I did.

"Well, why don't you just borrow it for a while? It looks better on you than me."

I agreed, so I did. When Elva and I returned to New York, I wore the cashmere cape edged with row upon row of sable tails – several hundred of them, to be precise.

Elva and I made many more trips to California to visit our new best friends, the Basses.

Ruth Dubonnet Enters the Picture

It was at about the same time that I met the celebrated Madame Ruth Dubonnet. Ruth was an elderly, rather frail, and rather charming New York socialite. Her first husband had been Walter Goldbeck, a famous American painter of the 1920s, much older than she. Ruth had invented the jet set. For the most part, she had resided in Paris.[*]

---

[*] Dubonnet was born in America as Ruth Obre. She took up residence in Europe in about 1920. In 1925, she was widowed by Goldbeck. Three years later, she married Count Paul Manca de Mores de Vallombrosa, a Harvard graduate of Sardinian origin. Later she married the Frenchman André Dubonnet. During the German occupation of France, Mme Dubonnet did ambulance work for the French Red Cross, temporarily assuming French citizenship to evade internment in a Nazi concentration camp. In 1951, she unsuccessfully petitioned President Truman to restore her American citizenship without the usual formalities.

Ruth went through several counts before marrying André Dubonnet, the primary figure in the Dubonnet apéritif empire. She divorced him, returned to New York, and moved into a five-storey brownstone at 43 West Sixty-third Street. She went on to conquer Broadway and became the long-time, live-in lover of Jule Styne (of *Gypsy* and *Gentlemen Prefer Blondes*). There was a secret passage through her front hall closet that descended into Styne's basement apartment.

It was through Ruth that I started to meet all sorts of groovy, fancy, important people in New York. How I impressed her on the first night, I'm not exactly certain. She claimed that her poodle, Gickie (who loved Marilyn Monroe but hated Jayne Mansfield), liked me, and that tipped the scales in my favour. Ruth fell for me hook, line, and sinker. Not only did she fall for me, but she caught fire when she saw me skate at Sky Rink. The Hurok connection impressed her, and she started to raise money and put people together, as she had so often. She was one of those women who dig show folk and know everybody who's anybody – or everybody who's going to *become* anybody. She had been around show business for many years.

Elva and I needed a New York apartment again. I took the first one that I saw. It was shown to me by Ruth. To this day, it is among New York's most desirable.

It was on the corner of West Fifty-seventh Street and Seventh Avenue, opposite Carnegie Hall. The elevator stopped at only one door on each floor. Barbara Walters lived directly upstairs. Anita Loos lived directly downstairs. Earl Blackwell lived under the roof, in an apartment that allegedly had a ballroom. Candice Bergen was around the corner. Obviously, it was exactly the right place for me.

I had a sixty-foot living room, a large dining room, an immense kitchen, three bedrooms, maid's quarters, and four bathrooms. What more did I need? I said that I'd take it. It was perfect. The price was $900 a month. When New Yorkers came to visit me in my new abode (furnished at auction for $2,000), they fell to their knees. They gasped. They couldn't believe it. I didn't know what all the fuss was about. It was the first apartment that I looked at, and I had never heard of rent control.

Elva Meets Her Match

Dennis Bass was intrigued by Ruth Dubonnet, but I think that Ruth was even more intrigued by Dennis. She likened him to Mike Todd, whom she had known well.

Dennis, it seemed, was going to resurrect The Ice Show and catapult it onto Broadway.[*] A lawyer, Tony Barash, drafted a contract. Because Dennis was going to turn me into the most major star of Hollywood, if not the world, I might as well sign it – for The Ice Show and the future.

The contract that I signed contained a phrase to which I paid no attention. Months afterwards, when I asked my own lawyer to extricate me from the contract, I came to understand it only too well. The phrase was *in perpetuity*. That means that, even after you're dead, they still have you by the short and curlies. Dennis was going to sponsor me, he was going to help me, but he was also going to control all the salaries, all the money, every conceivable aspect of my life (or death).

Since Dennis was the patriarch of Toller Cranston's The Ice Show, he thought, "Wouldn't it be fun if we flew all the kids to L.A. so that we can bond with each other?"

---

[*] According to *Playbill*, Bass, while still in his twenties, was the youngest Californian to hold a real estate license. Through his Bass Financial Corporation, he became a major developer of shopping centres. After "an intense study," he plunged into the entertainment industry "with the same boldness that marked his prestigious career in real estate." He and Robin Cranston (already, at twenty-nine, a former teacher, environmentalist, producer, lumber company owner, and Kennedy campaign worker) were the executive producers of The Ice Show.

I agreed that that would be considerate. The whole cast was flown in for a little party at the mansion – with the pool, the Jacuzzi, the Great Danes, and the multiple Rolls-Royces. Robin Cranston was somehow involved, and Elva was there as well. But not for long.

Dennis announced that she was fired. From now on, it was just going to be *us*. He brought in a pretentious drama coach from L.A. who swore that he was the best friend of Richard Chamberlain and had taught him everything he knew.

There was a frightening moment when Dennis Bass, Broadway's newest sensation, claimed that he had left his briefcase containing $50,000 in cash in a taxi. Lo and behold, the $50,000 was miraculously returned the next morning. The taxi driver (perhaps having seen too many gangster movies and suspecting a mob connection), passed up a wild shopping spree for fear of being dropped into the Hudson River wearing cement shoes.

Then Ellen Burka got into the act. That certainly was because Elva was *out* of the act. I summoned Ellen from Toronto to help choreograph and restage the show for Broadway. She stayed in my lovely apartment. I must admit that she couldn't quite believe the splendour in which I lived. Dennis Bass rather charmed her, too.

We had a send-off party at Ruth Dubonnet's sumptuous brownstone. John Glenn arrived, not to mention Ruth Ford, Ruth Warwick, Miles White, and other New York trendies. (Margaret Trudeau, of Studio 54 fame, was invited but did not appear.) We were on a roll. This time we *really* were going to Broadway.

Would You Like to Swing on a Star?

We added some new members to the cast: another pair, Mark and Janet Hominuke from Canada (both of them blond and gorgeous); the American Wendy Burge; and also, something that we really thought was a coup, JoJo Starbuck's partner, Ken Shelley. He had been the American champion.[*]

We rehearsed at Sky Rink, every night from midnight until 6:00 or 7:00 A.M. I had never seen New York in those early-morning hours. It was strangely peaceful. One day when Ellen and I emerged from the rink en route to breakfast, we saw a young thug across the street brandishing a pistol. We turned on our heels and scampered into an alley.

The show had a publicist, and we started to make waves: posters, television, "The Today Show," all sorts of things. Then came the opening night.[†] My entrance was one of the all-time greats. The rest of the cast entered the stage conventionally, swirled around, and presented themselves in shades of canary yellow. *I* arrived from the ceiling, unseen by the audience until I floated down on a gigantic starburst made of Mylar, covered with glitter and twinkles. I stood on a platform behind the starburst, holding an invisible rope, and entered slowly with my back to the audience. Once on the ice, I turned, skated towards the audience, and froze in a crooked arabesque. Theatrical agent Lillian Libman was overheard telling Leo Lerman, then editor of *Vogue*, that nobody had made such an entrance since Louis XIV.

Of course, the audience whooped and hollered. If they didn't know who I was, if they didn't recognize my face, they still knew that I was the star of the show. At last the black peacock costume made its New York début.

Many friends came from Toronto, as well as representatives of the Toronto press. After all, how many Canadians perform at the Palace Theatre on Broadway (and use Judy Garland's dressing room)?

While such luminaries as Andy Warhol, Jerome Robbins, and Alan Cranston were in the audience, Elva Oglanby and her lawyer

---

[*] Shelley, three-time U.S. pairs champion, won the men's title as well in 1972.
[†] Toller Cranston's The Ice Show opened on May 19, 1977.

were there, too. Elva was suing me now for thousands upon thousands of dollars. She was never allowed backstage, but she did sit in the front row and watch the entire show with an intensity that I found distracting.

The irritating drama coach spent the entire opening night on the basement floor, a great supine penguin in his tuxedo. His back had whipped out of joint. I had to step over him to reach the ice.

After the show, we all went to Sardi's and waited for the reviews. If I had written them myself, they couldn't have been better. Sir Ralph Richardson read them to vociferous hoots and yodels and wails and many clinking champagne glasses. We were all quite giddy and gay with the certainty that we were about to become great stars.

The last line of Clive Barnes's *New York Times* review was, "Go and see *Toller Cranston's The Ice Show*" – an imperial command. Anna Kisselgoff, who wrote the dance review, was completely intoxicated by the show.* Gene Shalit, that moustached "Today Show" reviewer, rhapsodized about it to the nth degree.

Strangely enough (perhaps the same thing happens when one wins the Olympics), I felt a distant sadness, an aloneness, a sense of anti-climax. Although there were congratulations all around, I didn't feel happy, and I didn't know why not. I looked forward to getting to bed.

The Price of Shoes

In spite of the superb reviews, business was not particularly good.

I was forever asking Dennis, "Where's my money?"

"Now, don't worry about it," he would say. "Everything's under control. What do you need?"

---

* Under the headline ICE SHOW: CRANSTON, A NUREYEV ON SKATES, Kisselgoff wrote, in part, "He has the bold-faced appeal of a successful rock star and the virtuosity of a great dancer. He is Toller Cranston and to say that he is an ice skater is not even the half of it."

"Well, I sort of thought that I might like to buy a pair of shoes."

"No problem. Here's fifty dollars. Go out and buy them."

"But where's my money?"

"Don't worry. It's all under control."

At about the midpoint of the show, I realized that something was up. I expressed my fears to some of the other skaters.

"You're not going to believe this, but I'm not getting paid."

"You're not getting paid? We've seen your apartment, you know."

"No, seriously. I'm really not getting any money."

When I called Dennis on the money question, shall we say that there was a falling out? I had two options: stop skating in the show altogether (and the show would close on the spot) or continue skating without being paid a dime. I opted to continue.

Things started to become quite grave. In the contract *in perpetuity* that I had signed, I had also agreed to a million-dollar life insurance policy, naming Dennis Bass as the sole beneficiary. I was so penniless (even though I was, of course, the toast of New York and a star on Broadway) that I could not afford to take a taxi to the Palace Theatre. I had no alternative but to walk every night. Each time that a passerby accidentally bumped into me, I imagined that he was a hired assassin. Such was my state of mind that I was becoming paranoid.

One evening, Dennis Bass, Robin Cranston, and others invited me to join them at Luchow's, a famous restaurant on East Fourteenth Street, near the Village. During dinner, my hosts announced that Ellen Burka was an evil snake. We had to get rid of her. I was never to see her again.

That was the straw that broke the camel's back. I ran out of Luchow's in my wolf coat and cried all the way from Fourteenth Street to Sixty-third. I walked through extremely frightening areas, hoping to be mugged, raped, and murdered. For some strange reason, none of that happened – at least not *that* night.

I got to Ruth Dubonnet's brownstone at midnight and knocked on her door. She crawled out of her apartment in her little night-gown and asked, "What is the matter, darling? What has happened?" I cried for probably five hours, because I couldn't *say* what had happened. The only thing I *could* say was, "I hate myself. I hate what I have become."

Then things truly started to get worse.

I broke contact with Dennis and the fatuous drama coach and almost everybody else. One night, near the end of the run, I invited the other skaters up to my apartment and tried one more time to tell them, "Look, I am not getting paid. *I am not making a dime.* I am skating for free. I have no money."

Not one of them seemed to believe me.

After the show one night, we were summoned to the garret of the Palace Theatre where Dennis Bass humiliated and excoriated me in front of the other skaters. Not one member of the cast rallied to my defence. Dennis announced that Colleen O'Connor, Bob Rubens, Jim Millns, and some of the others didn't need me. They would take the show on tour by themselves. My days were over.

Elva always said, "Tell people what they want to hear, and they'll go for it every time." I assume that, for those cast members, all the perfumes of Arabia could not have smelled so sweet. Of course they wanted to be great stars – the greatest ever.

Closing night arrived. I thought that, as often happens, people would play practical jokes to make the show especially memorable. It was, but not the way I had planned. Above and beyond wanting never in my life to have met Elva Oglanby, my second greatest regret is the crime that I perpetrated that night. In theory, it was funny. I realized later that it wasn't funny at all.

I dropped two raw eggs from the rafters just before floating down on my starburst. They plopped onto the ice with tiny Humpty Dumpty explosions. The skaters had absolutely no idea what was happening. All they knew was that eggs had suddenly started falling from the ceiling.

Several of them thought that some great eagle was entrapped in the rafters, laying eggs. When I wafted down on my Mylar starburst, I realized that they were all flabbergasted. A couple of them had actually tripped on the eggshells, and Mark Hominuke sort of clenched his fist at me – so the egg thing hadn't gone over well.

After the show, I went out with Ruth Dubonnet and Anita Loos, my neighbour in the apartment building and a legendary American writer. She was a mousy, teeny, itsy-bitsy thing. For her to come out to the final show had really been quite a tribute, because she was more than half blind.

We went to a restaurant called Mortimer's, and I started to cry. Tears rolled down my cheeks and splashed into my soup and onto my shirt. Then Anita taught me a lesson. She stood up, a frail little woman soon to die, and told me, in her Minnie Mouse voice, "Nobody can take your talent away from you. No matter what happens to you, no matter what people say about you, that is something that you will always have, and it will save you in the end."

I cried and cried and cried. I cried all the way home. What was I going to do? My rent was seriously in arrears. I had barely a cent to my name. I was flying by the seat of my pants. I phoned a lawyer friend of mine, Bill Graham (who has since become a Canadian MP). I said, "Bill, I'm in serious trouble, and I don't know what to do."

"I'll be there in a minute," he promised, in the way that one hopes good friends will. He was on the next plane.

Bill told me, "We have to get a lawyer here in New York." He gave me a number of choices, and I selected one based solely on the connotation of his name: Stanley Plesent. The name was not misleading.

Stanley was the chairman of the board of the Alvin Ailey Company, so he had a simpatico relationship with artists and performers. I explained to him that I wasn't getting paid. He figured that I should have made well in excess of $250,000 in six months – but it seemed that I had accumulated $100,000 in personal debt. He kept asking, "Toller, where is the money? Where is the money?"

I told him, "I have absolutely no money, but I do remember that I bought these shoes." He thought that was very funny.

Almost Murdered

Stanley Plesent lived in Larchmont, New York. One Sunday, he called and said, "Come up to the house. We have to go over some papers, and why don't you stay for dinner?"

I took a taxi to Grand Central Station. While I was dialling the phone to tell Stanley the time of my train, I turned around and an enormous black fellow took a coat hangar and wrapped it around my neck. "Give me your wallet," he demanded. Everything started to go in slow motion. I obeyed. The mugger took $300, then politely returned my wallet. I walked all the way back to Fifty-seventh Street and phoned Stanley.

I told him, "You're not going to believe this, Stanley, but I really cannot make it. I was almost strangled and murdered in Grand Central Station."

"Oh, my God! Thank God you're alive."

When Stanley said the word *alive*, I burst into tears, crumbled onto the floor, and had a complete breakdown.

Penniless

Elva was still suing me. Her case was that *she* had invented that rare and unique concept, The Ice Show (which was basically a series of exhibitions with costumes), and that I had benefited from all her contacts in the skating world.

Stanley Plesent warned me, "Toller, I'd love to try this case, but it will cost you more than you might recover in damages –

probably at least $60,000. You may want to consider settling out of court."

It seemed unthinkable to settle and pay Elva $25,000 (or any amount, for that matter), particularly since I didn't have a nickel – but I did.

My apartment was in Elva's name. She had signed the papers. All of a sudden, she was pulling every string to get me out.

Bill Graham advised me, "Remove everything from the apartment as quickly as you can and send it back to Toronto." Movers came, and suddenly rugs and furniture and paintings started going out the door.

The superintendent of my building said, "You're moving out! You're moving out!"

With frosty *politesse*, I replied, "Certainly not. I'm changing the décor. I've decided to go Chinese."

More paintings and more furniture left the next day. He said, "No, really, you're moving out! You're moving out!"

I responded, "Don't be silly. I'm simply changing the art collection."

Finally, when he walked into my apartment and saw that there wasn't a stick of furniture left, he fell to his knees and whimpered, "You're moving out! You're moving out! How can you do this to me? I'll lose my job. I have a family."

By chance, I had received one $2,000 cheque for my second book, *A Ram on the Rampage*. I signed it over to him there and then. At that point, I was, in a word, penniless. I then, with my little passport and my little wallet, walked down Seventh Avenue to the Canadian Consulate, demanded to see the consul, and said, "I am Toller Cranston. I am the star of New York. I don't have a dime. I have no place to go. You must send me home to Toronto." He did.

I went straight to Ellen Burka's and did not emerge for forty days and forty nights. I was in a state of shock.

We found out, after the demise of my show, that Dennis Bass and company were not what they seemed. The grand house, the Rolls-Royces, the Great Danes, the rugs – we were told that basically everything was rented.

Elizabeth Freeman wrote a rhyme about the last days of The Ice Show. I recall that it went, "Something, something, something, Dennis Bass demented. Who would ever have thought it? Even the Great Danes were rented."

Some years later, I got a call from Senator Alan Cranston. Robin had been killed – or perhaps murdered. He was the victim of a car accident, but it may have been a hit.[*] I was invited to his funeral, although I didn't go – perhaps I couldn't afford to.

The tragedy of Robin's death created an overwhelming sense of sadness in both Alan Cranston and me, though for different reasons. Senator Cranston leaned on me for almost familial support in his time of grief. I leaned on him because I felt another kind of loss: the loss of the father, and of the family, that (at least at that time) I did not feel that I had.[†] It is almost impossible to articulate the state that I was in. We used each other, each for his own reasons, without either of us fully understanding our intense emotional bond.

Exhuming The Ice Show

I might have been a lamed king, an emperor without an empire, but, without me, there was no Toller Cranston's The Ice Show.

---

[*] According to the *New York Times*, Robin Cranston died on May 17, 1980, "of injuries he received when he was hit by a van in front of his home last weekend. Mr. Cranston, who was 32 years old, suffered head and internal injuries in the accident in Beverly Glen Canyon and never regained consciousness."

[†] Although Monte Cranston was, as Toller claims, "a very nice man," Toller was so different from him that the two remained strangers. Stuart Cranston, a true eccentric, was the dominant parent. Toller was driven from the nest by what he perceived, correctly or not, as a chronic lack of parental support and understanding.

I heard during my self-imposed incarceration at Ellen Burka's that there were plans for The Ice Show to go on another Canadian tour, and I knew that the telephone had to ring. I would call the shot. Either I would do the show or there wouldn't *be* an Ice Show. A few days before The Ice Show was scheduled to open in Ottawa, the phone did ring. I'm sure that I made some demands – but I was young, I had energy, and I really wanted to salvage the wreck and go on to another adventure.

We rehearsed for one day and opened on the next. Everybody was rusty, but like riding a bicycle, it kicked in pretty fast. Although we were madly ill-prepared, we were determined.

We rehearsed in Windsor until perhaps nine o'clock at night. Everyone was very tired. When we boarded the old, beaten-up bus and set out for Ottawa, we simply collapsed. The bus driver, an American named Bob, was not very familiar with Canadian geography. In the middle of the night, Elizabeth Freeman, the brightest of the group, asked, "How can it say 'Windsor, fifteen miles'?" Her little question pierced the silence of the bus.

She kept on. "Bob, how is it possible that it says 'Windsor, fifteen miles'?"

We were back in exactly the same spot that we had left five hours earlier.

We drove right to the building. There was no time to stop at a restaurant or hotel. The crew had already set up. We got off the bus just in time for the show. The reviews were, "Oh, Toller Cranston's wonderful show! Great! A must-see!" Obviously, the reviewers knew nothing about skating.

The Ice Show limped across Canada to more spectacular highs and lows. It blew up in Calgary, but the trauma of digging up all that sewage I'm saving for another book, another day.

The Viennese Waltz

After the 1976 Worlds and Olympics, I rode my high horse and damned all existing ice shows as grotesque, vulgar, and cheap. An artist of my stature and taste would never stoop so low as to skate in one. Of course, never say never – because never is just around the corner.

Following the demise of my own show in 1977 (I still run the other way when I see double sevens), I was invited to perform in a special Christmas show in Garmisch-Partenkirchen, West Germany. It took place in the 10,000-seat Olympic stadium, which, until recently, was unheated. In the depths of winter, 10,000 people sat in the audience swathed in furs, drinking great quantities of schnapps to keep themselves warm.

I wore my famous black peacock costume. It was a mystical thing. I could wear it and all would be well.

The show was televised live. I skated one of the numbers that I had performed in my show on Broadway, a number that, for whatever reason, had never gone over too well. In Garmisch, the tape skipped forward, and I don't think that I skated for more than thirty-one seconds.

It was in Garmisch that I introduced the concept of running, diving on my stomach, and sliding on the ice in an exotic pose – unheard of at that time. Now sliding on one's stomach at the end of a number is so much copied and so *passé* that one can almost dock marks for it. (I do, anyway.) However, I invented it, and in those days it was quite shockingly original.

Coach Jutta Müller let out a *shriek*. She thought that I had had an accident, because I had done a mad, sliding dive and then just lay there. Since it was live television, and since I'd only skated for thirty-one seconds, I knew that my moment could not end there. I got up, did twenty-five split jumps, and saved the day. I'm sure that I hold the world's record in the splits department. The splittier I splat, the more wild the audience became. In those bygone days, they were impressed by that sort of thing. I had no music, just a roaring, half-drunk audience to galvanize me into yet another split.

Lovely Breasts

That night, I had Ruth Dubonnet in tow. Ruth was seventy-nine – or maybe she was eighty, or even ninety. She was, as she said herself, like Wallis Simpson: another American with perfect Chiclets teeth who married one of the crowned heads of Europe.

Something that was to haunt me for many years was the clutch of eccentric, rich, domineering older women who pursued me all over Europe and wherever else I was. Ruth was the queen of all that. She had come to West Germany with me and couldn't understand why we didn't share a bedroom. There were major scenes and major fights and major make-ups.

I was too nice. Instead of saying, "Leave me alone," I always left the door open an inch. That has been one of my major hang-ups in life. I can never say no to anybody or anything, which has gotten me into a lot of trouble, not to mention some embarrassing situations.

The day after the Garmisch show, Ruth and I flew to France, where we stayed with the daughter of the French ambassador to the United States during the Kennedy years and her husband, Michel. Ruth and I resided in their vast, quite unbelievable penthouse. It was completely decorated in cream wall-to-wall carpeting, with red lacquer walls and black granite floors. I had never seen anything remotely like it. The décor, very à l'orientale, had been done by a contemporary of Frank Lloyd Wright. Every room was sunken.

There I was in that penthouse palace in Neuilly, just outside Paris, as the I-don't-know-what of Ruth Dubonnet. I have no idea what people thought I was, and I used to be rather mortified about it.

I certainly wasn't a gigolo. As I said to Ruth, "One good thing about us travelling around Paris together is that everyone knows you're too cheap to have a gigolo."

Ruth would talk about Wallis this and Wallis that, and Wallis would be the Duchess of Windsor; Yves this and Yves that, and Yves would be Saint Laurent; Pierre this and Pierre that, and Pierre would be Cardin. It went on and on and on. I didn't believe her – until I started to meet all those people. Many of them literally bowed at her feet. Bernard Lanvin genuflected before her.

She told me that she had once had a fling with Artur Rubinstein during a transatlantic steamship crossing. I subsequently made a film with Rubinstein, and I wanted to test her story. I asked him if he happened to know a Ruth Dubonnet.

"Mmmm," he said, licking his chops. "Lovely breasts." So it was true.

Saying It with Wolf

There I was in Paris with a bubble in my career, not at all sure what to do. The telephone rang, and it was Skee Goodhart, president of Holiday on Ice. Would I like to be the guest star in Vienna? Of course I said yes.

Ellen Burka helped me with music designed to take Vienna by storm. It was Strauss's "Tales from the Vienna Woods," which, in its original state, was far too long. Not knowing any better, I started with the beginning, cut out the middle, and ended with a shortened version of the end. For the Austrian *Putzfrau* crowd, as it turned out, that was an egregious cultural *faux pas*.

Before leaving for Vienna, I stopped at the Bristol hotel, the most chic of the chic, the most expensive place on earth, equal only to the Plaza Athénée and the Ritz, to get a haircut. André Dubonnet had recommended his barber. I stopped him midway. He had hacked my fine, delicate, sensitive hair with a razor. I was a raped guinea hen. I immediately had myself recoiffed for my Viennese début, but then my hair was even shorter, and I looked even worse.

I descended from the plane in Vienna in a floor-length, silver-fox coat replete with a small train and went to greet two members of Holiday on Ice, who gasped audibly when they saw me. For me, it was the decade of entrances and exits, a skill that I had honed to the finest edge. I was into stardom, and, I confess, I did throw people on a good trip. If they believed it all, truly that was *their* problem.

So there I was, and I thought, "How nice. I'm being met at the airport by two of my Canadian friends. How kind of Holiday on Ice to have sent them."

That wasn't the case. The Canadian girls were there to meet two Hungarian studs they had picked up in Budapest. When I ran over in my fur to embrace them, they were more surprised than I was.

Holiday on Ice believed in the star system much more than any comparable North America company. There was a banner slapped across every poster in the land that proclaimed: *And with Special Guest Star, Skater of the Century, Toller Cranston.* I thought, "God, I'm a Canadian from the suburbs of Montreal, and here I am, flying down the Mariahilferstrasse in furs, with my name plastered all over the place. That's pretty good."

I was still feeling rather fragile from the collapse of my own show and not at all sure where the future was going to take me. Before the show opened, I was summoned by the general manager of the Stadthalle. I made an entrance, this time in a full-length wolf coat with fifty-five wolf tails in a boa that swirled around my neck and a Niagara of wolf tails that spewed down my front. Although today that approach might seem like *Sunset Boulevard*, then it was all taken quite seriously as the last vestiges of old-fashioned stardom.

So I arrived, and I was the *star*. The former Olympic gold medallist Wolfgang Schwarz was also in the show. It was to be his last professional performance before he evaporated into the unknown – his last fling. He was not really presented as a major star, but then he took it as kind of a joke. He never practised, and I was practising like mad, still doing my hours of Olympic training.

Wolfgang Schwarz was also summoned into the general manager's office. He arrived in a wolf ski jacket, but my wolf had fifty tails and dragged on the ground. He did a double-take. He knew who he was and where he was, and he knew who I was and where I fit – and it was all said in wolf.

Demel Café

I had arranged to meet Ingrid Wendl, once second in the world to Carol Heiss, very attractive, very Viennese.* She had always liked

---

* Wendl was the world bronze medallist in 1956 (behind Heiss and Tenley Albright) and in 1957 (behind Heiss and fellow Austrian Hanna Eigel) before winning the silver medal in 1958.

me. I was the first guest on her new television talk show, kind of "The Tonight Show" of Vienna sports programs.

To celebrate after the show, we went to the most famous coffee house in the world, the Demel, at 14 Kohlmarkt, the "cabbage street," in the depths of downtown Old Vienna. It was a *Konditorei* that had been much patronized by aristocrats for some 300 years. Its décor reminded me of *The Nutcracker Suite*.

The Demel was a gilded petit four inside, with mirrors in gold leaf and little serving ladies who looked as if they had been there forever, old and not of this era, who spoke a kind of German reserved for nobility. Instead of "Would you like a cup of coffee?" they would say, "Would *we* like a cup of coffee?" They couldn't be sure that it wasn't a prince or an emperor they were addressing. The serving ladies were all in black satin, white starched frills, and little bonnets, and they all had little spectacles and grey hair in little buns – what you'd imagine Mrs. Claus to be like.

The cakes and pastries were the most famous in the world. People flew to Vienna just to have a piece of cake at the Demel. It cost a veritable fortune. In 1978, you could have your little slice of cake or pastry for ten dollars American – and it was worth it. The manager, Herr Meingast, told me that a French gourmet magazine had given the Demel the highest ranking in Europe, saying that French pastries and cakes looked great, but it was the Viennese that tasted so good.

So there I was. I think I was wearing fox, although it might have been wolf. I had a variety of hats: Russian sable and sheared muskrat and, I think, a few minks, all in different sizes and shapes. I could change my appearance just by changing my hat. The get-ups were shades of Czar Nicholas II of Russia or, in a pinch, Ludwig II of Bavaria: mad, eccentric, dramatic, and way over the top.

I was having my ten-dollar cake and my ten-dollar coffee in that glittering café, making the Viennese scene. The most interesting and beautiful people of Vienna were there. So, as it turned out, was the

owner or head honcho (his position wasn't quite clear to me), Udo
Potsch. He was about five-foot-five. I later found out that he thought
he was Napoleon. Potsch was part of the new generation of Vienna,
the groovy, hip, trendy, almost Studio 54 Vienna. He was a designer,
an entrepreneur, and a promoter of avant-garde theatre – the
Austrian Andy Warhol.

He seemed to like me, or maybe he liked Ingrid Wendl (or maybe
he wanted us both – I'm not sure). He asked me, "Where are you
staying?" When I told him that I was not at all happy with my hotel,
he suggested, "Would you like to stay here?"

I said, "You mean, sleep in the kitchen?"

"No, this is a twenty-two-room *Palast*."

He was cohabiting at the time with a countess of some sort in
her winter *Schloß* in upper Austria, so it was just going to be me in
the twenty-two rooms. Naturally, I said yes. Udo then showed me
up a grand back staircase with red plush along the side and bronze
sculptures in many a niche. It led to the residence of the Baron von
Demel, who had long since faded out of the picture.

The Saga of Prince Pallavicini

What really impressed Udo was not my status as a matinée idol in
Holiday on Ice, but the fact that I knew a former owner of the
Demel, Prince Pallavicini*, a Hungarian prince who was quite the
gayest thing ever. Years before (because the Demels, I believe, were
Jewish), he had agreed to marry the Demels' spinster daughter to
save her from wartime persecution. He was a gentile and an aristocrat of the bluest blood.

I had met him through Ruth Dubonnet. He was the Hungarian
answer to Erté, a glittered and bejewelled ancient poodle with dyed
hair that I thought at the time was either mauve or pink. Extremely

---

* The spelling could not be confirmed.

noble, stupendously gracious, and a flaming queen – but with oceans of charm. He had been brought to my apartment in New York and had given me some of the books he had illustrated – very similar to the daintily iced pastel confections in the Demel.

According to the story that he told me, shortly after marrying the Demel spinster, Prince Pallavicini had run off to Paris, under the terms of their agreement, to live a poor, artistic life in a garret – a heady, giddy, and gay experience when Paris was the centre of the art world. Sometime after the war, there had been a knock on his garret door, and three stiff, bespectacled, magisterial men in black had announced, "We regret to inform you that your wife is dead."

"My wife? What wife?"

He didn't remember having one. Nonetheless, he inherited her family business. Overnight, he went from pauperdom in a garret to proprietorship of the Demel palace and the famous *Konditorei* and tearoom on its ground floor. When I announced that I had run into him in New York, Udo asked if I would like to stay at the Demel.

We passed through a labyrinth of rooms and passageways, up a winding staircase, into the highest, most secret part of the building – a kind of attic, but a very swanky one, which (I found out after I moved in) had provided a venue for the sexual indiscretions of one of the Lord Mayors of Vienna. I was thrilled. I was even more thrilled when Udo presented me with what looked like the key to an ancient castle or a treasure chest. As it turned out, it was more valuable than either. He had given me the key to the kitchen in the Demel. Whatever I wanted, whatever I chose to eat, was *compliments de la maison*.

Of course, when you have the key to the kitchen, and you can ingest as many ten-dollar pastries as you want, invariably you don't eat any. I do confess that it was divine to wake up every morning to the smell of fresh *Apfelstrudel*. I think that I was responsible for many a fall on a double Axel by Wolfgang Schwarz. When he heard that I was residing in the Demel and that I had the key to the kitchen, I can only say that it was like telling Robin Cousins that I had the key to Buckingham Palace. Wolfgang Schwarz, the Olympic champion, had to buy the ten-dollar cakes, but I could wave the key under his nose.

In the Night Café

The first night that I went home to the Demel, I was wearing the Russian sable hat and the wolf coat. The Demel at night is quite different from the Demel in the daytime. The Kohlmarkt was much frequented by ladies of the evening. When I swooshed out of my cab, an apparition in fur, I do not know what they thought. They might have taken me for a customer, or they might even have seen me as competition.

I didn't waste any time slipping into the palace of the Baron von Demel. When I got to the grand staircase, all of a sudden it became quite frightening and ominous. As I reached the top, the lights went off. I was convinced that someone was following me. I ran for my life through the palace. Periodically I stopped to listen for footsteps. When I didn't hear any, I naturally assumed that the thugs were lying in wait for me. I finally reached my garret, frightened to death. The twenty-two-room palace with its corridors, ballrooms, and stairways was feeling very *Sleeping Beauty*esque, and there I was – alone in my furs.

The next day, I was enlightened about timer switches.

The First Monkey Incident

In German, *Putzfrau* means cleaning lady. Holiday on Ice is kept alive to this very day by the *Putzfrau* contingent. They were bussed in from all over Austria, thousands upon thousands of them. Stampedes of *Putzfrauen* poured in for the matinée, only to be trampled by the *Putzfrauen* arriving for the evening performance. I don't think that there was ever one male in the audience. When I opened with "Tales from the Vienna Woods," it was like playing the national anthem with the middle removed. It didn't go over too well. I began with a tremendous entrance and ended with many split jumps and butterflies, but the number was on the short side, and the *Putzfrauen* could never hum along because the main theme was missing. It was almost an act against the state.

My number-one hang-up in life, my number-one beef, the nightmare, the unthinkable, was to skate with horrid monkeys and vulgar comedians. God had positioned me in the show to follow the comedian and precede the monkey.* An ape. A skating chimpanzee. The comedian was a tough act to follow, but the monkey was impossible. He was clearly the star of the show.

The monkey and I were not on friendly terms. He knew that I held him in disdain. The custodian of the apes looked like someone who had been training wild beasts for a long time and had had a few unpleasant incidents.

Holiday on Ice doesn't make a fuss about openings. You show up and pretend you're the big star, but you take a taxi home, and that's it – and you'd better show up for practice tomorrow. I was in my cubicle – not a star's dressing room, but we all had our little places – and was preparing to leave for the night when the chimpanzee escaped. I heard a screech from one of the chorus girls: "Ape on the loose!"

Wouldn't you know it, the creature started to chase me. I was running for my life, my furs flying behind me, when the monkey leapt onto my back, grasped me, and rode piggyback on my wolf-covered shoulders. Streaking through the backstage area, yelping and screeching and howling, I was eventually rescued by the trainer.

---

* The animal was a chimpanzee. "Monkey" is used generically.

That was my first monkey experience. In the months to come, I was to have a much more severe encounter with a monkey, far more threatening and frightening. I tell you this because forewarned is forearmed. I developed a great fear of, and aversion to, monkeys, not to mention a bit of jealousy, because, to be fair, they could spin faster than any of us. In fact, they defined inertia: furry little bodies in infinite motion. Sometimes the trainer had to stop them. There's really nothing quite like a monkey doing a sit spin. It's far beyond anything Denise Biellmann could manage. What they lack in artistic impression, they make up in velocity. That may be due to their low centre of gravity.

The monkey was not the only animal in the show. Trainer Ronnie Boxer had a herd of boxer dogs that played balloon volleyball, eating whatever was inside the balloons (along with the balloons themselves), which, I think, was the incentive. I never went into direct competition with the dogs, because they were in a different part of the show.

Life in Holiday on Ice was like life in a gypsy camp. No matter what happened, or who was in the show, or how many different nationalities were represented, backstage was like a gypsy bonfire with brewing pots and unidentifiable food that I consumed ravenously without wanting to know what I was eating.

Usually it was some jaded, tainted skater who had once achieved renown but was now third string who made extra money by running the coffee stand, a thriving business. He had to be conversant in at least five languages: Russian, Czech, French, English, and German.

I made a point of never mixing with the riffraff of the show. I sacrificed personal happiness and lived a solitary life in the swankiest hotel I could find. Holiday on Ice wanted its stars to be stars. They did not want their stars to hang around with chorus boys and stay at the *Bahnhof* hotel. I didn't have to be told. I knew. So even though I lived a lonely existence, I adhered to the discipline of stardom.

Leonard Bernstein

Vienna was an extremely long run: three and a half weeks. The closer we got to the end, the more packed the house was and the more *Putzfrauen* were jammed in. I was the toast of Vienna, second only to a much greater star: Leonard Bernstein, who was in Vienna conducting *Fidelio*, supposedly the definitive performance of the century.

I had first met Leonard Bernstein at the time of the Jimmy Fund show – a benefit that was created by John Misha Petkevich, an American skating god and one of the most talented skaters I have ever encountered. Petkevich, while attending Harvard, had started the famous benefit to help young children with leukemia. He had put it together and invited his friends to help out. It was (and is) a great success.

Although, as a Canadian, I was the northern relation, I had been invited to skate in the second edition of the show. I hadn't visited Boston before.

I'm never on time, but I'm never late. In other words, I don't arrive when I'm supposed to, but I never miss a performance. I missed my plane to Boston, so there wasn't anyone to meet me when I finally arrived at Logan airport. All I knew was that I was going to Harvard. When I told the taxi driver to take me to Harvard, he was confounded. "What Harvard? Where Harvard? Who Harvard?"

I arrived at dusk with autumn leaves falling all around me. I remembered that I was to be billeted at Eliot House, one of the main Harvard residences. I knew that there was to be a dinner to honour the skaters. That particular year, Leonard Bernstein had been invited, too. It was very exciting to think that we were going to meet him.

When I ran into Eliot House, the only person I came across was the janitor.

"I am Toller Cranston," I said. "I am a skater. I am supposed to be staying at Eliot House. I am supposed to be going to a dinner with Leonard Bernstein. Where is it? How do I get there?"

He was Portuguese and spoke no English.

I dashed across a sort of park and saw a shadowy figure passing under the trees.

"I am Toller Cranston," I tried again. "I am the Canadian skating champion. I am supposed to be going to dinner with Leonard Bernstein."

"But *I* am Leonard Bernstein," the shadow said.

"Well, could you please help me with my luggage, because I really can't lift it by myself. Leonard, do you mind if I call you Len? Len, when we go to the dinner, could you pretend that you know me? Everyone thinks that I'm late and that I screwed up yet again, but if we walk in together and you pretend to know me, all will be well."

We walked into the room arm in arm, and I introduced my new best friend, Len, to all the skaters. Some of them were in a state of disbelief. I think some were angry, but most had their chins on the ground. That was my introduction to Leonard Bernstein.

So Bernstein, or his secretary, phoned Holiday on Ice in Vienna to ask if I would dine with him. Holiday on Ice is a hotbed of incest, gossip, and I don't know what else. Everybody knows everything. When Leonard Bernstein phoned, news of the invitation spread like wildfire. I managed not to bat an eyelash, but I thought, "This isn't bad. This is what stars do."

Of course, I couldn't go to the dinner until quite late, which was fine with me. I would be making another entrance. I left after the show, encased in fur, and arrived at the Countess something-or-other's apartment. I took a glass-caged art nouveau elevator up to the fourth floor, knocked on the door, entered, and was presented to the dinner party. There were about twelve people, in gowns and black tie, in a fancy-shmancy apartment.

Leonard Bernstein, the guest of honour, got up from the table, ran over to me, hugged me, then pulled up a chair at his end of the table. He turned his back on the other guests, who were already having dessert, and started talking to me as if we were alone. While I was served a late dinner, he told me, to my utter shock and discomfort, how horrible it was to grow old. He couldn't find love any more. Love was the only thing worth living for. He was totally depressed. He was explicit about his sexual life, so explicit that I stopped eating and turned purple. There was a deafening silence in the room, because every single guest could hear him. I was not enjoying our tête-à-tête – not a bit.

After dessert, he made a suggestion. I didn't know exactly what he had in mind, but red lights were flashing in my head. I grabbed my furs and flew out of the apartment with Leonard Bernstein in hot pursuit. Instead of taking the glass cage, I plunged down the circular staircase, around and around and around, my fur coat bouncing off every step. Leonard took the elevator, which wasn't quite as fast as I was, so I just kept going and flew out of the building.

I dove over a snowbank and leapt into a taxi. Bernstein ran up, panting, and tried to open the door, but the taxi took off just in time, and I sped away into the Vienna night.

Twice after I returned to the drudgery of Holiday on Ice, the maestro invited me to the Hotel Sacher. Although I knew him to be one of the greatest geniuses of the twentieth century, I preferred listening to his records to joining him for *Sachertorte*.

4

Berlin

*I*f you were going to West Berlin twenty years ago, you could either take the long way around, travelling from Vienna to Frankfurt and then on to Berlin, or, for half the price, you could go from Vienna to East Berlin and then take the bus to West Berlin – half the price and certainly the worst thing you could do.

That was at the time when East Germany was about as East German as it could get. Of course, I made another terrible mistake. Rather than try to pack all my furs (with the trains that dragged on the ground), I wore one of them. When I got to customs, I was singled out and told to sit down. Then the customs officials simply disappeared. Three hours later, I was still sitting there – being punished, I think, for looking too rich.

When the officers finally returned, I was feeling a bit fragile. (Part of that was the residue of a previous East German misadventure when Robin Cousins, Emi Watanabe, and I were hauled off a train at gunpoint.) Then I had an almost Benny Hill experience that was so flummoxing I barely knew what to do.

I had five or six suitcases. The turnstile in customs was some distance from the exit door. If the door closed, it closed so that you could never get back in to reclaim your luggage. By sliding on my stomach (in my furs), I was just able to keep my toe on the luggage and hold the door open at the same time. Five or six guards watched with stony faces as I struggled. No one would help me. As I got on the bus, I thought to myself, "Well, *that* was unpleasant – but I'm leaving this country, and you have to stay here, so that's your punishment."

I arrived at the Hotel Kempinski, which was and still is the place to be, the grandest of the grand, the best that Berlin could offer. It was designed for entrances and exits. As the Skater of the Century in Germany, that was exactly what I craved. Of course, one night there would have cost a week's salary for a chorus skater, but I plunged in, thinking, "I'll never be able to stay there again, so I might as well do it while I [maybe] can afford it."

You walk in off the Kurfürstendamm, probably the most densely lined avenue of upper-class hookers on the planet. Then you pass through three reception rooms between the front desk and the elevators. People gather in these rooms to eat cake, drink coffee, and watch other people, particularly the famous guests. It was absolutely perfect for me.

My image was slightly tarnished right off the bat because I walked in off the Kurfürstendamm and not from the side entrance, so the manager at the reception desk realized that I'd taken the bus rather than arriving by plane. We both knew that the *real* stars didn't take the bus.

The manager was very Teutonic, small, short-haired, impeccably dressed (in tweed, as I recall), with a Hitleresque moustache. He was extremely attentive. He helped me carry my luggage to my

room, and, in the days that followed, developed the habit of bringing me chocolates, something that I strenuously encouraged.

Charlotte's Leg

I performed in the Deutschlandhalle. The manager of the building
was Willy Schilling, a name well known among skating people in
Europe. He was kind to me.

In Holiday on Ice, you were in for the long haul. The day that
you arrived was the day that you started to skate. There were three
shows on Saturday and often three on Sunday. That was called a six-
pack. I've even done a nine-pack, but let's not talk about it.

One afternoon, during a matinée performance, the famous
Charlotte was a special guest of Holiday on Ice. She had been an
international star before Sonja Henie and was the sensation of a great
show that was held in the Hippodrome in New York. Her claim to
fame was the Charlotte spiral or, more precisely, the Charlotte stop,
a backward spiral in which you try to raise your leg 180°.

When I met her, Charlotte was an invalid in a wheelchair. I presented her with flowers at her seat. Later she was brought backstage
to meet me. I may have been one of the few active skaters who could
pay her the proper homage, because I really knew who she was and
what she had done, and I was thrilled to meet her. I saw a frail,
white-haired, wrinkled-up woman who could have been any frail,
white-haired, wrinkled-up woman, except that she had fire in her
eyes. When those penetrating blue eyes met mine, I knew that she
was one of the chosen.

She said to me in English, in a deep, husky voice, "You skated
very well. In this show, only you know how to skate – and only you
and I know how to skate, as far as most skaters go." I was pleased
to be included in her group.

"Take my leg," she ordered.

I thought, "Do I have to? And if I do, will I be arrested?"

"Take my leg," she said from her wheelchair.

So I took her leg.

"Pull it," she said.

So I pulled it, and it went straight to the ceiling.

"You see," she said, "I still have it. Like you, I can still do it. Nobody else can do that."

She was wheeled away. Although I knew that I'd never see her again, I was inspired by the realization that although she was encased in an old body, she was so very youthful.

Tweedledum and Tweedledee in Leather

I had tons of clothes in those days, and I always affected the look of the artist/martyr as I made my entrances and exits at the Kempinski. Pale and interesting was the look of the 1970s. Anyhow, I was working hard. The workload was torture. As I was going out one night, the manager politely asked if he could have two tickets for the show, one for himself and one for a friend.

"Yes, I could arrange it."

"Would you like to have dinner with us afterwards?"

"Yes, that would be just fine. I'll see you tomorrow."

I had almost forgotten about it when I finished the last show on Saturday night and went back to my dressing room. A chorus boy knocked on the door. He said in a rather smarmy, smirky way, "You have guests."

Two seconds later, someone else said, "You have people here to see you." (Same smirk, same rolling eyes.) If it happened twice, it happened eight times. I began to think that something was up.

Since we were going out to dinner, I swathed myself in black velvet, a black cashmere turtleneck, and one of my furs. My make-up had been removed (but not absolutely all of it), and I looked pretty good. I went to meet my guests. *Toute la compagnie de Holiday on Ice* was arrayed at the coffee stand. There was deafening silence. I spotted my guests and blanched.

The little Teutonic man in tweeds was dressed, like his friend, from head to toe in studded black leather. Handcuffs dripped from their belts, and the two men were outfitted in chains, motorcycle caps, and high leather boots. Identical twins, except that one had spurs.

I sized up the situation, approached them, and said with a perfectly straight face, "How do you do? How kind of you to come."

The manager and his friend in no way alluded to their gear. They were perfectly nice. In fact, they were excited about the skating. They thought that I had been good but that the dogs had been better.

Then they escorted me to their vehicle. Each grabbed one of my arms, and they swooshed me out of the building. I was hurled into the back of a Jeep, and off we went to dinner.

We drove to a fine Berlin restaurant filled with all sorts of respectable people. When the lords of leather strode in, not an eyelash was batted. That sort of thing was normal in Berlin, a most progressive city. Our conversation centred on show life. I did manage to stammer, between the main course and dessert, "Do you dress like this often, or is this a special occasion?" They made light of their appearance.

At the end of the meal, they announced, "Now we're going to a 'fantasy club.' Do you want to come?"

The costumes they wore are usually associated with sado-masochism.

"No," I told them. "I think I'll go back to the hotel. You two go on to the fantasy club without me."

We parted ways, and that was that.

Holiday on Ice and skating in Europe were part of my education in life: about human beings, values, and lifestyles. You strike out if you become judgemental.

John Curry was inclined to be attracted to that particular world, the world of the hotel manager and his friend. Curry's beautiful figure, his sensitivity to music, and his skating talent were all things that he disdained. He waffled between loving and loathing skating, because the kind of person he was on the ice was the very kind of person he hated most in his private life.

Berlin pulsated with sex. The Kurfürstendamm, which is to Berlin what the Champs Elysées is to Paris, had dozens upon dozens of the most chic hookers in the world, twenty-four hours a day. They all wore leather boots that came up to their hips. There was omnipresent decadence. There was a disturbing rhythm to the city, unlike any I'd ever experienced. It was in the air.

Berlin was a tormented and tormenting place. The West German skyline that the East Germans could see (but not touch) was like a midway or the Land of Oz. It was a forbidden fruit that beckoned to them, tried to suck them in, and seduced many to defect.

I once was invited to a private club where fifty-year-old men in tuxedos danced to Strauss, accompanied by a piano and violins. That typified a certain side of Berlin that is long gone. In 1995, I went to Berlin to make a movie with Katarina Witt. I stayed at the Kempinski, but the Berlin I saw then was not the same as the Berlin of the late 1970s.

Elevator Music

Once when I was wearing my furs, I got stuck in an elevator at the Kempinski with an interesting-looking fellow in a multi-layered, down-filled canvas coat. I pretended not to notice him, but he spoke first.

"That is an incredible coat."

"Well, I was actually just admiring yours."

"Do you want to trade?" he asked me.

That exotic specimen was Seiji Ozawa, the conductor of the Boston Symphony Orchestra.

Terry Bradshaw in Tights

The dancer Alexander Godunov was performing in a Berlin production of *Swan Lake*. He had an imposing physical presence on the stage. He was like a tall Arnold Schwarzenegger or a Terry Bradshaw in tights, though he had infinitely more hair than Bradshaw – platinum blond, as I recall. He had such peculiar make-up that, even from where I was sitting, it was shades of the Ballets Russes de Monte Carlo. Great black wings sprang from the corners of his eyes. His dancing was competent but, because of his bulk, rather earthbound. He was certainly not on the level of Rudolf Nureyev or Mikhail Baryshnikov. But he was the token defector-of-the-year, and everyone was eager to see him perform.

I went backstage to meet him. Seen up close, in his dressing room, he was even more muscle-bound and gigantic than I had imagined. I thought to myself that, even in skating, there are people who, in many ways, are miscast in the sport. I wished I had known him well enough to suggest discus-throwing or football.

5

Le Patineur du Siècle

While in Bremen, West Germany, I learned that I had been selected by Holiday on Ice to be the star of Paris. The long-time manager of the Palais des Sports was an expatriate American named Charley Michaelis. He knew everyone, had seen it all, and was an intimate friend, as I found out later, of Joe Louis. He looked like a boxer. He was stocky and bald, but possessed a perfectly honed Parisian charm that made my stay that much more delightful.

Charley Michaelis invited me to Paris for the press conference to announce the new season of Holiday on Ice – and, by the way, would I be so kind as to design the poster? I did so, on my hands and knees, in my room in the Parkhotel, an absolutely divine hotel set beside a large pond in a formal park setting in Bremen.

I arrived in Paris. At first I was surprised, then thrilled, then rendered almost speechless by the omnipresence of the little poster that

I had executed on my knees in Bremen. Holiday on Ice in Europe blanketed entire cities with posters ranging in size from little bigger than large stamps to monumental forty-by-forty-feet billboards. There was the dancing figure in skates that I had drawn; there was my name; and there, following my name, were the words *Patineur du Siècle* – the Skater of the Century.

Fame is truly an illusion in other people's minds. Even though I, the total failure, didn't believe the description, the Parisians, at least at that moment, accepted it at face value.

The Palais de Glace

While I performed in Holiday on Ice, no matter where I was staying or how many shows I had per week, I spent every other waking moment drawing and painting. I confess that I became sickeningly rich. The sale of my artwork subsidized my extravagant life in five-star hotels. Without it, I could never have managed.

It was decided that I should have an exhibition of drawings in the Palais de Glace, the most incredible rink in the world, a rink known to people such as Dick Button, Tenley Albright, Sonja Henie, and to the actress Eva Gabor, who did a skating scene there in the movie *Gigi* (simulated, mind you – her feet were never visible). The rink was round. The brilliant feature of skating in a round rink, the real advantage, is that you can never run out of room, and you can never get stuck in a corner. All you have to do is turn a little, cheat a little, and off you go in another direction. I recommend it. Incidents like Midori Ito running off the ice could never occur in a round rink.[*]

The Parisian skating world came out in droves. Many judges who had been hideously cruel to me when I was an amateur met me

---

[*] At the 1991 World Figure Skating Championship in Munich, Ito jumped too close to the boards and fell through a TV camera opening.

as a long-lost friend. Instead of making a scene and saying, "You fucking so-and-so, why did you give me a 2.3 on my double three change double three?" I let it slide and was quite happy to see them as well.

I had both a skating exhibition and a painting exhibition. This was to become almost a ritual over the next twenty years. We drank champagne and dined upon hors d'oeuvre of lobster, shrimp, and foie gras, all those incredible things one associates with Paris. The next day, the building was converted into a television studio, so one of my claims to fame is that I was the last skater to perform in the Palais de Glace.

Of Ostriches and Capes

Holiday on Ice played in a somewhat ramshackle building at the end of the subway line. It was called, rather grandly, the Palais des Sports. In the world, on the entire globe, no building could have been more perfect for a skating show. The total seating was about 6,000, not large by North American standards, but rather grand if one thinks in terms of theatres. It felt like neither a stadium nor an arena, but more like a large Parisian nightclub such as the Alcazar or the Lido de Paris.

I can't possibly explain what it is to experience Paris. You have to be there to understand what the light is, what the magic is; nor can I explain the enchantment that I experienced every night in that wonderful building. The world stopped the second one entered. Magic and enchantment were conjured by the very first note of the orchestra.

I was afforded a rare privilege. While all the other dressing rooms were down in the bowels of the building, mine was up in the air. In reality, it was an appendage of the building superintendent's apartment. He and his wife spoke not a single word of English, but they became great friends of mine. I had the pleasure of sharing whatever *Madame* happened to have cooked for breakfast, lunch, or dinner, because I was included as part of the family. I loved running up the stairs, smelling the smells that were coming out of that kitchen.

I also had, in that secret, lofty dressing room – like Rapunzel in the tower – access to a passage that led out along the catwalk. I could watch the show from the uppermost row of seats, which, in those days, was punishable by a severe fine. The other skaters' quarters were in the cellar. No one was allowed to watch the show – but I watched it every night (and was never caught).

I did not enter at the beginning of the show, as most stars do. The Parisians had to wait for my entrance. Because I had been rehearsing entrances for months, if not years, this was the entrance to beat all entrances. In my opening number, a Viennese waltz scene, there were twenty or twenty-five women in ball gowns made entirely of diamonds and pure-white ostrich feathers, with ostrich feather headdresses that shot up in the air and tumbled down like Niagara Falls. The set had chandeliers and a ballroom backdrop in red, gold, and black.

In that number, the girls in white gowns were matched by girls in identical costumes of black ostrich feathers and diamonds. With a veritable flotilla of ostrich feathers on the ice, there was scarcely enough room to skate – or to breathe. (Has anyone ever suffered from plumophobia?) When the girls finished their Strauss number, they formed a phalanx (alternating black and white) so that there was a narrow diagonal passage across the ice. With great fanfare, I descended a staircase and alighted onto the ice in the middle of the column.

My entrance was equal to, and surely no less dramatic than, the heroine's death scene in *Tristan and Isolde*. It must have lasted a good ten minutes. Every time I took a step forward, I acknowledged both black and white ostrich ladies on my right and left, down the whole line. Then I struck a pose of such breathtaking hauteur that even if there were members of the audience who knew neither my name nor my credentials, they knew that I was the *Patineur du Siècle*.

I skated in my black peacock costume. I was an exotic creature. Although it is out of fashion today, I wore that extreme make-up, that Rudolf Nureyev make-up, that way-beyond-Alexander-Godunov make-up, that was *de rigueur* at the time. It made sense, because the whole production was exotic, flamboyant, and unworldly – and so was I.

I'm not certain if anyone could relate to me as a human, either male or female. Androgyny was another aspect of the 1970s that I cultivated to the max.

After my entrance, I skated three different numbers, including a finale in which all the white and black ostriches fluttered around and made a huge pinwheel, with me floating in the air at its centre. Few people in the skating world, or in any kind of show for that matter, have had the luxury of being presented that way, and it was fun.

That ended the first half. Then I slithered out of my peacock costume, changed my make-up, and donned my Spanish costume. I opened the second half with a Spanish number that went on for a good fifteen minutes. It was while doing this number that I learned to work a cape, and I will challenge anyone anywhere to a cape-twirling contest. First, I have had the practice. Second, I have the feel for it. Third, I have the theatrical sense. I don't think anyone can compete with me in the cape department.

Then there was a New Orleans jazz finale with people such as Katie Walker Baxter, Atoy Wilson, Greg Taylor, and Kirk Wyse. Kirk was also his masterful self in the Charlie Chaplin number. He out-Charlied Chaplin. That was a case where a corny idea was parlayed into an artistically brilliant act – with a dog that was the perfect show dog. Scrapette, a charming white mongrel, had a flawless sense of drama and followed every cue. She may have been the most professional of us all.

Altogether in that show, I had three numbers in the first half, a fifteen-minute number in the second, another full solo before the finale, plus the finale number. That was happening three times a day, sometimes without a stop. Holiday on Ice always had costumes that were easy to get out of, with zippers up the inside of the leg. For my perfectly stretched, beautiful lines, I adamantly refused them. Being the vain creature that I was, I supplied my own costumes. Every time I had a number, I had to change my costume, which meant taking off my skates. Well, if you take off your skates and put them back on thirty times a day, that's a total drag.

Nervousness is not necessarily a direct reflection of the magnitude of an event. I remember watching a torch-carrier in the Sapporo Olympics in 1972. While he was carrying the torch, people were skating on the speed skating track not far away. There were perhaps 70,000 spectators, and I thought to myself that if I were carrying the torch, I wouldn't mind at all. The hugeness of the event made the participants look incidental and the audience invisible. On the other hand, you might be tremendously nervous if your mother were sitting in the audience in a pre-juvenile competition. Because Paris, for me, was not Maple Leaf Gardens in downtown Toronto, I had no nerves at all on the opening night.

The Paris opening was grand and exciting. I didn't realize yet how many shows I would skate in the next three and a half months. I was marching onto a perpetual treadmill.

The evening ended with my famous stomach slide. That night, I fell too hard and broke a rib. I got up and took my bow, but for the rest of the night, I thought that I was going to die. By the next day, that was an attractive option. However, with his name in every métro station in Paris, how could the *Patineur du Siècle* not perform in the opening week of Holiday on Ice? Surely that would have been *un grand scandale*.

There have been a number of things in my life that have been difficult to do: skating for six weeks with a broken rib was excruciating. God obviously was trying to teach me a lesson. I'm not sure quite what it was, but I was being tested.

Every night, I was tested anew. The music would be playing. I knew that, in thirty seconds, my name would be announced. I would tell myself, "I can't, I can't, I can't, I won't, I shan't." Then I'd go out and somehow do it. Alone backstage, I often had a good old cry – yet I performed. That was almost the only downside of Paris.

The show had been designed around me, and I worked harder than any living skater has ever worked. The amateur training, even the poisonous period before Worlds in Göteborg when I was so nearly broken, was a holiday by comparison. I'm not sure that any contemporary skater could handle it.

The number of shows per week was astounding. Prisoners in Siberian salt mines might have preferred their lot to that of skaters in Holiday on Ice in Paris. We skated a show on Tuesday night, two shows on Wednesday, one show on Thursday, two shows on Friday, three shows on Saturday, and three shows on Sunday. Life was a question of day-to-day survival. In the good old Protopopov way (something that I adhere to myself but would have learned from them), your longevity as a skater depends entirely on how much you train and if you train every day.* On a three-show day, you had to arrive several hours early to practise before the first show. The third show always ended late, because Parisians are basically nocturnal. To finish at midnight was the norm.

I adored every single second. Every single moment of that experience was wonderful.

Business was so incredible that one day Charley Michaelis came to my room and presented me with a set of Louis Vuitton luggage. I wasn't the least bit impressed, because in those days North

---

* Oleg and Ludmila Belousova Protopopov, twice Olympic and four-time world pairs champions, proved the value of hard work by continuing to perform nearly thirty years after winning their last amateur title.

Americans didn't know about Louis Vuitton. To my ultimate regret, I sold it to a chorus boy for one tenth of its value.

Discovering Paris

When I arrived in Paris to begin my reign as the *Patineur du Siècle*, a familiar figure greeted me at the airport: Ruth Dubonnet. She said that she had come over to go to the dentist, but I learned, not too long into the run, that she was there because she *totally adored me*.

Imagine Wallis Simpson meeting you at the airport and showing you around the City of Light. I had been to Paris before, but I had never seen it the way I did through Ruth's eyes. Because of her, I saw things that most people will never see. I also found her completely exhausting, and I lusted for the private moments that she denied me.

Ruth Dubonnet, through a real estate agent, found me a fabulously expensive and totally wonderful apartment in the Seventh Arrondissement between les Invalides and the Latin Quarter. It was at 24, rue de Bellechasse, between boulevard Saint Germain and rue de Grenelle, which is in the centre of the most historical part of Paris – *très révolution française*. I was happy there. If I had wanted to, I could almost have jetéd across the Seine and landed on the roof of the Louvre. So I began to live my Parisian life as the *Patineur du Siècle* on the *rez-de-chaussée* of my grand bourgeois apartment.

I spent a vast amount of money on telephone calls. I understood instinctively that I was in the middle of a unique experience. I invited many people to visit. It was fun to show my friends Paris. Unlike every other skater in the show, I lived quite some distance from the Palais des Sports and was able to navigate on the subway, which gave me a somewhat superior feeling and was useful to me in my role as tour guide.

Because I arrived at the end of February, I experienced and discovered Paris as springtime arrived by degrees. On Monday, I was so tired that I could barely walk, but I had to go to a dentist whose office was across the Jardin des Tuileries. I would drag myself out of bed and walk, half asleep and half dead, across the Quai d'Orsay and slip into the Tuileries. My appointments were always at 8:00 A.M. One day, at 7:00 A.M., en route to the dentist, I had an incredible experience.

I stopped in my tracks. The sun was coming up behind the trees. In the diffused light of the mist, surrounded by slightly out-of-focus images, I thought, "I'm walking in an impressionist painting. Now I understand what they are."

Tired as I was, I looked forward to that morning stroll. I discovered Maillol, whose sculptures of big, fat bronze women used to decorate the Tuileries garden. At seven o'clock in the morning, in that light, in that setting, I understood what he was about, too. So it was both a painterly and a sculptural experience, going to the dentist.

There is no end of visual treasures in Paris. I frequented every museum that I could find. In the Musée des Arts Décoratifs, I came upon a glass bed by Gallé that lit up. I wondered if there wasn't a way that I could buy it or acquire one like it.

I discovered the Jardin du Luxembourg and the former palace of Marie de' Medici. As an amateur historian, I found that those things made great sense. I went promenading along the rue du faubourg Saint Honoré and breathed the expensive air that you don't have to pay for when you pass Hermès. It wasn't until I discovered the shop itself that I came to appreciate the conservative designs of Hermès. Years later, I met the chief designer, a German ex-skater named Joachim Metz.[*] To this day we correspond, artist to artist.

My Portuguese maid, Pepita, looked like a benevolent witch, but she was so charming. She spoke French, and finally all my years of pretending to speak French in high school (resisting all the while) kicked in. The French, snobs that they are, are convinced that theirs

---

[*] Metz was an ice dancer of the late 1960s.

is the only civilized language. My French, which is not at all Québécois, spoken slowly and with an anglo accent, was perceived as aristocratic. That suited me just perfectly. That was exactly how I wished to be perceived.

Airs above Notre-Dame

For a photo spread in *Paris Match*, I was persuaded by the publicity people to set out on my day off, resplendent in my peacock costume, and jump on a trampoline in front of the cathedral Notre-Dame de Paris. The plan was to photograph me from ground level, flying in a stag jump over the towers of Notre-Dame.

The day dawned. I put on my skates and costume, not to mention full stage make-up, and began to promenade around the cathedral. Even *I* felt just the tiniest bit peculiar. I suspect that no one else on earth has ever jumped on a trampoline wearing skates and guards. It's ever so difficult. Although it cannot be seen in the photograph, there was a substantial cloudburst, which added to the absurdity of it all.

As the photographer took the picture, the sirens of the gendarmes started to blare. The entire crew (including me) was arrested on the spot. One was not permitted to commit such flagrantly indecent acts in front of France's most sacred shrine.

It was slightly odd to be in the police station on that bleak Monday morning in a pair of ice skates, a sequined costume, and full stage make-up, but I hoped that the French were used to that sort of thing.

Dayle Haddon

It was Ruth Dubonnet who introduced me to the wonderful dentist on the avenue de Montaigne. One day as I leafed through the magazines in the waiting room, I recognized the face on the cover of *Vogue*. Then I recognized the same face on the cover of *Elle*. It went on and on and on – a curious coincidence.

When I was thirteen years old and attending MacDonald High School in the Montreal suburbs, I would often take the bus to the Lachine arena, an hour's ride away. The bus stopped at every single little suburban centre. There was a girl one grade ahead of me who was also able to get out of school a smidge early, and we would sometimes take the bus together. She was a dancer, and I was a skater, and on that bus we fantasized about who and what we were going to be. I lost touch with that girl after she became runner-up in the Miss Canada pageant, but she rose to a certain stardom again when she made the cover of the swimsuit issue of *Sports Illustrated*. Lo and behold, there she was again, on the cover of *Vogue*. She had made it, and I had made it.

She must have had a few little nips and tucks. She obviously had had her teeth capped. She must have had the bump on her nose removed, and she certainly would have had her hair straightened (it was sort of a black frizz in the early days), but the memory of that beautiful, extraordinary, green-eyed girl always floated through my mind in the dentist's office. Her name was Dayle Haddon. I mention this because, you know, dreams do come true.[*]

Now, fast-forward to the finale of my Parisian trip: I went to the airport, a bit sad to be leaving Paris, but resigned to the fact that that chapter of my life was over. I knew at the time that I'd never repeat that performance. But who should I be sitting next to in first class, flying back on Air Canada? None other than Dayle Haddon.

A good twelve years had passed since I had last seen her. She had become a movie star and a *Vogue* model; I was the *Patineur du Siècle*; and we both were sitting there in first class. The stewardess and even the pilot came back to meet me, say hello, and ask for an autograph. Yet from the economy section came hordes of French

---

[*] Haddon, while still in her teens, was the cover model of the 1973 *Sports Illustrated* swimsuit issue. She danced with the Bolshoi during its tour of Canada and began her film career opposite Nick Nolte in *North Dallas Forty*.

fans who knew who *she* was, so the score was even. We vowed to
meet again and exchanged private numbers and addresses, but it
was not to be. I never saw her again.

Artur Rubinstein

I was contacted by somebody who wanted to know if I would be
interested in doing a film with a famous French filmmaker who spe-
cialized in documentaries. It was to be a three-part film on the theme
of improvisation. He planned to combine great musicians and great
performers, thus creating a higher art. Nureyev and Baryshnikov
were involved. I'm not sure with whom they were partnered. However, I think that I pulled the plum out of the pie when I was coupled
with the great pianist Artur Rubinstein, who lived in Paris.

There were few people in the world I respected more. I
selected Chopin's Piano Concerto No. 2, a favourite of mine. Artur
Rubinstein did his bit in the recording studio. I filmed my part in
the Palais des Sports. Tired as I was that Monday, I was also exhila-
rated. Spontaneous expression is my forte. I'm probably one of the
worst people on earth to remember complicated steps, not because
I can't, but rather because I get bored and forget everything – which
used to infuriate Sergei Grinkov in Stars on Ice.

I wasn't paid to do the film, but Rubinstein sent me a five-gallon
cut-glass decanter of a priceless Guerlain perfume for men. You
could not use that much cologne in a lifetime, so before I left Paris,
I took a bath in it.

The other perk was dinner with the maestro. I was instructed
to arrive at the Élysée Matignon, a restaurant at the bottom of the
Champs Elysées. I made a point of being early. I was escorted to a
table for six at the centre of the room. There I sat by myself, await-
ing Rubinstein. The restaurant was rather full. It didn't take me long
to figure out that the who's who of Paris was present. Could that
really be Elton John over there? It was. And was that possibly Tina

Turner? *Mais oui.* Although I didn't know it at the time, Madame Nina Ricci of the perfume empire was there as well. Anybody who was there was a definite somebody on a certain scale of international celebrity.

Mr. Rubinstein arrived fifteen minutes late. As he passed through the entrance, the entire restaurant froze. The Elton Johns and the Tina Turners were forgotten in a New York second.

It was the first time that I had ever seen anybody with a conspicuous aura. I sensed something akin to a neon light beginning at his feet and encircling his body, like an all-encompassing halo. He appeared to me like someone from a different century, moving very slowly, wearing a long black opera coat, black bowler hat, and extravagant white scarf. He was accompanied by a much taller, attractive (yet not beautiful) woman with ginger hair, and by an older woman who, as it turned out, was his wife. (The ginger-haired woman, I subsequently found out, was his mistress.) Beside him, at least in my eyes, everyone else was nondescript.

Rubinstein appeared to have a blind side; one eye looked to the right while the other looked left. His ninety-two-year-old skin had a certain glow. He looked neither old nor frail, but rather like the last bloom of summer. Feature by feature, he was an ugly man. He had a large nose, tiny little raisin eyes that twinkled (at least one of them twinkled), and a receding chin beneath a small mouth set in an ever-present Mona Lisa smile. I had never seen anyone so beautiful in my life.

It dawned upon me that beauty is truly internal. Artur Rubinstein radiated a beauty that eclipsed that of all the other stars in the room. I might add that all the other stars gasped when he entered, but he came straight over and flopped himself down beside me. That certainly worked miracles for my ego.

I was prepared for anything, but what I got was not what I had expected. He was great and grand and humble at the same time. He sat down and took my hand in his hands, those world-famous hands, the hands that created magic on a global stage. He kept touching my hands and saying, "It's so nice to meet you. I love to watch skating, and I'm so flattered that you are performing to my music." He kept caressing me right up to the elbow with those hands. I can't remember the rest of that evening, but I felt that I was levitating off my chair. I ate very little.

As I left the restaurant and walked home that Paris night, I was higher than a kite on the sheer exhilaration of having come nose to nose with true greatness.

I never did see the film.

Stuart and Monte Hit Paris

Because I knew that the Paris dream wouldn't last forever and that the end was coming faster than I wanted, I broke down, raised the white flag, and invited and paid for my parents, Stuart and Monte Cranston, to fly over and stay with me in my apartment.

On the morning after one of my shows, I staggered into the bathroom. (One is always sore and stiff after a day of performing.) The mirror I used for shaving was on the back of the door. I turned towards what I thought was the mirror and began the ritual of my morning shave. I was shaving, but the reflection wasn't registering the fact. It dawned upon me that my mother had opened the door and was standing where the mirror should have been. Instead of looking at myself, I was looking at her face. It came home to me how truly I am my mother's son. In many ways, we are diachronic identical twins. Everything good about me, but particularly everything bad about me, comes directly from her.

My parents had arrived at a convenient moment, for a reason that was yet to be revealed. Paris being one of the main *entrepôts* of the world for tourists and travellers, who should pass through while my parents were in residence but Don Fraser and Candy

Jones, ex-members of The Ice Show? They had just won the world professional championships in Jaca, Spain – skating to music from *Company* yet again, the program that never lost a competition.

Don Fraser is a mensch, a tough little guy with a big heart. My mother always had a crush on him. At what must have been about three o'clock in the morning, the telephone rang. I never answered the phone if I could help it. My French at that point, and particularly at that time of night, was not at its best. I passed the phone to my mother. It seemed that Don had been tipsy in public and was languishing in the slammer. I was permitted to stay in bed while my parents darted off into the night to rescue the errant champion.

The Black Widow's Web

Holiday on Ice was the last really extravagant production. Of course, I saw myself as a serious skater and performer, but I also had an inclination to be over the top, profoundly melodramatic, and slightly absurd. That vehicle provided the perfect showcase.

Holiday on Ice combined the positive and the negative, the good and the bad, the wonderful and the ridiculous, not to mention the cruel. In some ways, it reflected everything that I was. I fit in somewhere between the trash of that show and the melodrama of certain operas. The pageantry, the exaggeration, the absurdity in opera – Holiday on Ice mimicked all of that in a cheaper fashion. It certainly was not for purists.

Europe, for the most part, doesn't have resident skating stars, so a Stars on Ice wouldn't make sense there. There are neither the kinds of fans who exist in North America nor the stable of skaters. Every European star, whether it's Oksana Baiul or Katarina Witt or Viktor Petrenko, has come to America. So Holiday on Ice manufactures a distinctive brand of glamour that appeals to the *Putzfrauen* and survives. I suspect it even makes money. It also goes where top skaters would fear to tread – such as the jungles of South America. It goes into areas where it's the only skating show in town. Holiday on Ice could never again in a million years hope to put one toe in the North American market.*

It was both a cut above and a cut below Ice Capades. I preferred the cut below. Slightly refined art is flawed in many ways. I like gourmet trash. I enjoy the bad much more than the almost good. Holiday on Ice as I knew it – much has changed since then – was a catch-all for freaks, gypsies, tramps, and thieves. Most of them had ulterior motives: to escape their grey lives. Whether it was a Czechoslovakian bus driver, a transvestite from Amsterdam, a Brazilian guitarist, or a South African soccer player, he might, like a barnacle, affix himself to the itinerant show and hold on for a while. It was an extremely diverse troupe. You could find just about anybody there.

The Americans (except for a certain breed, the tough ones) were known to the cast and crew as "tourists." Many Americans arrived at Holiday on Ice one day, tried the show the next day, and left on the third. North Americans could rarely adhere to the Spartan discipline. As for myself, I used the negatives, the inhumane treatment of people, as something to push against. (Of course, my lot was preferable to most.) My creed was, "I may die on the ice, but at least they will say I did a good job." If you died in one city, when the show moved on to the next, not only were you replaced in one second, but you also were forgotten in two.

The positive aspect was this: When you're young, travelling with a circus on ice, there is excitement. Gee, I'm in Vienna! Gee, I'm in Paris! Gee, I'm wherever I am! It's a passport to adventure. The truly

---

* Holiday on Ice began in North America in the 1940s. In 1973, Arthur Wirtz took over control of the North American productions, while Morris Chalfen retained International Holiday on Ice. The North American branch merged with Ice Follies, which then became Walt Disney's World on Ice.

smart people used the show to go to every museum in Europe, used it to meet interesting people, used it to their own advantage. The danger was that it could eat you alive. It was the black widow's web that you could never escape, because, whoever and whatever you were, the show was the safest place for you, the place where you could be with your own kind. It certainly attracted, in many ways, the lowest life form in the human gene pool.

Holiday on Ice was the twentieth-century answer to slaves in Roman galleys. It was so cruel, so unthinkably harsh, so mean, so inhumane, that no one has ever really disclosed the truth. I've never before been quite so outspoken about it, but it's so far removed from me now that I'm only being pristinely accurate.

At the time of my German tour, I was the featured skater with both Ice Capades and Holiday on Ice (unique in this century). In the American show, there would be a note on the bulletin board. "Dear skaters: The bus will pick us up at such and such a time; dinner will be served at such and such a time; we will all be staying at the such and such hotel, and these are the rates." They would give every possible consideration to the cast; make it easy for them to survive and get around.

Holiday on Ice was a little more rugged. After you had limped off the ice, say, in Frankfurt, after the third show on a Sunday night, the manager would say, "Next show Munich, eight o'clock, Olympiahalle." That's all you got.[*]

We scrambled like rats. Instead of getting *off* a sinking ship, it seemed as if we scrambled *onto* the sinking ship. Holiday on Ice had an evil device to force people to remain with the show. The cast was paid off, not in the city where they performed, but in the next city. Many people plodded on to avoid starvation. Once they were at the next stop, they thought, "Oh well, I might as well do another week."

---

[*] In today's Holiday on Ice, the arrangements are humane.

Many were little more than nuts and bolts in the great machine. Sometimes you'd be backstage, ready to go on, and suddenly you realized that the head girl in the white ostrich plumes was someone you didn't know. You would say, "Where's Jeannie?" Well, Jeannie never made it to this city. It didn't matter, because there was always another girl to fill that three- or four-thousand-dollar white ostrich-plume costume. The new girl might arrive in the city, be summoned by the show director, rehearse the number, and skate two shows – before she could even *think* of getting to a hotel.

There was a girl whose name I've forgotten who came from Red Deer, Alberta. She had sent a picture to the head office of Holiday on Ice in Amsterdam. She was accepted, and (oh, my God!) she was even sent an airplane ticket to Paris. She was excited. Obviously, coming from that provincial city, only in her wildest fantasies could she have imagined skating in an ice show in Paris.

She flew from Red Deer to Saskatoon, from Saskatoon to Winnipeg, from Winnipeg to Toronto, from Toronto to Montreal, and from Montreal to Paris. She was not met in Paris, but she had the address of the Palais des Sports. She had flown all through the night – I'm not exactly sure how long she'd been travelling – for someone to say to her, "So nice of you to come. You know, you can just fit into the back end of the caterpillar costume – and, by the way, we have three shows today."

She skated the three shows blind, in the back end of the cater-pillar, and then, as a total and complete stranger, had to find a hotel and come to terms with the reality of three more shows the next day. That was the glamorous life of Holiday on Ice.

If I sound bitter, I intend to be bitter, but I also see the whole experience as something remarkable. I don't know if *privileged* is quite the right word, but it was something I fell into that was the right thing at the right time. I am happy to have experienced it. But when I left – and I had been there, drawing thousands and thousands of people – no one said, "Thanks a lot. We really enjoyed having you." I was just one more person who had fallen off the vehicle as it went ploughing on to the next destination.

Many years later, Holiday on Ice celebrated its fiftieth anniversary in Nice, France. I would have loved to have seen so many people that I toured with all over the world. The management invited all their top stars, but not me. I guessed that it was an oversight, but when I phoned the office, they said, "We're not inviting you and paying your way, because you weren't a world champion." I was only the Skater of the Century.

So I told them to fuck off. I had been beyond the star level. I had been a major attraction in major cities and had generated thousands and thousands of dollars. It was perhaps a just and poetic *point final*. In their complete indifference to people who had given their bodies and souls, at least they were consistent from beginning to end.

The Millionaire

My thirtieth birthday, April 20, 1979, was among the best I ever had.

I had made a point of inviting certain people to come over to Paris for the occasion. Ellen Burka came from Toronto. Haig Oundjian, competitor to John Curry, my oldest skating friend and a good friend of the family, came from London. I've known Haig since I was eight years old, and we competed in the Olympics together in Sapporo in 1972.[*] He brought with him his cousin, Nigel Wray, and Nigel's fiancée. Nigel Wray today is among the most respected and financially successful entrepreneurs in Britain.

My mother came from Pakenham, Ontario, where she and my father lived after leaving Baie d'Urfé. Her trip was paid for by an intellectual groupie from Berlin who also attended. Ruth Dubonnet was certainly present as well.

---

[*] Oundjian was ninth in the world in 1970; sixth in 1971.

In those days, the phrase "jet set" was still fresh, and people were jetting in to see me. It wasn't Maria Callas and Aristotle Onassis, but it was good. I received flowers from all over the world, including a profusion of azaleas from Japan and three dozen flesh-coloured roses from Montreal. I had almost become the person I had always hoped to be – but I didn't really believe it, and I didn't feel any different. I was still the same old provincial little I-don't-know-what from suburban Montreal, but there I was.

I broke down and invited a large number of skaters, including members of the chorus. The comedian came, Atoy Wilson came, management came, and even, I think, some of the crew.

Then something happened that, in a way, changed my whole understanding of people. Ellen Burka brought an item that she had found on her basement floor: a cheque from Elva Oglanby, made out to me for a million dollars. Of course, Elva would have done that as a joke, but Ellen brought it and enclosed it in a birthday card.

When she handed it to me, instead of saying, "Oh, for God's sake, where did you get that? This is ridiculous!" and then explaining it, I opened the card without flinching and said, "Look! Look what this person has sent me!"

When many of my guests looked at the cheque and neither rejected nor made light of it, I said, "Oh, she's an heiress, and she wants me, but if she thinks that she can have me for a million, she's out of her mind." I embroidered the lie.

Well, everyone was somewhat flabbergasted. Some pooh-poohed it. Some said, "No, it's true!" Some didn't believe it but really did, and some believed it but really didn't. It became the main topic of conversation. I never did admit that the whole thing was a fraud.

The next day at the matinée, there was a queue at my dressing-room door. I didn't even recognize some of the faces. Everyone wanted a loan or a piece of my fortune. I conducted an interview with each person in the line. One man asked if he could have a Cadillac, because he had always wanted one, and it was only going to cost $12,000, so could he please, please, *please*? I didn't say, "Guys, you don't understand." I kept the charade going.

One of the principal skaters and his wife invited me out for lunch at a splendid restaurant, then hit me with, "Could we please have $25,000 [and, by the way, you are paying for lunch]?" The list of demands went on and on. It shocked me, and yet it was funny, but from the time that I received the million-dollar cheque, my position in the show changed. Some people never spoke to me again. Others wanted to be my new best friends. It affected my whole mystique. Because I was not close to anyone, I allowed them to think whatever they wanted to think. I followed one of my rules of life: neither confirm nor deny anything.

How Do You Solve a Problem like Marlene?

God had made a mistake with Marlene (I never knew his real name). He had the most Garboesque face, the finest features, a mane of hair, a perfect nose, and a body that could easily have replaced any Las Vegas showgirl's. He had long, muscleless legs and a wasp waist – yet he was a man.

Marlene, like many others, used Holiday on Ice to wear make-up legally. The queens in the show were always of artistic bent. Whereas Ice Capades and Ice Follies were appalled if male skaters (and even females) wore too much make-up, Holiday on Ice opted for a *laissez-faire* attitude. Many of the men in the chorus were infinitely more glamorous than the women. False eyelashes, glitter on the lipstick, rhinestones glued onto eyelids, elaborate shadings of powder and eye shadow: those were quite normal.

I think Marlene won first prize as the most over the top. When everything was on, he was gorgeous – if you happened to like men who dressed as women.

He skated in the chorus as a male. He couldn't wear a dress: he had to wear a pair of pants and a jacket. One morning while I was practising in my sweatsuit, Marlene was rouging up for the first of three shows. I had always openly disdained those people. I never spoke to them. To say that I acted with a certain *froideur* is an understatement.

When I returned from my practice, Marlene was fully made up. In my most sarcastic way, I said, "Like, why the fuck are you putting on all that make-up?"

He sat down, crossed his legs, and whipped out a cigarette. (He did have a certain ability to smoke a cigarette à la Bette Davis.) As he blew elegant smoke rings, he said, "Look, I am an entertainer. I am a fantasy for anyone in the audience. When the show starts, I eyeball the butchest man in the front row, and I stare at him. No matter where I am in the rink, I stare at him. Then, when the number's over, I blink my eyes with the electric-turquoise-blue eye shadow, and he gets a tremendous jolt – and it's really good for him, because he needs that excitement. It's people like us who give people like him a thrill. We make their banal little lives interesting. I do it for them."

I said, "You know, I think you're great, and I appreciate it. I'm sorry to have been so mean to you, and I understand everything. Let's be friends."

I had made a mistake. Yet those people find comfort in Holiday on Ice. They can't push groceries out of Loblaws. But they can be entertainers. With a modicum of talent in the skating department, they can be in showbiz. Holiday on Ice provided a stage and a little nest for many of those characters.

The Lobster's Lament

During the Paris production, a British boy named David became ill with the flu. He arrived in the morning and told the line captain, "Look, I'm really not feeling well. I can't do the first show, but I think that I could do the second and third."

The line captain said, "Put that bloody costume on right now. We don't accept missing a show on a three-show day. We'll dock your pay completely for all of Saturday."

"But I don't have any money."

"Take it or leave it. You're either going to do three shows or no shows."

That particular boy had to do the lobster part in "Alice in Wonderland." The costume was so huge, heavy, and unpleasant and so hot and sweaty that I'm sure it was difficult for him. But he did it – and he would have received no sympathy. No one would have said, "You know, David, I'm sorry. Gee, that's really too bad." It was every skater for himself.

Money and Sex in Holiday on Ice

Champions of the skating world had few professional career options in those days. Holiday on Ice, Ice Follies, Ice Capades, the Vienna Ice Revue, and some lesser productions were the only shows available. Today there are professional competitions and television specials, but then it was a case of, "Boy, am I lucky. I've been singled out as the lead in Holiday on Ice. Too bad *you're* not. Why don't you just go back into private life or teach skating or do whatever it is that you do?"

It was also the case that, no matter how big you were, they had you where they wanted you economically. Although I wasn't fired by Holiday on Ice, my contract wasn't renewed. Often, if a skater expressed a desire to stay with the company, they said in honeyed tones, "Why yes, we think you should – and, by the way, we're only going to pay you a fraction of what we gave you last year."

Those who were desperate enough stayed, and the following year their salaries declined even further. Ondrej Nepela, 1972 Olympic champion, fell to a very low level in Holiday on Ice. In spite of his Olympic credentials, he was paid just the tiniest smidge above chorus level. He was also one of the first skaters to die of AIDS.

Something that was always disconcerting, particularly for a North American in Holiday on Ice, was the casual homosexuality that permeated the show. It was entirely devastating for a naïve young man to arrive and discover (at least in his own mind) that he was the only straight boy in the chorus. A new boy on the line was new meat on the block, and he would be chased, harassed, and pursued. Somehow, some way, someone was going to seduce him.

Of course, for financial reasons, no chorus skater could live by himself, so the option was either to stay with another guy in the chorus (who was probably gay) or to stay with a girl. Although I believe that, for the most part, homosexuality is congenital, the environment was so thick, so abnormally normal, that sooner or later he was going to be seduced – and once he was, the word was out. Then the predators lost interest and waited for new blood to come to the dressing room.

Young heterosexual women, meanwhile, joined the show during the prime of their lives. They yearned for love and romance and sex, but they were flowers blooming in the desert. There weren't any men for them. They'd go out with the boys – to gay bars. They'd pretend to have fun, but while every boy would go home with a guy, those girls would go home alone.

Many of them developed a definite disdain for men, yet they could never show it because those men were their friends. Some actually grew to hate men, because it was men who took other men away from them. There were certainly many skaters with emotional scar tissue, even the stars.

Over and over again in Holiday on Ice, women skaters, including Olympic and world champions – one who comes to mind is Sjoukje Dijkstra – discovered that in order to love and marry someone, they had only one or two options: crew members such as the electrician or the animal trainer were prime candidates.

Ellen Burka attests (as does her daughter, Petra, who was in Holiday on Ice at the time) that Sjoukje Dijkstra, the Olympic champion, the two-time world gold medallist, the one the Queen of Holland came to cheer, ended up backstage at Holiday on Ice assisting with the toilette of the animals in her husband's mule act.

As for myself, I was as disciplined in the show, and as impervious to emotion and to outsiders, as I ever had been as a serious amateur. That was what I believed to be right for the time, and it may even have been the correct behaviour. Nevertheless, I always (though I never could admit it) hoped to find love – the kind that you hear about in songs, the kind that you read about, the kind that you see in movies. I was hoping to experience the emotion that, until that time, had been denied me, and I began to live a life that set the stage.

The Existential Dilemma

Within Holiday on Ice, I had a symbolic, structured, well-honed image that I had never allowed to slip through any indiscretion or scandal. People may have talked about who I was and what they thought I did. No doubt they speculated about my love life, my imagined or presumed affairs. Yet for years, even decades, it was *only* speculation, nothing more. In actual fact, there was little of any consequence to talk about.

Nobody knew whom I saw, what I did, or who my friends were. I was mysterious, elusive, a self-created enigma. I might have dined with Leonard Bernstein, but I might also have been going out with Yves Saint Laurent or Ruth Dubonnet. It was a world that was unknown to other skaters. They suspected (and I'm imagining this, because no one ever discussed these things with me) that I lived on a different planet, and my planet never collided with theirs.

That was rather painful for me because, even today, I'm lonely, and I have no family life. As the years have gone by, I feel, more than ever, a different kind of loss. The Olympic gold medal is long gone. Now I worry about other things. I feel sad that my family is so dysfunctional, that some members are so hostile to others. Once, I took it for granted. Once, I took it in stride. Once, I may even have cultivated some, or most, of the antagonism, and perhaps I was insensitive.

As you grow older, your family becomes more important, but I can't seem to make it right. Strangely enough, I'm no longer centre stage where the antagonism is concerned, but it bothers me greatly that there is so much turbulence and outright contempt.

My father was a very gentle man. The only thing that he really wanted in life was *not* success, as we usually measure success. All he wanted – *all* he wanted – was for his family to get along. We have never done that. The discord is so bitter that it seems to be past the point of no return. I'm afraid to initiate the healing process, lest I get bitten before I even begin.

The fact that I have no children of my own bothers me. As in the book *Charlotte's Web*, there are cycles of life. One starts to live vicariously through one's children, and to pass on knowledge to another generation. It saddens me not to be a part of that cycle.

Virtually every skater – it could be Robin Cousins, it could be me, it could be Scott Hamilton, it could be Brian Boitano – is an egomaniac. Let's face it. We are all stars in our own lives. I'm not saying that we're bad people, but on one level we are stupendously selfish.

The selfishness that I am trying to cure, certainly in the last decade, has absolutely nothing to do with money or possessions. I could quite happily give you whatever you wanted. I could give you a painting, money, a coat, a plane ticket. But don't ask for my feelings, and never ask for my time. That is what I *can't* give you, because I'm too selfish.

I was speaking to Oksana Baiul at the second AIDS benefit in Toronto. She told me that she did not like living in North America and that she loved Europe. She had no real friends, no real affection in her life, and no boyfriends. She was unhappy. Yet that afternoon she went out and bought $40,000 worth of Versace clothes. I don't have $40,000 to spend on Versace clothes these days, but when I was flying high, I might have done exactly the same thing. For one little moment, you freeze your emotions, and you think that money and clothes will make you happy.

I don't know Oksana well. I don't know if anyone can help to show her the real meaning of life. I also suspect that even if there had been someone to show me when I was in her position, I would have been reluctant to learn, because, when you're a star, *you* call the shots.

If you don't have a massive ego, don't even *think* about making it to the top. This is the age of television and publicity and fans and world championships and TV specials that are sometimes broadcast to 300 million people. You must have the components. You need the slickness of Paul Wylie, who is savvy and smart and amusing, a perfect instrument to entertain the press; or the extreme self-effacement and the "Gee, I'm getting too old for this game, and I don't have a triple Axel" of Scott Hamilton; or the far more coarse approach of Philippe Candeloro. We all have equal and massive doses of ego, and they are necessary.

However, life is a question of balance. You may lose during this decade but win during the next. This decade you're ugly, but you can become beautiful. This decade you're fat, but you can become thin. There are people who have screamed in their own silence at the injustices that they feel have been committed towards them during their skating careers. Some of them have gone for the second round. Those not-world-champions and those not-glittering-ice-stars have children and love, something so much more solid and meaningful. They win, and the winners lose.

Is it possible to have it all? Yes, but for the breadth of human understanding, you have to step out of the glass bubble. Whether or not I'm out of my bubble, I am aware of my limitations, and I am struggling, like every other person, to fix what went terribly wrong.

I have never had what I would call a serious relationship in my life. I created the cool veneer of a certain kind of performer. The older I got, the thicker the veneer became. If there were people I knew who really delighted me, I'd never realize it, because they couldn't penetrate my hard surface. It's too bad. I lost the game.

I have been luckier than many. I try to enjoy what I do have, and I also try, much more than ever before, to give pleasure to other people if I can, but I am so aware of my faults now that even if I try to do something nice, I feel guilty about it and wonder if I may be suspected of ulterior motives. I know that giving of oneself or giving materially can often be a selfish act.

I'm a different kettle of fish. I have been so removed from other people. I have had a life that is, by many standards, quite unusual; compared, for example, to living in Kalamazoo and driving a bus. I'm not saying that my life is better, but I'm saying that mine has been different – even in the context of the skating world. Who out there is really going to relate to me?

That, at least, is the mantle that I wore. I'm just so unusual as a person that no one can possibly know or understand me. That was a mistake, because it doesn't really matter what you are or what you do if you can open yourself to other humans, but you have to make that step. Now I feel that I'm ahead of the game, because I'm trying to undo the damage that was done. I can acknowledge what I am and what I've become (good, bad, or indifferent) because my values have changed, and what I want is different from what I thought or dreamed that I wanted.

Twenty years ago, even as I was skating my twelve shows a week, I was also getting up in the morning and painting passion-ately. I was sending work back to Canada to be sold in the galleries. I was visiting museums, then going home and trying to be a better artist because I had just seen Leonardo da Vinci.

Could that possibly be the energy that one has in massive doses when one is very young? I never questioned it, but that's what I did: two jobs at one time. Yet, as I was ploughing into the second and third months, my Parisian adventure (although unique, spectacular, and wonderful in many ways) was a desert in the land of emotions.

There I was, flying so high. I was, after all, the *Patineur du Siècle*. Why couldn't I have all the rest? In truth, I did not know how to go about getting it. To this day, I still don't.

Becoming Ruth-less

Ruth Dubonnet was driving me insane. I was beginning to lose my manners and a whole lot of other things. She was taking all the little bit of free time that I had. She did it because, like me, she was selfish. She wanted me for herself. Ruth was jealous of everyone and wouldn't allow me ever to be around younger women (or men). I was only permitted to hang out with people over seventy-five. Then she didn't feel threatened.

By the second month, when my rib started to heal, Ruth was encroaching upon my privacy. She had a key to my apartment. On the pretence of bringing me a croissant, she could barge in without ringing the bell. There wasn't any need for privacy, but the fact that I didn't have it began to bother me. On Friday nights, while other people in the show went out to discothèques or the Lido and did things that younger people did, Ruth knocked on my door and off we'd go. I was being dragged around by an eighty-year-old woman who at one time had been the queen of Paris. I was seeing it through her eyes, but something was missing.

On the upside, she always took me out to lunches that one of her rich friends was obliged to pay for. I saw the dining room in the Ritz at the Place Vendôme. I went to a totally chic place called le Relais in the Plaza Athénée. I dined with the Lanvins. I met Pierre Cardin. I went to the apartments of rich, savvy, cosmopolitan people. The experience left quite an impression on me. I didn't know that table settings could be so splendid. I didn't know that food could be arranged so beautifully. I didn't know that interiors could be so dramatic.

The designer for Josephine Baker took me to his apartment. Every single thing in it was black marble, fluorescent burnt orange, and white.

I went to Madame Carven's (of Carven fashions and perfume). Her apartment was a rhapsody of Eastern spice colours.

I went to dinner at the palace of one of the Rothschilds on the rue du faubourg Saint Honoré. I achieved a certain status at the dinner table – not because of being me, and not even because I was with Ruth Dubonnet, but because I was Canadian. The topic of conversation was Margaret Trudeau. What was she really like? Since I knew Margaret, I became the centre of attention. Something happened that was rare in those circles. The conversation melted from French to English.

I went to a designer's apartment on the boulevard Saint Germain, an Indonesian-style apartment with twenty-foot ceilings, smoke-grey walls, and more gilt than I had ever seen in my life. You sat on Indonesian pillows, engulfed in incense, and sipped peppermint tea at low tables.

There was another apartment on the place des Vosges that belonged to an actress who didn't speak a word of English. You entered an Arabian tent that she had imported from the desert, and you never did see the living-room walls or ceiling. The tent was full of divans, satin poufs, and perfumed I-don't-know-whats. I thought I was in the middle of *Arabian Nights*.

I saw the bathroom of the man who conjured all the perfume scents. It was madly impractical but sensationally original: the floor, ceiling, walls, and bathtub were all made of black mirror.

Ruth showed me an apartment that she had designed in the 1920s. There were two bathtubs joined side by side but facing in opposite directions, with a backgammon board inlaid between them.

These were the brush strokes and colours that started to form impressions in me. They were visually, artistically, and culturally a huge influence. I started to learn about taste and refinement in a way that one could never possibly begin to imagine in Toronto.

But I had absolutely no love in my life. My good buddy and travelling companion was an eighty-year-old, domineering, jealous woman, and I felt like a lucky zombie.

The time was coming for Ruth to go home. She realized that the climate had changed, that I was becoming recalcitrant. Anyway, she had her huge brownstone in New York. Her attitude was, "I have many friends who really adore me. If you like me, you'll want to spend every single second of your time with me."

I was trying to say, "I *do* like you, but I *can't.*"

The final day dawned: one more Monday to spend with her before she left the next morning for New York. It was my day off, and I didn't really want to pay court any more, but it was the last time, so okay.

Paris was grey and drizzly and cold. My body ached. I lay in bed until almost four o'clock in the afternoon. I might have eaten a tiny bit of yogurt and fruit. I was so tired from the weeks and weeks of giving every last smidge of energy and passion that I had, and I was going to give a bit more to her.

I wore a pair of grey flannel slacks, grey socks, a grey casual sweater, and a grey jacket, because I was feeling emotionally grey. I walked down the boulevard Saint Germain en route to the Café de Flore, made famous by Stein, Picasso, and Hemingway. Three of us were to have a drink there before going to dinner. The third was Thomas Quinn Curtiss, a very pleasant man, the expatriate theatre critic for the New York *Herald Tribune*. He was a brilliant and eccentric fellow who had written a generous article about me.

I was late. Because it was raining, I walked in looking like a drowned rat. Ruth and Tom were sitting across from one another at a little round marble table, so I had to sit one table over, facing an empty chair and the sidewalk beyond. Their conversation was brisk and chirpy. I was constantly being thrown remarks that I didn't parry well. I was too bloody tired.

It dawned upon me just then that the gentleman in a trench coat and scarf sitting nearby with a newspaper in front of his face was listening to our conversation. It was in his body language. Our eyes never met. He was dark and Mediterranean (I thought maybe Cypriot or Turkish). I became two people at once. I fulfilled my social obligation to Ruth and Tom, yet somehow stretched my antenna diagonally towards the mystery man behind the newspaper.

If you can catch my drift, a sort of energy was flowing between the tables, but not in the direction of Thomas Quinn Curtiss and Ruth Dubonnet.

Precisely then, the entire Japanese skating team walked into the Café de Flore. The team was headed by an old friend, an ex-competitor of 1972, Yutaka Higuchi. I waved. We chatted. His group went to the far end of the restaurant.

Ruth was becoming fidgety. Tom was not going to dine with us, and Ruth wanted to leave. "Let's go," she said. I got up. She got up. Thomas Quinn Curtiss got up and made for the door.

I took it upon myself to go back to the Japanese team and have a farewell chat. On my table, there happened to be a piece of paper and a ballpoint pen. Like a beast operating on intuition, I snatched them as I headed to the Japanese table. While saying my goodbyes, I wrote a note: *ce soir*, my telephone number, and *neuf heures*.

I walked out of the Café de Flore and never looked back, but the tiniest little scrunched-up ball of paper plopped onto the empty table where I had been sitting.

Ruth and I got into a cab and went to some sort of fishy restaurant on Saint Germain. The conversation became tedious, and I became even more tired. Ruth clearly wanted to have a fight, or wanted to play, well into the late hours of the night. I wanted to go home.

"Let's go to the Moulin Rouge," she suggested. "Let's go to the Paradis Latin. Let's go and drink champagne."

"Let's go home," I said. "I'm so tired."

"What do you mean, you're so tired? It's my last night. How ungrateful of you. How can you do this to me? I would never have gone out with you if I hadn't thought –"

I said, "Please, *please*, don't do this to me. I just want to go home. I just want to leave. I'm tired."

Well, we didn't drink champagne, and we didn't go to the Paradis Latin, but we did have a fight. We got into a cab. All the while, I was glancing at my watch. When the cab arrived at the door of 24, rue de Bellechasse, I didn't want a prolonged hug hug, kiss kiss, when will we meet again? I wanted out. She wanted a passionate, romantic, eighty-year-old farewell. We hugged. We kissed. I thanked her.

As I ran into my apartment, the telephone was ringing.

I answered the phone. I spoke in a perfectly calm voice. All the tension that I had experienced for the last two months had dissipated when Ruth Dubonnet finally gave me back the key to my apartment.

I said, *en français*, "Where are you? I'm ten minutes away. Why don't you drop over?"

The doorbell rang.

Last Tango

Not many words were exchanged. The person whom I will call J spent the night. We talked in the morning.

Whatever it was, whatever happened, there was a kind of affection or warmth or *something* that I needed at the time. It had, perhaps, not a lot to do with sex. It had to do with something else, another need.

An affair started, you might say, yet there were rules. As in the film *Last Tango in Paris*, only first names were exchanged. He withheld his telephone number. There were all sorts of restrictions. It was a while before I discovered what he did. He was a South American ambassador who lived in Paris with his wife and kids. Perhaps that was what appealed to me most: the intrigue of a forbidden rendezvous. We snatched moments whenever we could. We met once or twice a week, and all of a sudden the dreary Paris spring became brighter.

Paris is quite disgusting. Everywhere you look, people are in love. I had found it to be offensive and depressing, until, of course, I had my own little dose. Suddenly I, too, had something that every other person in the Parisian streets had: *romance*.

The ambassador went on a diplomatic mission to Poland. He was away for about three weeks as Holiday on Ice wound down. He came back. We spoke on the telephone. We got together. He announced to me that he was very sorry, but he had met somebody else.

I took it in my stride. We continued to see one another, but we never slept together after that. He said, "Well, you know, there's no future. You're going away in a week, and I'll never see you again. What's the point of becoming involved?"

It made sense, but it wasn't what I wanted to hear.

I had one free day before I had to go back to Toronto. J said, "I would really like to see you before you go, so could we please meet tonight? Let's go to the Paradis Latin." I said that would be fine. "And we could have dinner afterwards." That would be fine, too.

Now the one thing that J hated about me more than anything was what he regarded as my inability to be punctual. I waited the whole day in my little apartment, getting ready and looking forward to the evening. I allowed a good one and a half hours for a twenty-minute cab ride. It was around six o'clock, or maybe it was seven. I could *not* get a cab. All of a sudden, I was slightly concerned, then more concerned. Then I became desperate. I knew that if I were late, the evening would be a shambles. Somehow, some way, I did get a cab, but of course I was late. The words shot through my mind before I uttered them: "I'm sorry I'm late. I'm sorry I'm late." But the damage was done.

"Well, you've ruined everything," he said. "The show has already started. Now we can't go in."

I had been through three and a half months of twelve shows a week. I was fragile. I was worn out. I had no more passion. I had no more energy. I had no more strength.

I said, "I understand what you're saying, and I'm so sorry." Then I turned and took off as fast as I could into the Paris night, and I never looked back. First I ran. Then I slowed down and walked. I was crushed.

When I got to my apartment, the telephone started to ring. It rang all night, but I didn't answer it.

In the morning, I grabbed my bags and went to the airport. As I was flying across the ocean with Dayle Haddon, I thought to myself that it had been a poetic way for an artist to end a sojourn in Paris that had been so Parisian in every way.

That episode was entirely out of character for me. I blame Ruth Dubonnet completely. She had the eyes of a hawk. She knew everything and was fifty times smarter than I was. I think that the real kick for me was that the affair was begun right under her nose.

The last time that I saw Ruth Dubonnet, I was chasing her down Fiftieth Street in my *Firebird* costume because she had driven me into a rage. I ran her out of the theatre and barely made my entrance onstage at Radio City. I'm not sure if it was unusual for that part of the world, but as far as I know, Fiftieth Street and the Avenue of the Americas had never before seen a firebird on skates chasing an eighty-year-old woman down the street.

6

Tokyo

I had bought a house at 217 Carlton Street in Toronto, and I was looking forward to seeing what all the money I had been making in Paris was doing for it. I had become addicted to red and green. Without going into detail, at that particular phase of my life, my house was a temple to red and green.

I had been back in Toronto for a short time when the telephone rang, and I was summoned to Tokyo. Japan is reputed to be one of the hardest markets in the world to crack. Shows that were a hit on Broadway – *A Chorus Line*, for example – died in Japan, while others, like *Beatlemania*, a minor hit on Broadway, became block-busters in Tokyo. Ticket queues wrapped themselves around sky-scrapers. Nobody knew how to tap Japanese gold. It was hit or miss. With Holiday on Ice in the summer of 1979, it was far more of a miss than a hit.

I was ensconced in a B-class hotel in an area that even the Japanese had never heard of. Harumi was in the dockyards, completely uninhabited by humans. There was a baseball diamond and a large, isolated, covered stadium that was to be the site of Holiday on Ice for the duration.

The Japanese culture embraces something that North Americans have never entirely understood: the "saving face" syndrome. You must stick to your word, no matter how awful the situation. Get the hell out and cut your losses is unheard of in Japan. Once you commit, you commit, and everyone involved has to save face. We were booked in Japan for ten weeks, and we stayed for the full ten weeks – which was about nine and a half weeks too long. Whoever had advised Holiday on Ice was so completely out of touch that even neophytes in the business could have figured it out. Nevertheless, we marched consciously to our doom.

On opening night, the nicely papered house gave us the illusion that we were about to repeat the success of Paris.[*] The building never again held that many people collectively over ten weeks. Of course, business was terrible for a reason. The silly mistake for a company that seemed to know the business better than anyone else was that they had booked skating in the middle of the summer. A fool knows that skating does not enter anybody's head in the heat of summer, particularly in a non-skating country like Japan.

Besides, the scheduled performance times were absurd. Show time was either at ten o'clock in the morning or at six o'clock in the evening. It was not exactly holiday time. The Japanese worked – and anyone who worked couldn't get to that ridiculously remote location by six o'clock.

Occasionally, if they gave away tickets and there were more than 100 people in the 10,000-seat building, backstage we all started to

---

[*] A "papered house" is a theatre (or similar venue) that one has filled with spectators by distributing free tickets.

get terribly nervous – which was so silly, considering that several months earlier, we had skated three shows a day for full houses of 6,000 without the tiniest tremble of nervousness. In Tokyo, we were used to audiences of under twenty. The cast could have pooled their salaries and paid the audience not to come. You might think that I am exaggerating (something that I'm known for), but, on this particular point, I am not.

The *Toronto Star* reporter Sid Adilman, who was married to a Japanese woman, interviewed me at the Imperial Hotel in Tokyo. His article ended with a quote that got me into trouble with Holiday on Ice. I said to him, ". . . and business is so bad here that if the phone rings in the office and someone asks, 'What time is the show?' the pat response is, 'What time can you come?'"

Holiday on Ice did not think that was funny. I simply thought, "Well, it's true."

Earthquake!

The second day after the opening, I was lying in bed in a T-shirt and underwear when, all of a sudden, my bed began to shake, then the walls. I didn't have to be told that it was an earthquake. As smart as I was, I jumped out of bed, rushed out of my room, plunged down ten flights of stairs, ran into the lobby, and continued on into the street. The building did not fall down. When it seemed to me that the shaking had stopped, I yelled from the parking lot, "Excuse me, but didn't we just have an earthquake?"

"We have earthquakes every day," people assured me.

The fact that I was outside in my underwear at ten o'clock in the morning then dawned upon me. I slunk into the hotel and returned to my room somewhat wiser.

The Second (and Absolutely Final) Monkey Story

My running feud with the resident chimpanzee was resumed in Tokyo. It was not the same animal that had affixed itself to my fur-draped shoulders in Vienna. Nevertheless, this chimpanzee and I vied for practice time. For some reason, I always got the second-rate slot. Several times the creature spotted me in the seats as I waited for her to finish her sit spin. She invariably scrambled across the ice in my direction. I wasn't sure why, but I always assumed that the objective was to attack.

The building in Tokyo was rather horrible. The place where the audience sat was fine, but backstage was prison-like grey cement. The muggy heat of Tokyo in the summer is insupportable, and often there were two-inch bugs crawling on the cracked walls of the carbuncle that was my doorless dressing room. Whenever possible, I (and many others) stripped almost naked while we waited for our numbers, and delayed putting on our costumes until the last possible moment. A lot of time was spent in the carbuncle reading a book in one's jock-strap.

The day of the final simian showdown arrived. I was sitting reading *Confessions of a Mask* by Yukio Mishima when, completely out of the blue, the baby chimpanzee skittered into my dressing room, scurried between my legs, scuttled under my stool, and hid at the back of my carbuncle. That in itself wasn't too upsetting – until the mother chimpanzee ran in looking for baby.

She snarled, bared her fangs, and charged me. Then she reached her hairy mitt into my jock-strap, grabbed my testicles, and started to squeeze them. She didn't squeeze them hard, but sort of played with them, shall we say. I let out a shriek that easily exceeded in volume anything Pavarotti could have accomplished. Many members of the chorus assumed that a terrorist attack had been launched backstage, since there had been a number of terrorist incidents at the time.

With the mother chimpanzee holding my testicles, the baby behind me, and the trainer in hot pursuit, I said through clenched teeth, "Get this animal away from me!"

The trainer replied, "I can't. It's too dangerous."

And it *was* dangerous, because the chimpanzee saw me as an obstacle to getting to her baby. My memory blanks out at this point, but I had the general impression that she was going to eat the testicles – at least, that was what I feared.

Somehow, the baby was coaxed out from its spot. When that happened, *maman* let go of my testicles and the trainer was in control again.

I gathered enough composure to run out of my dressing room (with my testicles still hanging out of my jock-strap) directly to the office, where I demanded that either the chimpanzee go or I go, but the two of us could not possibly continue to perform in the same show.

The management made something of a concession. The chimpanzee was never again to be allowed on the loose. Henceforth, *maman* was always tied up. Every single night, that chimpanzee went for me, straining against her rope, knowing that I had been the one who had cost her her freedom. I always made sure that I was *just* out of reach.

The trainer and I were really not on speaking terms. However, one day at the coffee stand I asked him, "Can you tell me why that chimpanzee grabbed my testicles?"

He said, "Chimpanzees like anything smelly."

The Pachinko Wizard

The show in Japan was one of the hardest I'd ever done. The ice conditions were horrible. It was a kind of ice that exists only in tropical climates: hard granite with a layer of sticky frost. It impeded any kind of glide, and was, in quality, somewhere between real ice and the Teflon substitute.

It was week after week of two shows a day with no one in the audience. I often coaxed cast members to peer through the flimsy, disintegrating grey curtains. If they could please just watch me, maybe I'd try harder. Near the end, I had to pay them.

The oldest show poodles in the history of ice were brought together in Japan. Some had been in Holiday on Ice for twenty-five years, a professional life span unheard of in North America. That particular company was made up of anyone who could be persuaded to go to Tokyo, in the pollution and heat of summer, to skate in the dockyards.

The *Patineur du Siècle* was out of his milieu. I was lonely and isolated, and I became increasingly introverted. I spoke only when spoken to and had all my meals alone. Perhaps this was appropriate. I was perceived as being just as strange as I perceived my fellow cast members to be. I timed my arrival at the arena down to the second and appeared just as the show started. As the last note of the music played, I was already fleeing the building.

I'd go to my hotel to change into a pair of shorts. Then I performed a ritual that persisted for the entire ten weeks. I walked from the dockyards into the Ginza, a hike that took slightly less than an hour. I walked from ice cream stand to ice cream stand, buying green tea ice cream, finishing one in time to have another. That was my green tea ice cream promenade.

I didn't wander around the Ginza, because I knew exactly where I was headed, to Tokyo's remedy for people who can't afford psychiatrists: the pachinko parlour. Pachinko is one of Japan's national pastimes. The parlours are similar to pinball arcades, but the machines are perpendicular. You go to the counter and get a basket containing dozens of little silver ball bearings that you put, one at a time, into the top of one of the machines. They trickle down through little wheels, ledges, pins, and holes, and if a ball bearing gets through the maze, a rush of ball bearings comes out to replenish your supply. If a bearing doesn't quite make it, and is eaten up by one of the electric tongues, you may find that you've run out of ball bearings.

Conversation is impossible. All you hear are thousands of ball bearings making their way through mazes. It is therapeutic in the short run, like shock therapy. After playing pachinko for an hour or two, I came out numb, paralysed, and at peace. Then I retraced my steps back to Harumi, often succumbing to more green tea ice cream.

In the long run, the more rattled I became as a result of playing pachinko, the more depressed I became – and the more lonely. Although Tokyo had many attractions, I felt that I was in the right place at the wrong time.

The Fortunetellers

I have consulted fortunetellers three times in my life: once in Montreal when I was fourteen, once in Tokyo when I was thirty, and recently in Mexico when I was forty-five. Yutaka Higuchi, the Japanese skater who provided my alibi in the Café de Flore, enabled me to visit the fortunetellers of Tokyo who sit in lotus position holding little gas lights over which you extend your palm. They read it without looking at your face. I hadn't gone alone because I needed an interpreter.

Remarkably, the Japanese fortuneteller told me exactly what the East Indian had told me when I was fourteen in Montreal. He said, "This is an unusual hand. I haven't seen one of these for many years. This hand has on it the cross of fame in sport. It suggests world renown in sports, national renown in art" – exactly what I had been told before. He went on to say that my real talent, my real contribution, would be teaching. Something equally revealing: he had never before seen a hand so completely devoid of love or emotion. It was blank. Up until that time, and even today, that remains true – although I'm fighting it.

He also told me that I was too negative with people. Because of my inherent talents, I was too hard on others. I expected them to be like me, and I imposed the same standards and discipline on them.

"But when you have been given that ability," he said, "you can't expect the same thing from other people."

I had rarely spoken to anyone in the Holiday on Ice cast. After I left the fortuneteller, I was determined to be more polite.

Maya Plisetskaya

I had one encounter in Tokyo that affected my life profoundly.

There was a program at the downtown concert hall called Ballet Festival. Nureyev and Baryshnikov weren't there, but truly every other dancer of renown was on the bill: Vladimir Vasiliev and Ekaterina Maximova from the Bolshoi; Alicia Alonso, a blind prima ballerina from Cuba; Patricia McBride and Cynthia Harvey from the United States; Jennifer Penney, Carla Fracci, and more. The program also featured the sublime Russian prima ballerina Maya Plisetskaya, the Soviet Union's answer to Margot Fonteyn.

In reading a biography of Plisetskaya, I learned that she had undergone great difficulties. She was Jewish at a time when being Jewish in the arts in the Soviet Union was not cool. When I found out that she was on the bill, my memory was tweaked. I remembered my dear friend, the lawyer who had bailed me out of The Ice Show, Stanley Plesent – or Stanley Plisetskaya, as he turned out to be. Maya was his cousin.

After all the other stars had danced, it was Maya Plisetskaya's turn. At the time, she was nearly fifty-five. She gave a lesson in theatrics, a lesson in stardom, a lesson in enchanting an audience.

After the performance preceding hers, the applause was allowed to recede to a deafening silence. We sat for what seemed like a considerable time (I suspect it was about two minutes) while every light

in the room was extinguished. Not even the exit lights were left illuminated. As we sat in blackness, it was natural to expect that something incredible was about to happen. We were primed for it, and
something incredible *did* happen.

As the music began, a spotlight perhaps two or three feet in
diameter started to move slowly across the stage from left to right.
Then, instead of disappearing, it reversed direction. It swept to
centre stage, hovered there, then got larger and larger. The curtains
opened in a swag to reveal Maya as a swan, dancing with her back
towards the audience in front of a huge oval mirror. I recall a liq-
uidity of arms. The rest of her body was stationary on pointe.

Maya held that position as the curtain drew apart. Then she
turned and faced the audience. Her body was unlike anything I'd
ever seen. She had a certain proportion of torso, leg, and head, a car-
riage and presence, that set her apart from all the other dancers. I
discovered, years later, that her body was precisely like the
Hieronymus Bosch depiction of Eve in *The Garden of Earthly Delights*,
painted circa 1504.

As Maya began to dance, Jorge Donn, an Argentine dancer, ran
onto the stage wearing an electric-blue silk cloak that fluttered at
least thirty feet behind him. He crossed the stage, circled Maya
once, then vanished. Maya continued balancing on pointe, making
swanlike movements in front of the mirror. Jorge then ran out in an
imperial-Chinese-yellow silk cloak and circled again with the cloak
billowing behind him. He returned a third and last time in a
crimson cloak of identical design and length. As he circled, the cloak
fell to the floor, revealing a loincloth.

Every time Jorge appeared with the cloak, he tore off a piece of
Maya's clothing. First, he ripped off her swan sleeves. When he
returned in yellow, he ripped off her tutu. When he appeared in red,
he ripped off the bodice of her dress, revealing her in a flesh-
coloured bodysuit painted with red and blue lines (which suggested

to me that she was naked, but you could see her veins). My interpretation of Jorge's actions was that the male had stripped the female of any defence, disguise, or façade, reducing her to the essence of womanhood. Jorge, in a loincloth, represented the essence of masculinity – without either of them actually being naked.

I can't remember Maya's dance. However, when she finished, she took bows the likes of which I had never seen in my life. Each deserved another. The bows themselves became a performance. That fifty-four-year-old prima ballerina had flaming red hair and a head that accentuated her profile. The way her neck was set back, her head appeared to be mounted on a pedestal. First, she honoured the Japanese public by affecting a Japanese style of bow: hands on the knees, bending from the waist to both sides of the stage. As the applause receded, she suddenly became Tina Turner. She stroked her hair, strutted across the stage, and froze in an incredible pose. With her back to the audience, she became living sculpture.

The audience screamed and yelled, but I was the loudest. The corners of my mouth got stiff and sore from smiling.

Melodrama is rarely perceived as high art, but Maya's bows, perfected over an entire career, were incredible. Her acceptance of flowers by embracing them, kissing them, dropping them into the orchestra pit, and throwing them out into the audience spoke more than words ever could. I felt as though I had been electrified. I had seen greatness at close hand, surely in a way that I had never seen it before.

Because of my connection to Stanley Plesent, the Japanese woman I was with encouraged me to go backstage to meet Maya. After the thirty minutes of bowing, I had cold feet. With some urging, and with a certain trepidation, I slunk backstage. The first person I encountered was a dancer I had met in New York, Cynthia Harvey. As we chatted, I mentioned that I was there to see Maya. She blanched and said, "Toller, even *I* can't speak to Maya Plisetskaya.

None of us do. The only thing we can do is take class with her."

Undeterred, I continued on my quest. Maya was taking her thirtieth or thirty-fifth bow. An entourage of supporters, groupies, managers, masseurs, and wardrobe people hovered in a cluster behind the curtains. I could see the dancer's impeccable silhouette. My throat ran dry, and my heart started to pound.

When she emerged between the curtains, the face that I saw was something I shall never forget. Onstage, she had exuded agelessness. However, the fact that I could now detect her age and see her make-up (it had heavy red lines, and there were red dots on the bridge of her nose) made her even more stupendous. I was looking at a Leonardo da Vinci under a magnifying glass – and I wasn't disappointed.

My Japanese interpreter ran to another interpreter helping Maya off the stage. Although there were large numbers of people around the star, the interpreter explained who I was, what I was doing there, and how I was connected to Stanley Plesent.

Maya stepped out of her entourage, ran to me, and grabbed my hand – my trembling hand. I spoke in English to my interpreter, who translated to Japanese. My words were then translated from Japanese to Russian.

What Maya did next is nearly indescribable. Words sully the vision. She danced a conversation. Don't ask me how, but she thanked me for coming backstage; she wanted me to say hello to Stanley Plesent for her; she loved skating, and she was happy to meet me. She *danced* it!

I left, five feet off the ground, and didn't return to earth for several weeks. I was thrilled. I was rendered speechless. I was in awe.

Maya Plisetskaya taught me two things: one, you can do whatever you do for as long as you wish to do it, providing you are prepared to pay the price; two (and this is one of the great basic truths of anything choreographic, compositional, or artistic), it is not what you do but how you do it.

In my B-class Japanese hotel during that wretched run, I had been seriously contemplating retirement. After meeting Maya Plisetskaya, I discarded the idea. I knew that I could skate as long as I wanted to.

A Japanese Tragedy

To amuse myself and to escape the boredom of the unpleasant Holiday on Ice experience, I made contact with Japanese skaters whenever they came to the building. Occasionally, after the show, they put on their skates, and I helped them. This was the case with two handsome sons of an international skating judge. They were one year apart in age – perhaps eleven and twelve. I was charmed by them, but I didn't speak Japanese.

The parents asked me if I would like to share a meal with them in their house. They picked me up, and we drove to a modest house in the Ginza. When the door opened, I thought, "How strange that there isn't any furniture." There were straw mats and perhaps a chair, table, and pillow. I subsequently learned that the house was probably worth three million dollars. *Nobody* lives in a house in downtown Tokyo. I was encountering extreme affluence, although it seemed to me to be abject poverty.

After the meal, they encouraged me to do a drawing on their dining-room wall with a felt pen. I drew a harlequin skater at least six feet tall, and I signed it.

The judge wanted his boys to become great skaters. Whether he was in love with her or not (I was told by Japanese sources), he had married his wife for the length of her legs. He wanted long-legged skaters. She produced two long-legged boys, which was even better.

I learned that the father had strict ideas about the kind of skaters he wanted his boys to become. At great expense, he insisted that they skate in an empty arena, that they never skate with their contemporaries, nor take lessons from a teacher. He was their teacher.

I was afforded the privilege of working with them because he felt that I, the renegade, might be a positive influence. I never saw the boys again, but I have a little photograph of them in my address book. On it I wrote, "These two boys will become world champions one day."

The years went by, and I didn't hear from them. When I asked about them, there was no answer. I learned later, from a source I dare not disclose, that what happened was tragic. The man went away to Europe for several months on a business trip, and the boys were left to train by themselves. Apparently they didn't really *want* to skate by themselves, so they invited other skaters to join them for their regular session (which probably, at the time, cost three hundred dollars an hour). The father came back and discovered that they had been influenced by other skaters. Although I was not told this in so many words, it is my belief that their father broke their legs, and they never skated again.

Sayonara, Pachinko

At the end of the Tokyo adventure, my Japanese fans presented me with a used pachinko machine. I was happy about that. It was with my other baggage when I went to the airport. Getting to Narita airport at rush hour is hopeless. I have never seen traffic like it. I thought that only if I walked on the hoods of the cars would I have a chance of making my plane. Somehow the jam cleared up, and I got there on time.

When I found out that my overweight baggage (I'd done a lot of painting) was going to cost more than two thousand American dollars, I left my lovely pachinko machine at the JAL counter for some lucky person to find. I could not take it with me. I hope my benefactors don't find out. I'd like them to think of me playing pachinko and remembering Japan.

It was while I was in Japan that I discovered Japanese aesthetics.

I discovered a different way of serving food: less is more, and infinitely more attractive. I discovered the beauty of the Japanese people, who, if appreciated in the context of oriental aesthetics, are the most beautiful people in the world. I discovered the Japanese concept of body hygiene. We have baths to scrub off the dirt, while they scrub off the dirt and then have the bath. I was impressed, too, by the texture and quality of their hair, which was eclipsed only by the perfection of their smiles and their teeth.

I had the strangest feeling in Tokyo. I sensed that I had been there before. It was like a hand fitting into an old glove. Japan is very familiar to me – even in the oriental flair that so many of my paintings have. I attribute that feeling to a reincarnated life.

7

Beijing

Dick Button can lay claim to a number of innovative skating ideas.[*] At a particular time in the 1980s, he played a major role in the skating world. He had the money to support his ideas, and the credibility which afforded him entrée into many international projects – including China.

One day in 1981, my telephone rang. Would I like to go to Beijing? Of course I jumped at the chance. There was to be a televised documentary incorporating live performances and behind-the-scenes footage of the skaters visiting historical sites. Ours was to be one of the first Western contingents to enter China, because skating,

---

[*] Button, five-time men's world champion and twice Olympic champion (1948 and 1952), formed Candid Productions. He produced many professional skating events, including the made-for-television Beijing exhibition.

unlike, say, the Beatles, had been culturally approved by the state. Many other sports and forms of entertainment were neither officially recognized nor welcomed.*

Being the stars that we were, we expected and got first-class tickets. I flew to New York from Toronto to join the other skaters for the trip to Tokyo. There we changed to China Air for a five-hour flight to Beijing, and to this day, I don't think that I've ever experienced comparable luxury. We were handed piles and piles of Chinese souvenirs. One stewardess offered to massage my feet. Another asked if I'd like a shampoo. Really, by any standard, it went beyond the call of duty.

To me, Beijing was rather forbidden and ominous and military and Communist. Don't look at anybody cross-eyed or you might end up doing a repair job on the Great Wall of China.

We arrived in mid-afternoon. I was delighted to discover in Tiananmen Square an enormous, absolutely monstrous crowd of people to greet us. I had not realized that our fame had spilled across the borders of China to that degree. Perhaps it hadn't. I was distressed to learn later that they were not there for me, nor for JoJo Starbuck, nor for John Curry. Someone important had just died, and we were gate-crashing the funeral.

We arrived at our modern, first-class hotel. I suspect that it has (but I hope that it hasn't) changed its name by now. The correct spelling I cannot be sure of, but it was pronounced "the Fuck-Sing Hotel." I relished the very thought of staying there and sent post-cards to many people, just letting them know that I was having a lovely time at the Fuck-Sing Hotel.

The first thing one does after a trip of that length is go to one's

---

* "International Skating from Peking" was televised by HBO in July 1981. The troupe of which Toller was a part was the second contingent of its kind. An earlier, unrelated exhibition was broadcast on ABC's "Wide World of Sports" on December 27, 1980, as "U.S. Figure Skaters in China."

room to sleep. If I had been asked for my immediate impressions of China, I couldn't offer them. They evaporated the moment my head hit the pillow. I do remember my first impression when I woke up the next day. (Actually, I'm not sure what day it was. I may have lain in bed for more than twenty-four hours.) I opened my windows and saw an enormous city with hundreds, if not thousands, of apartment buildings. They were all the same. They were all painted an odious urinal grey. My impression was that Beijing had no colour whatsoever. All Chinese people wore grey Mao suits. The shade of grey didn't vary. The overwhelming greyness of Beijing even muted the blue of the sky.

Bells rang throughout the city, signalling the time for t'ai chi. Grey, somnambulant figures performed movements the likes of which I had never seen.

One had a sense, early in the trip, that we were the ugly Americans. Probably the ugliest of all was Dorothy Hamill, not because she isn't a raving beauty, but because her face, her jewels, her hair, her make-up revealed an affluence that the people of Beijing could scarcely comprehend. They could not relate to her, I suspect, as a human, because she was so far beyond their experience. Instead of feeling good, as I would have in Moscow (where one can stroll around Red Square and feel superior in Western clothes), I felt guilty and decadent in Beijing.

John Curry, the 1976 Olympic champion and a self-professed enemy of mine, was part of the troupe.[*] For everyone else in the group, having the two of us on the bill virtually ruined the trip. At the time, JoJo Starbuck was a partner to John Curry in his ice show. She had to cling to John professionally and kowtow to his every whim, but my impression is that she did not like him. (Admittedly,

---

[*] Elva Oglanby wrote in *Black Ice* that at the 1975 world championship, John, in self-enforced isolation, quit speaking to Toller, who was baffled.

this is not the way she remembers it.)* She preferred me. So JoJo ended up between a rock and a hard place. To be honest, with John and me, the relationship was far more dire than a rock and a hard place. JoJo was caught between a land mine and a grenade, and at any second – well, you just never knew.

Every day, every hour was ruined by John's *froideur* towards me and my *froideur* towards John. As hot and muggy as Beijing was, each day was chillier than the last. If I wished to address Lord Curry, I needed an intermediary. Face-to-face conversations were out of the question. JoJo was the designated diplomat whose trip was completely destroyed by having to perform in this capacity. Yet there was also something very funny about it, as I realized many years later.

I would have spoken to John, but he didn't speak to anybody. He did not like himself – perhaps he even loathed himself – and somebody had to be punished for it. I think that one of the few occasions when John and I talked (which may have been our only conversation of the decade) was when we both agreed that, from a cultural standpoint, the Chinese adventure was among the best skating trips we'd ever had, and weren't we lucky?

We were all taken to a large Madison Square Garden sort of rink, a grey temple to sports that happened to have had ice installed. We were still out of whack because of the jet lag: dizzy, not feeling our legs under us. Even though I had slept so long, I felt tired. Then when we arrived at the practice session, we found 23,000 people

---

* Starbuck explains, "I dearly loved John. He meant a lot to me and impacted my life quite a bit. He opened doors and influenced me in wonderful ways artistically. . . . I respected and revered John for many reasons. On the other hand, John was very difficult. Anyone who dearly loved him will not hide that fact. He was scary sometimes, just because you didn't want to rock his boat. You wanted to please him. You wanted to be everything that he wanted you to be. Consequently, it could be stressful at times to be around him."

waiting to watch. That was disconcerting. Any performer knows that a practice is a practice and a performance is a performance, but that practice could only be considered a performance, which prevented any of us from ironing out the kinks.

None of us did anything difficult, because we were terrified of falling. As it happened, those members of the crowd who hadn't previously acquainted themselves with skating became quite fond of the accidental tumbles. Anybody who fell got a rise out of the audience. A triple Lutz went completely unnoticed. The practice was not memorable, but as skating was entirely new and foreign to most of the people looking on, the medium itself was a source of fascination. The next night was the actual performance. We were more rested, and the show went well. I do believe that our contingent was solely responsible for teaching the Chinese how to applaud. We applauded our own numbers and got the audience to join in. I'm convinced that we brought that sliver of Western culture to China.

A Different Scale

The show was televised. It was amusing to be told that our little performance claimed two times the viewing audience of Prince Charles and Lady Diana's wedding, an indication of something to be learned about China: the scale is different from anything we know in the West. We were mice on the Chinese scale. One felt inferior and insignificant.

We were visited in our dressing rooms by a group of dancers from the Chinese National Ballet. They were so thrilled to see us, so kind, so happy, so affectionate. They begged us to come to one of their classes the next day. When we arrived, the entire company met us at the front door. We later found out that some of the dancers were so famous throughout China that what really happened was that the Chinese answer to Margot Fonteyn had run out of the studio to meet our bus. Somehow, if we had arrived in England, I would not have expected Dame Margot Fonteyn to meet the bus and lead us up to the studio.

They did sequences taken from classical dances for us, literally gave us a personal performance. I think they wanted to reciprocate for our performances the night before. It was extremely moving. I'm glad I didn't do it, but I became so inspired (and I'm not at all a trained dancer) that I had to suppress the desire to run out and do an interpretive dance for them.

We visited the Great Wall of China. How is it that something begun more than 2,000 years ago is the only structure that can be seen today from space? The Great Wall was one of the follies of mankind, a monument to fear. The guide told us that it was a supreme embarrassment to the Chinese people, a mammoth, serpentine tombstone to the thousands who lost their lives building it. This impressed me in such a profound way that I thought about it for many years afterwards. The Great Wall of China changed my understanding of human potential and the scope of human accomplishments.

Like all tourists, we went to the summer palace of the dowager empress Tz'u Hsi, who had a mountain formed with the fill from her slave-made lake. A lacquered, marble palace was constructed on top. Compared to the Hermitage in St. Petersburg with its thousand rooms, the summer palace is tenfold – ten times the scale of anything Western. The empress also ordered a two-tiered white marble barge. When it sank like the proverbial stone, she was flabbergasted and had every worker beheaded on the spot. Truly it is those images that have contributed, in a major way, to my belief in magical imagery and enchantment.

Aesthetic Awakenings

Our visit to the Ming tombs still affects me greatly as well. A raised causeway, flanked by huge pairs of mythological animals sculpted in

stone, descended into a valley. Underneath a walled compound were
the tombs, only one of which had been excavated.* Its entrance was
remarkable because it was so un-North American. A large road
angled into the ground. At its end, we passed through a hole to a
marble staircase that zigzagged down to the antechamber of the
main tomb.

The emperor's sarcophagus (unlike the stone bathtubs in Egypt)
was a red lacquer box. So simple was its design that it struck me as
more modern than ancient. The emperor and his household effects
were contained in variously sized cubes and rectangles that had
been lacquered shut. The emperor's wife was buried in a similar box.
The overall appearance was not unlike a cubist painting in brilliant
red lacquer, peculiar in its contrast to the white marble.

So fantastic, so very the Great Wall, was the fact that workers
had built a separate chamber for the emperor's concubine, wife
number two, but the corridor to the burial chamber was too narrow.
The concubine's sarcophagus had to remain in the main chamber.
All that work, all that planning, all that expertise, to commit such a
primitive *faux pas*.

There was a museum of artifacts that had been found in the
tomb: gold, jewellery, materials, vessels. Nothing compared to the
Phoenix crowns worn by the emperor's wife and concubine. They
challenged my sense of the intrinsic value of things. The value of the
jewels of the Hapsburgs or Bourbons was measured in the materials
used to create them. The two Chinese crowns made me stop dead
in my tracks. They had a profound influence on my painting career.

They were made of gold as thin as aluminum foil. The wife's
crown was the less impressive. It was an elaborate headdress composed of hundreds of gold flowers, meticulously crafted so that it

---

* The Ting-ling tomb of Ming Emperor Wan-li, who died in 1620, was excavated between 1956 and 1958.

looked as though real flowers had been sprayed gold – every petal, every stamen. They seemed to be on invisible springs. If the empress had worn that crown hundreds of years ago, no wonder people thought her mystical and divine. The crown would have danced gently on her head, as though the flowers were magically floating above her.

The more impressive crown, the most enchanted object I have ever seen, was composed of hundreds of butterflies in varying sizes, in gold and cloisonné in shades of turquoise and jade green, again seemingly suspended on invisible springs. When the concubine walked into an imperial ceremony, it must have appeared as though butterflies had been trained to hover over her head, flapping their fragile wings.

I left the Ming tombs irrevocably charged with a sensitivity that permeated my body. They challenged me, tipped the scales, and threw my aesthetic understanding into a creative frenzy. Perhaps Beijing was the centre of the world, and New York was a pretender. China made me think about many things, of which skating was quite the last on the list.

The Horrors of the Lazy Susan

On the final evening in Beijing, there was a grand dinner in a private restaurant. The succession of dishes never let up. As soon as we sampled one, the chef whipped out another. The tables were outfitted with lazy Susans. When you whirled it around, whatever it was that you wanted appeared in front of you.

At one point in the dinner, the chef came to our table with a tiny, exquisite monkey cupped in his hands. He paraded the monkey around the table. Several even held it. Then, without warning, the monkey was placed in the middle of the lazy Susan. How cute. How sweet. How adorable. How unusual. The next thing we knew, the monkey had been plunged into a hole in the centre of the table, its head had been twisted off, and its brains had been plopped out onto the lazy Susan. To say that we were shocked is to say nothing.

Monkey brains are extremely gourmet and are served only to the finest people. I confess that those particular monkey brains were wasted on us. They were never sampled. The dinner ended precipitously on that merry note. All of us, without prompting, fled into the Pekinese night.

8

Ice

*T*here are certain opportunities that come along once in a lifetime. That was the case with Radio City Music Hall in February 1983. For the pleasure and prestige it gave, and because it was unique, that show would be at least one of the corners of my skating hexagon. Radio City had seen skating before, but the show that was about to open was highly unusual. It was to be called Ice, a title fatal in its own way, but little did anyone know what Mother Nature had in store along those lines.

Radio City is a temple to the arts, a temple of the sort that almost cannot exist in the age in which we live. It's too monumental. The costs of maintaining it are too enormous. Radio City must be one of the largest theatres in North America – if not in the world. Its interior represents the apex, in my opinion, of the art deco style begun in Europe but perfected by American architects.

Ice was to be the greatest show on earth. It *was* the greatest show on earth, because the cast was a who's who of its age. Almost without exception, every brilliant skater of the time was in the show.

The three stars of Ice were Peggy Fleming, Robin Cousins, and I. In addition, there were Sarah Kawahara, an old friend and a choreographer; Sandra Bezic and her brother Val, who skated as a pair; the American Allen Schramm (no relation to Norbert); Shelley MacLeod; John Rait; Bob Rubens; and Carol and Clive Phipson, an entirely miscast British adagio team, a bit long in the tooth, who had a whiff of bad taste about them and invariably brought down the house. But apart from those principal skaters were the greatest chorus skaters ever assembled. Just off the top of my head, they included Keith Green, Michael Shinniman, Tami Pennington, Carole Fortini, and Paul Douglas.* Many of them would have been principals in any other show.

Robin, Peggy, and I each had a chance to be showcased. We each also had a third of the creative control, which, in some ways, was stupid, but I think that the producers were afraid our egos were too big to accept direction. Ellen Burka, to whom I was loyal to the end, was hired to choreograph my third.

We were summoned to fly to California to work on the music for my numbers. I went that day saying (and this is so typical), "You know, this is really where we are going to be discovered. This is Hollywood!" I bought Ellen a burgundy cashmere cape with twenty burgundy fox tails around the edge. She looked quite good in it (though I looked even better in it).

Off we went, because we were stars, and we were going to show

---

* Others were Cindy Bartholow, Craig Bonsignore, Linda Davis, Gary Enos, Jack Frizelle, Gail Gilbert, Daniel Henry, Marlene Hogg, Louise Kirouac, Bob Knapp, John Knight, Aimee Kravette, Michel Lessard, Valery Levine, Deborah Lynch, Reggie Mack, Mitch Millar, Jill Schulz, Mary Lu Shipstad, Stewart Sturgeon, and Joan Wade.

Hollywood that we knew where it was at. We were picked up in a limousine and driven to some strange musical director's house where fox tails and cashmere and whatever else I was wearing didn't make a lot of sense. The music was being done in a suburban garage. However, Paul Walberg turned out to be a musical genius. He looked like a burned-out hippie, but he had a vast, photographic memory of all things musical.

Then I encountered Jef Billings, someone who, I think, still has a very chilly feeling about me. When we meet each other, we're always frighteningly polite. Jef didn't like me, and probably for good reason, because I did not like his designs. I think he must be a good designer, but it was Hollywood, it was Bob Mackie, it was sequins and beads and jewels, and I would have been thinking in terms of serious dance. I don't mean tights, but costumes with a modern art look. I scrapped all his designs for me and wore my own costumes, which I guess stars are allowed to do. Maybe I should have tried harder to work with him, but I dismissed him with a wave of the hand. I don't think he liked that.

I went back to the East Coast for what was going to be the break of my life, the jackpot, the big time. I trained and trained and slimmed myself down to sylphlike form. Then Ellen and I flew to Montreal because the troupe – *l'histoire se répète* – was being rehearsed in Lake Placid again; going to New York again; going to Broadway again (almost). But all the players were different, and the times were different, and it was legit. It was real money.

India Ink

An embarrassing thing happened to me at the baggage carousel in the Montreal airport. I, being the artist that I was, wouldn't have dreamed of spending my three and a half weeks in Lake Placid without my art supplies. When the luggage came down, everyone's Louis Vuitton and I don't know what else was covered in black India ink.

Not coincidentally, I had packed a large bottle of black India ink. Clearly, it had broken. That did not disturb me unduly, because all my clothes were black anyway. But, like a drug dealer whose contraband is discovered, I did not know whether I should seize the luggage and run or pretend that it really wasn't mine. One suitcase was definitely blacker than the others.

Everyone screeched and yelled, and I thought that I was going to be sued. When I pulled my suitcase off the carousel, I was immediately grabbed by security and marched into an office – but nothing happened. India ink, if you don't know about those things, is as indelible as you can get. I think that I destroyed an entire cargo hold of luggage, because it was a gallon of India ink. It wasn't a little bottle. It was *that big*, because I was *prolific*.

An Exercise in One-upmanship

We were picked up and driven to Lake Placid, where we were well looked after at the Holiday Inn. The stars, of course, had their own suites. The chorus had to share.

There were so many hungry and aggressive skaters that they virtually assumed a sprinter's crouch before bounding onto the ice. It was the professional Olympics. People were artists. People were intense. People were secretly watching other people for fear that they might be upstaged.

Peggy Fleming was the one exception. As we were all burning the midnight oil, jogging around Mirror Lake in the dead of winter, flexing, stretching, pumping, skating, Peggy was nowhere to be seen. I believe that she may have had personal problems at the time.

Katherine Healy's Dilemma

The question was asked whether or not Katherine Healy would also be starring in the show. She was officially invited, and money seemed to be no object at all.

Katherine did not have world or Olympic credentials, but she had a uniqueness that holds its own in this century. She was a child prodigy, a ballet dancer, and a skater of renown. She was torn between the two passions. As a result, neither the dance world nor the skating world could truly take her seriously. (I had a similar dilemma: I was torn between art and skating.)

Katherine arrived in Lake Placid. Although she was neither a Robin Cousins nor a Peggy Fleming, some of us – I can at least speak for myself – were rather in awe. As a one-of-a-kind property, she made all sorts of stupendous creative demands (that may or may not have been her right) because she was already a star ballerina. She could not – and it must have been so difficult – make up her mind either to be part of the unique and historical ice show that was going to devastate the world or to remain aloof because of her pure and integral commitment to dance.[*]

I believe that it was at a Superskates show that I saw Katherine Healy skate *Don Quixote*. To this day, I have never seen a performance like it: the quintessential best of dance applied to ice. She became the perfect character in her role. That performance ranks among the most incredible that I've ever seen. I felt intimidated and somewhat Philistine if I compared myself to her.

New York, New York

When we got to New York, Peggy Fleming chose to stay in the Meridian-something, which was like a health spa, quite grand. I resided in the Warwick Hotel on West Fifty-fourth Street, famous because it had once belonged to Marion Davies, mistress of William Randolph Hearst. I had a slightly dingy but large and comfy room,

---

[*] According to Healy, who became a prima ballerina with the Vienna State Opera Ballet, she wanted to appear in Ice but was prevented from doing so by Elva Oglanby.

like an enormous bedroom in somebody's summer cottage. Robin
Cousins had just bought a condominium that I never saw.

Robin and I were always friendly, but Robin and Peggy had an
entirely different experience at Radio City than I did. I had my own
circle of friends. Half the cast was Canadian. Peggy was not the least
bit interested in skating. Robin, who was always masterful – and I
can say this because I've performed with him many times – was not
as intense as he normally is. He was clearly one of the hits of the
show, but he wasn't the driven *artiste*. He was more interested in
having fun.

Robin's number with Peggy was a dreamlike Currier & Ives
tableau. Peggy was the snow princess and he was the snow prince.
They bonded. I suspect that Robin was good company for Peggy in
her times of trouble.

I think that Bob Shipstad, the producer, was particularly fond of
me (perhaps because I was intense about my work), so when it came
to assigning dressing rooms, I got the biggest and most sumptuous.

Of course, none of us knew what anyone else was being paid,
but I believe that I was being paid a fortune. It could have been close
to $20,000 a week, which was exactly what I had in mind. If they'd
offered me $500, I still would have accepted – but it was lots of
money.

Acres of Props and White Grand Pianos

The miracle of Radio City Music Hall is that it has an incredible
number of sets and props in warehouses all over New Jersey. If
you said, "You know, I think I want fifty-five golden chandeliers to
fly in during my number," it had them. If you said, "I want an East
Indian temple, because we're doing *Scheherezade*," it had that, too. It
was like going to the candy store and having whatever you wanted.
The cache of props was not dissimilar, I suspect, to the British Royal
Family's jewel collection. I've heard that, under Buckingham Palace,
in something resembling catacombs, there are acres and acres of

plain wooden shelves dripping with jewels, all numbered and cata-
logued on computer. That was Radio City.

Ellen Burka and I were driven artists. When we were coming up
with my number, we wanted to know the line that was going to run
through the show, the colour and texture. There was a director who
knew nothing about skating. I think she had choreographed "Sesame
Street" for a while and was quite well known. Sarah Kawahara did
the choreographic work. I believe Ice was her big turning point.
After that, she began to be taken seriously.

All that the director could say was, "I want ten white grand
pianos." We never really understood why, but she was the boss.
Many, many grand pianos appeared. For the finale, Robin, Peggy,
and I were pushed out onto the stage on top of white grand pianos.

There were also slides of artificial ice. For our final bows, Robin
and I went up into the balcony and came sliding down. Robin
invariably ended his slide with a back-flip, which I have always felt
was a cheap little trick, but it totally brought the house down every
time. As far as back-flips go, his is the best. I can do a back-flip. In
fact, I do them often – in my dreams. But I always thought, "Would
Rudolf Nureyev do a back-flip in *Swan Lake*? Would John Curry do
a back-flip?" Although I eventually did learn how, I thought that it
really was not in my image to do one.

There was a Slavic number. I don't know if Robin had ever done
a pair with a male before, but I was his partner. We did that whiz
around, you hold my hands, I do a butterfly, and then you do a
butterfly manoeuvre. The world had never seen such butterflies as
ours. I had to do them opposite from my usual way, so mine were
not in perfect form. I was less like a butterfly and more like an asym-
metrical moth, because one leg went much higher than the other.
Robin is strong. In another life, he would have been a tremendous
pairs partner.

Robin is equal to Scott Hamilton as a professional. Robin is a
master. Robin is the top of the line. He knows how to do everything.

He knows everything that there is to know about performing. Nobody's better. His numbers were a high point in that show.

Yet there were other minor highlights, or major highlights by minor stars. Allen Schramm sometimes skated so well that, on certain nights, he was the best skater in the world. He was better than all of us.

Since then I have never felt the kind of excitement and nerves that I felt at Radio City. It was larger than life. It was New York. It was the centre of the world. Robin skated first, and I skated second. He did a modern piece, "Homage to the Athletes." I did the Paganini violin concerto (No. 5 in A minor), and Peggy did "Rhapsody on a Theme of Paganini." I almost fainted from the excitement every time I went out, but all of us are larger than life when we're in larger-than-life situations, so we knew how to do it.

There was an opening-night party in some swanky restaurant high in the air, and we all dressed to kill. Peggy did something that was very professional, and perhaps I did something that was very *un*. She presented Robin and me with an opening-night present of a silver pen from Tiffany's. I didn't give anybody anything.

Prince of Thieves

My second-act number was extraordinary. I'm quite sure that it will go down in history as one of the most innovative and creative numbers ever staged. It was conceived by Ellen and me. The score came from many sources, one of them the film *Blade Runner*. I was a jewel thief.

When the number started, there was a huge scrim across the stage. You heard a cacophony of city sounds. Then I appeared behind the scrim. It was lit from the back, so my shadow hit the scrim and was magnified to a height of about fifty feet. I had jewels in my hand. Other people came up behind me, and the action moved in slow motion across the stage: people shaking their fists; me running, looking back over my shoulder. Eventually there was a screech, and the lights blacked out. I whipped around the scrim, and I had escaped. I was on the ice.

There were lights, like headlights from a car, their beams projected horizontally. I was in the headlights, running for my life. It was a dramatic opening. There was never a sound in the audience. (Incidentally, I borrowed the headlight idea from Maya Plisetskaya in the death scene of the Béjart ballet *Isadora*, but no one must ever know that.)

My character was all too much like me. I was alone in the city, tough but sensitive, greedy but generous; someone who would put a bullet between your eyes but wanted love. As I finished skating, all of a sudden, BING! Shelley MacLeod was at a dressing table on the other side of the ice. She switched on a light, and it illuminated her, framed in a window, as she was getting ready to go out. She powdered herself; pulled on a dress over her slip; tried on some jewels. I was the thief on the street, looking in.

The doorbell rang. I hid behind a pillar as she looked out the window, ushered in her lover, and let him put an incredible emerald necklace around her neck. They went off to the ball. I climbed through the window, grabbed some jewels, then followed them into the chandeliered ballroom because I wanted the emerald necklace.

The dresses for the ensemble had been done by Billings in turquoise and salmon net and black. Shelley was in strawberry ice cream net. I was in silver. The other men wore black tie. There was an eerie, Felliniesque feeling to the tableau. Rather than waltzing, the skaters performed strange, discordant fox trots and slightly vicious tangos.

Then (borrowed from the original production of *Cabaret*) the company froze in *tableaux vivants* so that the action focused on one person, and the audience could see what he was thinking. I began to oil my way around the floor. I noticed various women and their jewels, but my eye was never far from the emerald necklace.

Then I started to become overtly enamoured of Shelley, and vice versa. When we danced together, the rest of the company froze. At the end of our *pas de deux*, there was a moment that was among my favourites: we engaged in a violent, passionate kiss, a real one, the complete. As the spotlight hit us, I ripped the necklace from her neck, which ignited the company and led to a vigorous chase. I was captured, and (in a move borrowed from the Alvin Ailey company) I was picked up in the splits, carried in the air, then plopped down like a fish on the line until I was hanging upside down by my blades, a silver bass in skates.

I was allowed to slide down, as the snake in the Garden of Eden might have slithered down the trunk of the Tree of Knowledge. I was disgraced. In a frozen moment, I looked up at Shelley as she took the necklace that had been returned to her and threw it at me as if to say, "You can have it." At that, a black scrim came down, cutting me off from the ballroom. You could see by the shadows that the party continued, but I'd been ostracized. At that point, à la Giselle, I realized that I had made the wrong decision. I had sacrificed love for greed.

There followed a scene in which I went mad, because I had found something worth much more than jewels but had thrown it away. At the end of the number, I did multiple handstands, cartwheels, and somersaults, then lay suffering, leg outstretched. When I pulled the jewels out of my costume, only my hand was illuminated, holding the necklace.

It was not exactly Ice Capades, not exactly Holiday on Ice. It was very Ballets Russes de Monte Carlo, a slice of *The Red Shoes*.

Of Rave Reviews and Acts of God

The reviews were published, and the show was a rave. The show was a hit. The show was the best skating show that had ever been, with one exception: Peggy Fleming was roasted *en brochette*. Vivisected by the *New York Post*. She just didn't belong. Time had passed her by. The Olympic title and an incredible dress did not cut it. That reception jaundiced the entire run for her, I think, because she realized she couldn't suddenly make up for the time that she hadn't spent practising. It was too late.

Rex Reed gave us a sublime review, although he made a slight jab at me, saying that I had brought new heights to melodrama. I didn't think that I was being melodramatic. I thought of myself as passionate, like the Bolshoi Ballet, but I'm sure that I was totally over the top.

There was talk of going to the Dorothy Chandler Pavilion in L.A. Then we were going to do Europe. We considered South Africa. Then we thought Japan would be just the thing. But God did not want that to happen.

Two days after the opening in New York, there was a blizzard. The Antarctic does not have blizzards like that one. Many people in the show had to sleep on mattresses in the basement of Radio City. I managed to make my way through waist-deep snow to the Warwick Hotel.

The next day, the sun came out. Everything was twinkling and frosty and lovely, and New York was immobilized. People were skiing and snowshoeing down Park Avenue. That was the kiss of death for business. We started playing to near-empty houses. Towards the end of the run, the show caught fire again, but we had lost momentum, and the producers had lost money. The Dorothy Chandler Pavilion almost happened but didn't quite, and the greatest show on earth was not to continue.

It was a remarkable experience, thrilling and wonderful, but not the big break that I had hoped for. I was not on my way to Hollywood to become the male counterpart of Sonja Henie.

The Wayward Scrim

Midway in the run, a most unfortunate thing happened during my jewel thief number – my *pièce de résistance*, my launching pad for Hollywood, because you never knew. There might have been a director in the audience, waiting to discover me.

During that particular matinée, the stage manager, a decent man whose name I have forgotten, committed a *faux pas*. The scrim that should have dropped at the end of my number dropped at the beginning. The entire number had to be skated on a corridor sixty feet wide by two feet deep. You make do, so shall we say that there was a lot of attitude but very little skating?

I was wounded to the quick. As I was jewel-thieving my way around the ice, I started to boil. The words "towering inferno" hardly describe the heat that I was generating. Mount Vesuvius was ready to explode. When the number ended, I stomped off the ice and, in front of the cast, slapped the stage manager in the face and said, "You have the great pleasure of working with ardent professionals like me, yet I have been cursed by working with people as unprofessional as you." With that, I huffed away in my jewel thief costume.

I later went back and apologized, but I really think that part of me had done it not because of the man's mistake, but to enhance my reputation among the cast as a temperamental *artiste* who was ready to have a breakdown if the teeniest thing went wrong. It worked, because that story was bandied around for years afterwards.

A Day in the Life

Radio City was twenty-four-hour theatre. Walking down the street to the building was itself an act of theatre, because I was *someone*. I had a genuine reason to be in New York. I was one of the stars. My name was in the middle of the marquee: Cousins, Cranston, Fleming. Whatever you are, you at least have to fill the shoes.

When I arrived at Radio City, numbers of die-hards would be training. Robin rehearsed, but I would have been there earlier. The chorus always rehearsed, because it was the greatest chorus ever assembled in the history of the world. I never saw Peggy Fleming at a practice.

After practice, I drank a cup of coffee. I didn't eat lunch, because I had a show to skate. I was always at the theatre early for the matinée. I pretended that it was in the name of professionalism, but it was really just to savour the moment.

Then there was the ritual of applying make-up and getting ready for the show. I often received guests *à deux* in my dressing room, friends from the show, for little chats. Then the show started and I performed.

I went home after the first show and had the tiniest bit of sustenance, tea and maybe a muffin, but I didn't eat much because the evening show was still to come. Others took it casually, but I lay prostrate on my bed, saving myself for the next show. Then I changed into evening attire and made an entrance.

I didn't dress for the after-theatre crowd, and I didn't dress for the other skaters. I dressed in ever-greater sartorial splendour for the staff at the performers' entrance. They complimented me on how I looked, and I feigned surprise. "Oh, really? How kind of you to notice." A chauffeur once told me that chauffeurs driving limousines wish to be treated like professionals. They don't want, "Golly gosh, I'm in a limousine." They want, "Driver, pick me up at ten o'clock in front of Cartier, and don't be late!" That was how it was at the performers' entrance.

After the evening show, many of the skaters, I imagine, went out. I don't know about other people's New York experience. We were all tripping, each of us in a different orbit. I was autonomous. A good friend from Winnipeg flew in, so we might have gone to the Palm Court for an after-show thing, but usually I went back to my hotel, too tired to eat. I went to bed rather early, with few exceptions.

That was how, over a period of three weeks, I went from 155 pounds to 120, never realizing how thin I was getting. I was living on adrenalin and black coffee.

The Penthouse Brawl

My social contact was with people from outside the city, with one exception: friends of Alex Dubé, of the Hurok Concerts period, loaned him their vast penthouse apartment on Fifth Avenue while they were away, so he threw a party for Morgan Fairchild and me. I didn't really know who Morgan Fairchild was. She was performing quite successfully at the time in a Broadway play.

The penthouse was somewhat understated, but it had a large terrace that completely encircled the apartment. Its great claim to fame was that it looked down on Jacqueline Onassis's penthouse. The guests were, for the most part, Alex Dubé's friends: creative people, managers of creative people, or people on various arts councils. They were intellectually connected, hip New York people, but not glittering. If Morgan was to be the diamond at that party, I was to be the rhinestone.

Morgan, for whatever reason, never showed up. That was both good and bad. The bad was that the party was for her. The good was that I, by default, became the star. Because I was skating in Ice, and Ice was the flavour of the moment in New York, the talk at the dinner table turned to skating. Somewhere between the appetizer and the salad, Sonja Henie's name entered the conversation.

I was seated between a ballet impresario (charming but abrasive in her tough, New York way) and a male guest. I was not terribly involved in their conversation, because I was answering the questions posed to me by the swanky Fifth Avenue crowd, but I did proffer one little thing. I said that Sonja Henie was unique, for all her positive and negative attainments, and did anyone know that Sonja Henie, although she was partly Jewish, actually did the *Heil Hitler* salute at the Berlin Olympics?

If I had dropped a neutron bomb, the blast would have had less impact. An argument flared between the ballet impresario and the guest on my other side, who made far more sense to me than she did.

The gentleman maintained that, even though Henie had done outrageous things, her personality was unique. Could we at least agree that, like it or not, she had been an incredible person? The woman insisted that Henie was an evil snake. How could she have saluted Adolf Hitler?

The argument paralysed the dinner table. What was supposed to be an urbane Fifth Avenue party turned into a débâcle a few rungs beneath the Mad Hatter's tea party. It was an intellectual brawl. It was theatre of the absurd. It was a Genet play gone off the deep end. Before the main course was served, the woman jumped up and declared, "I cannot stand being here another moment!" She fled the table and ran out the front door. The man, upset and furious, scurried towards the service elevator. We were left minus two guests and never did get to the main course. Everyone left.

The Final Curtain

As the final night of Ice drew near, I felt mild desperation, some sadness, and a definite desire to make every performance even better than the last. Then it came.

After I chased Ruth Dubonnet down the street in my *Firebird* costume, I had a somewhat estranged relationship with her. I wrote earlier that I never saw her again, but that's not quite true. I didn't see her for a long time, but she rallied and came back for the closing night of Ice.

She was accompanied by George Faison, the unofficial choreographer of *The Wiz*, and an ex-Alvin Ailey dancer whom I had known. Faison had been one of Ruth's protégés until I came along and took over, probably to his great relief. He was well known for staging rock shows, choreographing the Earth, Wind & Fire show at Madison Square Garden, and helping Valerie Simpson and Nick

Ashford. Ashford and Simpson were very hot at the time, and they came to the show with Ruth and George, encrusted in furs and leather and dreadlocks.

Chita Rivera, a long-time friend of mine, also came on closing night and brought her daughter Lisa, who had just made her Broadway début. Liza Minnelli's sister, Lorna Luft, was there. So was Dick Button. Let's say that the final evening was fairly star-studded. My father and mother were also in attendance.

On final nights, there's always tremendous emotion – bravos, standing ovations, and that kind of thing. I had something of an emotional breakdown. I was in my dressing room, fully made up, ready to go out. Perhaps because Ice was coming to an end, perhaps because I was so thin, perhaps because of the hemorrhoids that I had developed for the first time in my life, perhaps because of my mother and father – who knows? – I had a good old weep. It was not wasted on the dressing-room walls. Many people were privy to it. I performed meticulously, comforted by the likes of Shelley MacLeod and John Rait. It was a cathartic release of emotion before I devastated New York with my final performance.

The closing night was a Roman candle that exploded, twinkled, then dissolved. When the show was over, it was over. There wasn't a big party. Everyone went his own way. I went back to my hotel. The next day, I returned to Toronto. Accompanied by my house-keeper and dogs, I limousined my way to my nineteenth-century country estate in Baltimore, Ontario, with its fifteen trout ponds.* Then I slept for a week.

---

* Toller used the estate for several years as a country getaway during the time when he owned the Carlton Street house.

، 9 ،

In the Land of the Mamba

One June, sometime in the mid-1980s, when it was extremely unfashionable to even discuss Sun City, let alone go there (because of guilt by association with the apartheid policies of South Africa), I was invited to a competition.[*] The fact that it was not cool to go to Sun City was of less concern to me than the fact that I was terribly out of condition, but I thought that maybe, once again, I could pull it off.

I boarded the plane in Toronto with a sense of trepidation. The trepidation may have been communicated by phone to the

---

[*] Sun City, a casino resort, was located in Bophuthatswana, an independent Bantu homeland within the Republic of South Africa, to which it was economically tied. Bophuthatswana was governed by its own president and legislature, although its independence was not generally recognized by the world community.

International Management Group because I was met in New York by two IMG officials and escorted bodily from LaGuardia to Kennedy. They didn't handcuff me, but if I had tried to bolt, I'm certain that I would have been shackled. My agent, Jay Ogden, saw me off. He waved at me on the plane: I was timid; he, relieved.

I decided that the only way to deal with the trip, even though we did fly business class, was to drug myself heavily with sleeping pills. I did so the very second that we took off. The plane landed at a refuelling station somewhere off the coast of Ghana. As I'd never been to that neck of the woods before, I decided to put my foot on African soil for posterity's sake. I was so drugged that I almost missed the flight. I managed to reboard the plane just before falling asleep. When I woke up, we were about to land in Johannesburg.

All of a sudden, things began to change dramatically in a way that thrilled me through every fibre of my being. Other skaters on the plane were told to go through customs. I was singled out and ushered through a special gate that avoided customs entirely. While the others waited at the luggage carousel, I was escorted into a private lounge and fed canapés, smoked salmon, and would I care for a glass of champagne? I said that I would.

Stevie Godsen, the entertainment director of Sun City, who was to become a great and dear friend, informed me that the bus trip would be much too arduous for me. Would it be all right if I flew in the private jet that belonged to the owner of Sun City? You can imagine what my answer was. Although I seethed with excitement on the inside, I recaptured the cool, blasé exterior of the Skater of the Century and pretended that it was exactly what I was accustomed to.

The trip took under a half-hour (compared to the two-and-a-half-hour bus ride endured by the other skaters). As the Lear jet grazed the runway, a large, violet-coloured Rolls-Royce pulled into view. The chauffeur swung open the limousine door as I came down the steps. I suppressed any expression of positive emotion, thinking that pale and interesting was what they expected. I got into the Rolls-Royce with Stevie Godsen and was driven to one of the most unusual resorts I had ever seen.

Sun City had sounded a bit like *Sin* City. I thought that it might be similar to Las Vegas. Not at all. Sun City was a family playground in an otherwise sparsely populated part of Bophuthatswana. That area did not subscribe to apartheid. Why it was boycotted by so many performers I don't know. We arrived at a compound in the middle of a very arid area. Yet, no sooner had we entered the grounds of Sun City than Paradise materialized before us.

There were two hotels. I, of course, was ensconced in the A-class hotel, the Cascades, while the others resided in the B. I seem to recall that at the *porte-cochère*, the asphalt melted into marble. There was marble, gilt, and glass in every nook and cranny. Fountains bubbled. Flowers sprouted. Doormen smiled. It was my kind of place.

I was escorted to my suite. The affable porter showed me into my rooms, opened the windows, fluffed the pillows, and asked if there was anything else that I needed – and, by the way, they had room service twenty-four hours a day (which was rare at that time), and if I wanted anything, day or night, I was to feel free, it was all on the house, good night, sir. He closed the door. With that, the suppressed euphoria that had been working up to a crescendo inside me erupted into a squeal of delight. I jumped up and down. I think that I might also have bounced on the bed a few times.

The view from my windows afforded a glimpse of many swimming pools, cascading waterfalls, twinkling lights in every patch of flora, and tropical birds settling down to nest. A few sapphire-blue and emerald-green macaws fluttered by. I believe that the title of the song from *Annie* is "I Think I'm Gonna Like It Here." If I had known the words, I would have burst into song.

The fact that I had been singled out and given superstar treatment while the others had to ride the bus and stay in the B-class hotel was a puzzle to me. I wasn't at all sure why I was being accorded preferential status. I cast about for an answer, and suddenly it became clear. Every single one of the television specials that I had ever done in my life had been aired there. I was a known commodity.

Toller's One and Only Golf Story

The cast of skaters could have been my guests on "This Is Your Life." I had known them all for years, had competed and travelled with many, and could truthfully say that they were a collection of the best friends I had in skating, spanning a period of fifteen years. Our only responsibilities were to perform a lovely exhibition in one week's time at the main concert hall/skating rink that adjoined the hotel and to compete on the following weekend. One could play in Sun City for at least two weeks without fear or trepidation.

Sun City became so intoxicating to me that when the entire group would say, "Guess what? We're going to the snake farm in Johannesburg," I would reply, "I'm sure you are, but I'm staying here."

High on the list of things to do (but new to me, I confess) was golf. There were many ardent golfers in that group: David Santee, Norbert Schramm, Scott Hamilton, and a great guy whose name is Chris Harrison, to cite a few. Flying rather high as I was, I thought that I would allow them to mull over an idea. I pronounced myself a splendid golfer. I said that I could not possibly golf with any of them because I had been taught by Arnold Palmer, and I wouldn't waste my time with riffraff.

As always, there were a few who believed me. There were also a few who thought it possible, and there were a couple who absolutely rejected the thesis and demanded to see me in action. The joke went on and on. Finally, there came a time of reckoning: I was cajoled onto the golf course. Really good jokes have to be played to the last second. Rather than say, "Guys, I've never held a golf club in my life," I proceeded to the number-one tee. Many started at the women's tee, but I insisted on starting at the men's, because, after all, I had been taught by Arnold Palmer.

I grabbed a wood. It's harder to hit with a wood than an iron, but I thought that it was the correct thing to do. Many took practice swings, but I declined to do so, because I didn't need the practice. Finally, I straddled the ball and raised my club. I was prepared for the worst, because I had never golfed in my life. With one vicious swing, I connected with the ball. It went straight down the fairway. I don't think two hundred yards is an exaggeration.

The entire group was awed by my drive and suddenly believed that I had been taught by Arnold Palmer. I pretended that it had been one of my weaker shots. I never hit the ball that well again. Several times I spun myself into the ground and lay on my back. At other times I pounded the ground so hard that I thought I had dislocated a shoulder. The one or two times that I did connect, the ball ended up on the wrong fairway. However, a great time was had by all.

After my introduction to golf, I became hooked (so to speak). Although few people, for some reason, wished to golf with me, I managed to coax a group to take me out the next day. I foisted my attention upon the caddies. I was the first person in Sun City history to demand two caddies. Why, you might ask? Because, I said, this is the land of the mamba. This is Mambaland (the mamba being the most poisonous snake in the world).

I had done a certain amount of research on local fauna and had found out that mambas did, indeed, live in the south of Africa. The green ones lived in the trees, and the black ones lived in the ground, and if one bit you, the only thing you could do is say goodbye and drop dead. The caddies, who spoke perfect English, had never considered snakes to be a problem, but because of my angst, and because one was required to walk in front of me and the other behind me, my angst became their living terror.

I walked with two clubs in my hands, one in front and one behind, as we promenaded around the golf course. In the event that one of my balls connected and went into the rough, I gave the imperial wave, and the caddies had to retrieve it – because there was absolutely no way that I would.

At the seventh hole, there was a gully full of fallen logs and dried brush. I had no intention of going down into the gully and up to the next tee. Therefore, in a skaterly way and at high running speed, I did a major split jump over the gully and made a perfect landing. The caddies were not equipped to follow suit. They had to decide (over a period, I'm sure, of five minutes) whether or not they would go down the gully and up the other side. They did. The fear of snakes still exists in those two caddies' minds because of the seriousness of my mamba knowledge. I also note that a mamba is supposedly the only snake in the world that will chase after you.[*] That added an additional peril to the game.

I thought I spotted prehistoric birds flying in slow motion over the golf course, but the sight of them might have been eclipsed by the baboons (that I was convinced carried rabies). One had to wait for them to go their own way before continuing. Then there were the wild boars. There were often little clusters of wild boars that could, we were told, be dangerous.

When it became known that my golfing ability was sub-kindergarten, the only person who agreed to be my partner was Richard

---

[*] Black mambas are considered the fastest snakes in the world. While they don't usually chase people, when they feel threatened, they speed to their burrows, attacking anything in their way.

Dalley. He didn't seem to mind my golf game. Instead of impressing him with my swing, I regaled him with the meaning of life while the prehistoric birds and wild boars frolicked around us.

Each day in Sun City was chock-full of laughs. At night, although we may not have spent the day together, we skaters always met in one of the ten restaurants, ordered the most expensive meals, and signed our room numbers to the cheque. After those splendid meals (usually hunks of roast beef and gigantic steaks that nobody could finish), we drifted over to the casino.

Blackjack, in truth, was not my forte. However, the pleasure of betting and the camaraderie of the blackjack table were well worth the price of any losses that I incurred. My gambling was so dreadful that one night, when I arrived at the table, hungering to place a bet, a fellow Canadian citizen said, "Oh my God, it's not *you* again."

I replied in my most haughty tones, "I interpret that as an insult. I just want you to know that I am extremely rich, and I love to lose, so fuck off!"

The week before the competition, the pressure began to build. I was convinced that David Santee was doomed. Although he was adept at drives, he crumbled on the putting green. I, however, was lucky to hit the ball from the tee, but when it came time to putt, it was always a hole in one. When I suggested to David that the game was a sure foreshadowing of what was to happen on the ice, he turned to dust. Sun City was not one of his finer performances.

Scott Hamilton and Norbert Schramm are ardent competitors. Their competitiveness is evident not only on the ice rink, but also in intense, rather bitter golf games. Scott Hamilton and John Evert (Chris Evert Lloyd's brother) became so inebriated during one of those golf games that both of their bags of clubs ended up in the lake. That, in itself, was probably bad manners, but when someone decided to go in after them, I cautioned them not to, because, don't you know, alligators live in that lake. The clubs were left for the caddies to retrieve.

The Last Hurrah

The competition drew near. I had been training, and I can adjust to situations quickly, so I was in a good position. We stood around in our costumes and skates, sipping minty drinks while waiters served hors d'oeuvres on silver platters in our red plush dressing room. Many of us were watching the television when it announced that martial law had just been declared in South Africa. We couldn't understand it, because we loved it where *we* were. As far as we were concerned, everything was just perfect. Of course, Sun City was not reality and not a reflection of South Africa at all. It was like le Hameau, the peasant village of Marie Antoinette at Versailles.

The competition, if I'm to be absolutely fair, was between Scott Hamilton and me, although the field included Brian Pockar, Allen Schramm, Norbert Schramm, David Santee, and several others. That night I gave one of my best performances of recent years. I skated to *Pagliacci* wearing the peacock costume. Since *Pagliacci* has never failed and the peacock costume has never fallen down, I was in rather good shape. Scott skated well also and won, but perhaps his Olympic gold medal was slightly shinier than my bronze. That didn't matter, because we'd all had such a great time. The competition ended with a cocktail party in one of the many pavilions on the Sun City grounds.

That wonderful trip cemented friendships of long standing. However, one more day in Sun City would have been a drag. When the two weeks were up, we were all happy to head home.

· 10 ·

Upstaging Joan Collins

I had known M since 1965, my first year at the École des Beaux-Arts. She was a girl from Munich who became a part of the demi-monde of Montreal, and she embodied the idea of the artist that an artistic boy from the suburbs would imagine. I felt a great affection for her, and I respected her.

I played a little game, with the best intentions, but with disastrous results over a period of almost thirty years. I tried to play Henry Higgins to her Eliza Doolittle. Even though M was ten years older, I was determined always to be loyal. If I did well, she would do well.

In 1986, I was asked by Herr Jann and his business partner, Herr Meinelt, from the J. G. Weißsche Druckerei in Munich, if I would like to have an exhibition. Similar invitations were often extended and often bore no fruit, but I was more inclined to go after the adventure than not. M went with me.

You couldn't be absolutely certain what sex M was. She looked a bit like Napoleon. She had dark hair, bullfrog eyes, a prominent nose, sensuous lips, teeth that were not at all close together, and rather creamy, rosy skin. She was somewhat corpulent, with tremendous breasts, a protruding stomach, and good legs: a chunk of a human being with a great sense of humour, stupendous arrogance, a sense of the absurd, and a discerning fashion instinct. She was not a *femme fatale*, but I thought of her as an artist through and through. That was the bond we shared. She knew nothing about skating.

M was an artistic sprinkle who threw people on a good trip. Oh my God, look at those two! They're obviously *somebody*. Socially, she could have been a liability. Although she had a certain naïve charm, she horrified many people with her outrageous behaviour, egomania, and rudeness – but it was all in the name of Art.

Flying High in Munich

One should always travel dressed to the max. Air Canada had almost never bumped me into first class, but with Lufthansa, the way that we looked – exotically odd – M and I were propelled into first class.

The deal was that we would book into the Bayerischer Hof, one of the top hotels in Munich. Two days after the exhibition opened, if nothing sold, we would move into the *Bahnhof* hotel next to the train station, at about twenty dollars a night. But, to start with, we were flying high. We were playing a game of theatre and adventure.

Things looked good as we floated through Munich en route to the Bayerischer Hof. On every telephone pole and billboard was a poster announcing my exhibition. We entered the hotel and saw a large poster in the lobby. We didn't have to check in. It had all been done for us.

Stars, but especially North American dignitaries, stay at the Bayerischer Hof. Chic, conservative Germans stay in the Vier Jahreszeiten Kempinski on the Maximilianstrasse. The Bayerischer

Hof may be overrated. The rooms aren't particularly large, but it is German service and German first class. M had a room and I had a room. We changed our clothes and went to check the Weißsche gallery on Altheimer Eck.

The gallery wasn't exactly a gallery. Herren Jann and Meinelt, two wealthy financiers, had a large building with two marble halls where they held special exhibitions. Both men were exceedingly baronial and polite. We were offered schnapps and coffee. While we hung the exhibition, there were workers to help us and champagne all around. We could play international *artiste*, as if we did this all the time. Of course, we didn't.

Herren Jann and Meinelt said, "We're having a special preview tonight and a five-course dinner in the gallery. We invited the owner of *Stern* magazine, the owner of *Bunte*, the this, the that. Do arrive at eight o'clock." Somehow we formed the impression that it wasn't going to be a two-bit operation. M and I decided to play it to the max. I can't remember precisely what I wore, but I think that I would have been pretty black, with many black scarves. I was serious and intense. M wore pants, a jacket, and a hat with a large veil that fastened around her neck. Although make-up was almost unthinkable to her, I insisted on red lips for the evening.

There were twelve of us in the dinner party, and everybody was *somebody*. After dinner, a few of the guests bought paintings. We could stay at the Bayerischer Hof for another night at least.

The next day, I started to do interviews and make television appearances. I felt that the only way to feel good about oneself in those circumstances was to buy clothes. I had to do it, and I thought that it would be greedy and rude of me if M couldn't do it, too. We went out and bought incredible clothes and started to look wildly aristocratic.

That night, the exhibition was very sardines-in-a-can. The gallery was jammed with mad, eccentric people. The Canadian ambassador and the whole ambassadorial staff arrived from Bonn. There were celebrities here, celebrities there, the paparazzi, the whole shebang, and things started to sell.

I didn't sleep well that night, because I kept thinking about what I was going to buy the next morning. We ate breakfast in the Bayerischer Hof's breakfast room overlooking the Frauenkirche, that famous, twin-towered, very phallic German church. When the stores opened, we dashed around Munich. Instead of thinking, "Gee, I'll never make this kind of money again," I thought, "How much is that coat in the window? I have to have it. In fact, I think I'll have two." I discovered a shop that is among my favourites in the world: the Loden-Frey shop that sells beautiful, chic, Loden green Bavarian clothes. The more purchases I made, the more suitcases I had to acquire.

In West Germany, there was a vast selection of woollen scarves in every shade and hue. Wearing two and three at one time, twisted together like a rainbow, was the look of the moment. One could change one's look by changing the colour of the scarves. Usually the basic outfit was black. That approach was *way* past fur. It was on to another thing – modern art clothes.

Adventures started happening at every turn. I made the scene. I met the Munich jet set. Money was incidental. M and I were middle-aged Babes in Toyland.

Head to Head with Joan Collins

Thomas Gottschalk is the Johnny Carson of Germany. He's an immensely charismatic blond fellow, very popular to this day, with a large nose, a great smile, and perfect teeth. I was to appear on his talk show. Joan Collins was scheduled for the same night.

The Gottschalk people said, "Wouldn't it be great if you could skate during the show?" They brought in a little plastic ice rink and put it down on the set. Then they said, "Wouldn't it be even better if we could have half of your exhibition on television as well?" They created a set where I could skate among my own paintings.

I had spied a black leather jacket with shoulders almost five feet across and one hundred thousand studs on the epaulettes. It was drop-dead movie-star incredible. When the night came, I looked rather good. I told the make-up person to ply her trade liberally; I was going up against Joan Collins.

First I skated. Then Gottschalk asked questions in German that were translated into English through my earphones. Fluke of all flukes, I found the questions so amusingly interesting that I could respond in German. So I skated, I painted, and I spoke German. I was definitely a glittering guest, and I was wearing a jacket that Gottschalk wanted to rip off my back on the spot. The audience was reverent.

Joan Collins had just married a Swede. (As it later turned out, that ended in complete disaster.) The Swede drove her onto the set in a huge car that she had just been given by BMW in Munich. She wore a voluminous, quite extraordinary, cut-on-the-diagonal mink coat that had also been a gift. She was flying high, because "Dynasty" was hot. The Swede jerked her as she flopped out of the car, so her entrance was askew. It was live television. The translating device kept falling out of her ear, and she couldn't hear the questions. I remember her saying, "I really do want to respond, but I cannot hear what the questions are, and I don't speak German."

Several people in the audience stood up and said, in essence, "We really don't know what all the fuss is about. You're such a bad actress. Why are we paying so much attention to you? Why are you getting BMWs and mink coats?" They all decided that I had pulverized Joan Collins. I heard that she rushed back to the Vier Jahreszeiten and left Munich the next day. I went on to have many more adventures.

Holy Shit!

M and I decided to go out and celebrate my talk-show success. I continued to wear my drop-dead jacket. M wore a purple velvet quilted coat (she looked like Henry VIII) and a Moroccan suede fez with a tassel. First we went to the bar at the Bayerischer Hof, where I demanded a zombie that came in a soup bowl. A zombie is the kiss of death. I'm not really a drinker, but somehow most of that zombie disappeared. Then we went out on the town. Since I was ripped out of my mind on the zombie, and M was as well, our movements were slow and deliberate.

The first club we hit was in Schwabing. We arrived and stood in the middle of the room. The restaurant was paralysed. Then people started to applaud. Someone in an upper balcony exclaimed, "Holy shit!" We took it as a compliment. We felt like holy shit. We sat down with some people and had a drink, which was the worst thing that I could possibly have done. Then we went on to Kay's Bistro, frequented by movie stars, and arrived looking like greater holy shit. The Red Sea parted, and we swooshed in. I had a tiny bowl of spaghetti that cost three hundred marks. It was made with truffles.

Kay's Bistro was typical of a special kind of club in Munich, what M called a glitter palace. It was a cheap version of my house in Toronto: lots of net draped on the ceiling; Christmas lights; cupids; twinkling things; glitter all over the floor. Glitter was also thrown on the waiters, who had turquoise and lavender glitter on their eyes. It was exotic and decadent, the way one thought Berlin to be, but a lighter decadence, more humorous.

We slithered off to another place that people had told us to visit. I don't even know how we got there. It was called Bei Roy, another glitter palace full of groovy model types and rich people. Someone pointed out Prince von Thurn und Taxis, the richest man in Germany, sitting in a corner. Because I wore the same outfit I had worn on

Thomas Gottschalk's show, our club-hopping was a continuation of the show. Bei Roy immediately overflowed with candied fruit and pheasants, and the owner whipped out magnums of champagne.

M and I climbed into a taxi and went to our last glitter palace of the evening, an extraordinary Studio 54-type club filled with the most hatefully attractive people I have ever seen. P 1, below the Haus der Kunst art museum at the back of the English Garden, was where the grooviest of the groovy went. I was starting to feel not terribly well, and I was nervous, as I always am when there is a queue.

But M is far more adventuresome than I, and we did look good – let's face it. I started walking like a zombie towards the front door. As I walked, the queue split open. The owner welcomed us with open arms. As we oozed our way into the back room, someone offered us exquisitely coloured little capsules on a plate. I declined and M declined. Who knew what they were?

M and I danced. We were making the scene. Then, while gyrating to a vicious tempo, I passed out flat on my back on the dance floor. I remember the back of my head hitting the floor with a hard *clunk*. I could feel the floor throbbing. Lights flashed on and off. In my lovely, drop-dead, stud-encrusted jacket, I was dragged off the dance floor and carried out like a sack of potatoes. I was put in a taxi and returned to the Bayerischer Hof, still completely out of my mind. M had the doorman carry me upstairs and lock me in my room. Then she left and rejoined the party. That was the end of the pleasant Munich night when I upstaged Joan Collins.

Vignettes

Somehow, at the age of thirteen, I went on a magical mystery tour to Port-au-Prince, Haiti, to do a skating exhibition.

A slightly older friend of mine at the Lachine arena was a girl named Raymonde Corbo. It seems to me that the Haitian connection was through her. The long and the short of it was, would I like to go to Haiti with her and two other skaters, a girl named Lise Gauthier and my friend Thom Hayim, to skate exhibitions for a week?

Haiti, at the time, was under the dictatorship of Papa Doc Duvalier. Few tourists, or anybody else, ever went there. It was forbidden territory, much more forbidden in those days than, say, Cuba is under the dictatorship of Fidel Castro. I had never travelled outside Canada.

First we were going, then we weren't. One Friday, at ten o'clock at night, Thom Hayim, a friend of almost forty years now, came over to my house and announced, "It's on." My parents never took the trip seriously, nor do I think that they understood (nor did I) the danger inherent in what we proposed to do.

I was picked up from my little suburban home by Thom's father, and we were driven to the airport. All we had to rely on was some sort of Haitian guide with whom we never had much contact. Off we flew to Haiti on Pan American. I had precisely twenty dollars in my pocket and no return ticket.

I have not really thought about Haiti for years. The memories have to be dredged up. Yet that experience was clearly imprinted in my mind. I knew even then that it was all part of the adventure that would run through my life like an enchanted thread. The uniqueness of that particular trip was that no one in the history of the world had ever skated in Haiti. It was virgin ice. I'm not certain that anyone has skated there since.

A gangster of some sort had somehow acquired a refrigeration plant. He could have continued freezing meat, or whatever it was, but instead – I don't know how it ever dawned upon him – he decided to bring skating to Haiti.

We arrived at Port-au-Prince at ten or eleven o'clock at night. It was my first encounter with humid, tropical air. Everywhere there was dampness and mildew. There was scarcely a white face to be seen. Everything was black. There were no streetlights in Haiti. It was shantytown after shantytown as we made our way to the hotel. It was all exotic, forbidden, and terribly exciting. We felt giddy and nervous.

We were not lodged in Port-au-Prince, on the coast. We were staying in the mountains, which was preferable, in a town called Pétionville that might have been at least half an hour outside the capital. We made our way up landscape such as I had never seen – nor have I since. One had the sense of a bygone age. Haiti must have been, at one time, a wealthy colony.

Many houses and villas hung by a hair on that lush, mountainous terrain. The architecture struck me as Haitian shantytown mixed with the grandeur that had preceded it: part Spanish, part French, with a dollop of Victoriana, so that one had the sense of diseased gingerbread houses in a hybrid architectural style.

Everything was falling apart, yet it had a certain tragic romance. It was as though the earth were eating those buildings alive. They were slipping into the ground, yet their scarlet-tiled roofs, hanging balconies, and pillars remained as testaments to what had been. From a distance, you might have thought, "How lovely." Then, if you got closer, you'd think, "How monstrous." It was *Gone With the Wind* gone terribly wrong.

We got to the hôtel Choucoune. It was a fine hotel, with a swimming pool and enclosed garden – impossible for any Haitian to stay there, I suspect. It was a Western hotel, but, as there were no tourists, we were the only people there. We had large, open, high-ceilinged rooms, meticulously appointed, with white marble floors and fans hanging from the ceilings. I roomed with Thom.

The next morning, we got up and had a sumptuous breakfast, served in an imperial way by white-gloved waiters in white coats. All of that was quite unusual for the kid from suburban Baie d'Urfé – and unusual for Haiti, the poorest nation in the Caribbean (in fact, in the hemisphere). We were living pretty high on the hog.

We went to practice. I had chosen a piece of music (I think it was "The Colonel Bogey March") that had a lot of whistling in it. In those days, choreographing a program was unthought of. You just played the music and skated. I was proud to have brought my only skating suit – made of royal-blue wool flannel. When I wore it during the practices and the shows, because of the perspiration, the heat, and the stickiness, it was as though my legs were being eaten up by army ants.

The rink, unlike any that I've seen since, had a low ceiling – maybe eight or nine feet. There was a chance that, if one did an

Axel, one might knock oneself out against the roof. There were no boards. It was just a square of ice plopped in the middle of the factory: tropical ice, which is like skating on chalk. There was a suggestion of a railing around the rink. It was as though we were Martians who had come to a strange planet. Barefooted people in sarongs or loincloths watched while we skated in our woollen suits.

There was also a peculiar French-Canadian comedian (they only make his kind in Montreal) who had no connection to the skating world. His one trick was to stand on his head on a stool with his skates on. Once, the stool slipped and he fell on his head and nearly killed himself.

I remember sitting on a little stool surrounded by huge bugs that buzzed around light bulbs: monstrous creatures, moths with four-inch wingspans. I sat there in my prickly royal-blue wool skating suit beneath a gigantic fan that blew our sweat, like horizontal rain, and splashed it onto the wall.

I recall dim, dim lighting, the kind of lighting one finds at night in the tropics. All we could see were the whites of people's eyes. We were skating for eyeballs.

We were driven around, and it was all quite pleasant, but it was like *The Chronicles of Narnia*, four kids in a fantasy world. People would return us to the hotel, but we basically existed on our own as the shows came and went.

Sometimes we were taken to the sea. The Haitian coast is very rocky. There were no beaches, so you would swim in the ocean, which was wonderful, but when you opened your eyes, you might meet a five-foot-long fish. I stepped on a sea urchin, which stung like crazy. I jumped out of the water. An accommodating Haitian climbed a tree that bore a sour pink fruit, then took a machete, hacked a hole in my toe, and squeezed juice on it. All was well within seconds.

We were taken to a remote, thatched-roof, middle-class house where we met a New York woman who had married a Haitian. We sat cross-legged at her coffee table. She was an intellectual, perhaps a journalist, who nonetheless feared voodoo. Of course I was interested. She had a total comprehension of how dangerous it was, and how real. She said that people who had been cursed could literally die of fright. I had no reason to disbelieve her.

In the market, the merchants sold wooden Haitian figures. Coloured bead necklaces were also in vogue. With ten of my twenty dollars, I bought about ten and a half pounds of beads. I thought that I would go into the bead business in suburban Montreal or else make a bead curtain for my bedroom, the kind in *Casablanca*. We found out that the beads were poisonous. If you put them in your mouth, you would be dead. That's why importing them into North America never really caught on. Those beads ended up as ten years' worth of Christmas presents.

The life indigenous to Haiti was so different from what I knew in Baie d'Urfé. There were herds of beggars. Someone told me that people maimed their children at birth so that they would become professional beggars. Begging in Haiti was so prevalent that it was sort of unionized. Whatever you netted went into a big communal pot that was divvied up at the end of the day.

One fellow shocked me. He had no hands, and his legs were snipped at the hip. He did have arms, and he skittered along the cobblestones at the marketplace with a lead plate strapped to his trunk and lead plates (for hands) on his stumps, so he could skate around and beg. I had never seen anything so grotesque and frightening, yet he often smiled and laughed, in defiance of his lot in life.

Thom and I were taken to a village outside Port-au-Prince. We were invited to go swimming there in a large, slimy, mossy, weedy trough, maybe thirty feet long, in the jungle. The water was black, so the bottom was invisible. I couldn't imagine swimming in that trough, but I encouraged Thom to have a swimming race with a six-and-a-half-foot-tall Haitian stud. We became the toast of the village when Thom won.

One night, there was a tropical rainstorm. It was unlike anything that we have in North America. We got into a Jeep and headed down the mountain for our little performance in Port-au-Prince. It was an extremely frightening and exciting ride. The driver could not see one millimetre ahead, but we were riding on the edge of a precipice. Several times we encountered mud slides. Once, the front wheel of the Jeep got stuck: one little push and we would have fallen hundreds of feet, but we loved it. We thought of it as a midway ride on an out-of-control roller coaster.

The rain continued to pour down in torrents. When we finally arrived in Port-au-Prince, we swooshed into the main square, where the water was four feet deep. Water started to rush in through the Jeep's floorboards. We were going to drown.

Several naked Haitians saved us by pushing the car to higher ground in the nick of time. When we trailed into the rink, soaking wet, to perform for the troops, there weren't any. There wasn't a single person in the audience.

Haiti was mysterious, foreign, exciting, and scary. There were peripatetic policemen with machine guns. The Haitian police were among the most savage and violent hit men of this century. There was an omnipresent sense of danger.

Even at thirteen, I sensed that the political climate was sinister. Haitians had an aura of doom about them. It was as though they were trapped and could never escape. North America was only a few hours away, yet Haiti was the end of the world.

Even our departure was dramatic. The show had not done well. People there couldn't buy a coconut, let alone a ticket to an ice show. They were starving, so how could they possibly? When the last show ended, the factory was either abandoned or went back to being a refrigeration plant, because no one, to my knowledge, has ever seen skating there since.

It was a growing concern that we had no return tickets. The Haitian mob leader who had sponsored our trip and planned to make barrels of gold from our appearance had vanished. We had no way to get home. I believe that the Canadian Consulate intervened, and somehow we got plane tickets. There were portents of something political happening. We didn't know what, and perhaps it was better that way, but we did know that we had to get out fast.

The day came when we were to leave, and we had all our belongings packed up. Thom had bought a large Indian sculpture, the largest and cheapest in the marketplace, but everyone – even the beggars – laughed when they saw it. What he had bought was an enormous colony of termites. Every morning there was a circle of sawdust around the statue on the white marble floor. However, when Thom got back to Montreal, he put the statue in the freezer and killed the termites. He still has that sculpture today. It is probably quite valuable.

On the final afternoon, we left in a taxi. We felt as though we were fleeing for our lives. (I would have contributed to that particular line of thought.) All of a sudden, the taxi's two front tires exploded. We lurched to a stop in the middle of nowhere. There were a few poinsettia bushes, maybe a rooster or two, and that was it. Our escape had come to an end. Lise and Raymonde began to cry.

Always resourceful in desperate situations, I took it upon myself to run in front of a huge transport truck carrying nine layers of turkeys and chickens in boxes in the back. The Haitians speak a French patois, so I don't know how we communicated, but somehow we paid the driver to take us to the airport. We had to ride on top of our luggage, which was on top of nine layers of turkeys and chickens, all pecking and squawking underneath us.

We arrived at the airport, and things were not going well. I don't know if it was a *coup d'état*, but something was happening. We got to Pan American without incident and boarded the plane. Later, we heard that it was the last plane to leave the country for several weeks.

Shortly afterwards, there were uprisings in Haiti. In our naïveté, we weren't absolutely certain that we hadn't contributed to the situation by being well-dressed white imperialists amidst abject poverty. Perhaps our presence had added a certain vitriol to the roiling pot of unrest.

My father met us at the airport. On the way home to the suburbs, I regaled him with my Haitian adventures, my first trip abroad as a skating star.

It has since occurred to me that if I were a parent, never in a million years would I have let my son, at thirteen, go marching off to Haiti. It's not a criticism; it's an observation. I would have said, at least, "Look, if you're going to Haiti, tell me where you're staying, your flight numbers, something." But we went off into the wild blue yonder.

Moving about Haiti was like walking among open cages of lions, tigers, and bears. We weren't hurt, but the atmosphere was ominous. I didn't think about it until years afterwards. At the time, it was, "Hey, we're going to Haiti. We have free plane tickets. Imagine, Haiti! International! The Caribbean! I'll meet Raymonde, Thom, and Lise, and off we'll go."

It isn't as though you can ask another skater, "Tell me your Haitian story." There aren't any others.

The Triumph of Bob McAvoy

The most extraordinary moments in skating have everything to do with drama, emotion, and the human struggle to excel and little or nothing to do with the technical elements of skating. Such was the case with Bob McAvoy, an unusual pairs skater who represented Canada in Ljubljana, Yugoslavia, in 1970.

Bob started skating at eighteen. Just slightly under the age of thirty, he went to Worlds. He probably could have been an exceptional skater had he discovered the sport earlier, but maybe he was even more exceptional for discovering it so late.

Bob was a smallish man, quite a bit older than I, who had skated at the Lachine arena with Thom Hayim and me. He came from a

broken family and was supported by his mother. He worked in theatres as an usher, or at whatever little job he could find, and spent
every single cent on figure skating. Certainly, when he started out,
I couldn't take him seriously as a skater, yet he trained hard and
dedicated his life to skating.

Bob acquired a technically strong partner, Mary Petrie, who was
the junior Canadian champion at the time. They trained with Wally
Distelmeyer, a Canadian teacher, and they qualified for Worlds along
with Sandra and Val Bezic.

Ljubljana was my first Worlds. We went to a training camp on
an army base in Lahr, West Germany, between Freiburg and Baden-
Baden. Now the idea of going to training camp several weeks before
Worlds is old-fashioned, but in those days you did. So there I was,
going to Worlds with someone I had known from the time I was
eleven. He had a strange way of getting to the same place as me, but
he had done it. He was a legitimate competitor.

We were all excited. When you're young, making the world
team is a big deal. We felt that we had arrived. Bob McAvoy wanted
nothing more in life, before he taught skating or hung up his skates,
than to be able to say, "I went to Worlds."

But he never got to the rink in Lahr. He became extremely ill on
the plane and went straight to the army hospital while the rest of us
trained at a hateful, glacial rink that had been built for the Canadian
Armed Forces. We trained and we trained and we trained. Bob, in
the evil way that the Ferris wheel has of continuing to turn without
you, was not on board. That was difficult for his partner, too, but
what could she do?

It is my belief that during our two-week sojourn in Lahr, almost
no one went to visit Bob in the hospital. I took it upon myself to see
him on the day before we were to fly to Ljubljana. What I saw on
the cot was a shadow of the person who had flown to West Germany
with me two weeks earlier. He had lost maybe fifteen pounds. He

was gaunt, grey, sick, and weak, and he was feeling sorry for himself – for good reason. He was about as low as he could get.

I sat beside him on his cot. We recalled the days when we used to dream about such things as Worlds. I said, "Bob, you know, you've just *got* to get out of bed. You've just *got* to go to Worlds. You've just *got* to go to Ljubljana." He kept saying, "I can't. I can't. I'm too weak."

I believe that my visit charged him up a bit. He joined the group, and we flew to Ljubljana. When we arrived there, he and his partner were virtually summoned from the airport to go to an outdoor practice in a snowy, freezing rink. They went. They practised.

The short program was the next day. How he galvanized himself to do it, I'm not certain, but he did. He and Mary even beat the Canadian champions, Sandra and Val Bezic.[*]

The long program in those days was gruelling. At five minutes in length, it wasn't so much a test of skating as a test of endurance – the very quality to which that unfortunate competitor couldn't possibly lay claim.

Everything appeared to be fine in Bob and Mary's warm-up and at the beginning of their performance. They did a number of difficult manoeuvres: double flips, throw Axels, and whatever else one did then. But right in the middle of the program, during an extended overhead lift, the fact that Bob had no strength hit him like a bolt of lightning. He was paralysed. He just stopped. His face turned green, and his arms buckled like spaghetti. Mary dropped flat on her face and lay there on her stomach, her legs splayed. Bob also fell on his stomach and lay where he landed.

The music kept going, which added a macabre touch. The referee – the person who was supposed to *do* something – did

---

[*] Petrie/McAvoy placed twelfth for the short program, two spots ahead of the Bezics.

nothing. The audience was flabbergasted. Somebody should have run out onto the ice and saved Mary and Bob, but no one moved.

They must have lain on their faces for at least thirty seconds. Bob then raised himself up a bit. His face was scraped, and he had blood on his cheeks. On his hands and knees, he made his way to his semi-conscious partner, put his arm around her, and pulled her up. Somehow they managed to stand. Her face was severely scraped. Blood seeped from the wounds. The audience remained in a state of shock. No one knew what to do, and the music played on.

Then, in an extremely masculine and noble way, Bob brushed the snow off the back of Mary's dress. Next, he made a gesture that the audience could understand without hearing his words. The gesture said, "Would you like to continue?" Mary said yes.

As they started to skate again, the audience began to boil like Mount Vesuvius. Within fifteen seconds, not a single note of the music could be heard. The spectators were so boisterous, so explosive, that whatever strength the skaters lacked personally they got from the crowd. The pair skated the performance of their lives.

As Bob and Mary ended their program, they received an ovation equal in emotion to any that I have ever heard. It was a moment when skating took a back seat to integrity, sportsmanship, and the belief that nothing is impossible to a willing heart.

The judges, bound either by fear or rules, gave them marks that reflected the terrible accident.[*] But if their technical mark was 3.5, as a skater, as a knowledgeable member of the audience, or as a judge, I would have held up a 6.0 and would have been damned for it – but that is what they deserved. Their performance completely eclipsed the brilliance of Irina Rodnina and Alexei Ulanov, the eventual winners. It was a triumph. My eyes mist over when I remember that performance, because I can still *see* it.

---

[*] They finished fifteenth (of seventeen competitors) in the long program and overall.

In December 1994, at his mother's home in San Diego, California, Bob McAvoy died of AIDS.

Craig Russell

Craig Russell was a phenomenally talented female impersonator. I met him in 1981 at the annual Christmas party of Gino Empry, his manager and publicity agent. (That was the same year his four-city tour of Western Canada was cancelled when he undressed on stage and threw wigs and jewellery at the audience.) I wanted to dislike Craig immediately, but I couldn't. The second that he opened his mouth, I sensed a superior intelligence; someone who could show-direct the room; someone who had been around; someone who knew the secret to many of life's quandaries; someone who had a broad understanding of humanity.

We shook hands, I in black velvet and a silver belt, he in a tuxedo and high heels. His face was nondescript, the quintessential androgynous face. His voice was neither masculine nor feminine. He was a different species altogether. He winked as though we were having a special conversation and said, "Tell me, Toller. Which one of us is really skating on thin ice?"

That was perceptive. I thought about it for several days afterwards, wondering if it was just a clever remark or if he possessed a certain psychological X-ray vision.

Whenever Craig and I ran into each other, he was friendly and nice. Perhaps more tragic in his own way than Judy Garland (whom he could imitate to perfection), his burden was multi-faceted: drugs, alcohol, a questionable gender, insecurity about who his friends were. He was a yacht without a rudder, and the captain was lying on the deck in sunglasses, getting a tan. That yacht, during Craig's rather brief life, got into a lot of rocky, troubled waters and sank prematurely because of his own neglect.

Outrageous, the 1977 movie that Craig had written and starred in, was done on a shoestring yet made millions – of which he didn't receive a dime.* A decade later, it went into round two: *Too Outrageous*. Of course, sequels of artistic, clever, real films rarely work. Once Hollywood gets in, starts dumping big money and hiring name actors, the charm of the original is lost. The whole thing was a blowout and had absolutely nothing to do with Craig Russell or with the intensity, true emotion, and torment of a transvestite drag queen. It was glamorized, gilded, and turned into a phony C-minus movie.

During the filming of *Too Outrageous*, Craig stayed in a hotel three and a half minutes from the house I then had on Pembroke Street. Like many stars – he was a star, and I was at least perceived as one – Craig and I each spent frequent nights alone. You will literally go out with your cleaning lady just to assuage the hurt and loneliness.

Craig phoned me on one of those Saturday nights when he was staying at the Jarvis Arms. We chatted. He was amusing in the way that Charlie Chaplin could be. He was profound and as funny as any person in the world, on any subject.

I suggested that we could have dinner at his hotel. That would be fine, he said, "but I must warn you. I've been playing."

I hung up the phone, not knowing what "playing" meant. Craig arrived in a costume that I couldn't quite identify. I think that peignoir is the closest thing to it: a diaphanous, floaty top, a pair of pants, and sandals. His hair was androgynous. Fortunately, the hotel staff was aware of his idiosyncrasies. As soon as he sat down at the table, he grabbed the centrepiece, a bouquet of chrysanthemums, and dropped it onto the top of his head without missing a beat. He wore a tremendous crown of flowers but made no reference to it. Many people in the restaurant fled for the exit.

Part of me (because I'm really not that brazen) was uncomfortable. But why should I have been? I was sitting next to an historical

---

* At the Virgin Islands Film Festival, Russell was named both best actor and best actress.

person who was one million times more hilarious, original, and fantastic than any of the lines in the movies he made. He had brilliant timing. He was a font of information. There was a genius in him that I acknowledged right off the top: genius on the wrong track, or maybe genius on the right track, but appreciated by few.

Craig Russell taught me something that became one of my golden rules of life. He had at one time been doing sold-out business in a theatre on the Maximilianstrasse in Munich, but he hadn't been getting paid. (That sounded familiar.) He had run down to the box office in the guise of Tallulah Bankhead as people marched in to see his show, and he had made a demand in German that he taught to me as we had dinner together. I am happy to pass it on to anyone who cares to listen: *Geld in Hand.* Money in the hand. Money in the hand before I do another show. I have told that to many a skater, and many have thanked me for it. I firmly subscribe to the philosophy of *Geld in Hand.*

At the end of the evening, Craig, in high heels and peignoir, offered to walk me back to my house through a rough park frequented by thugs, prostitutes, and drug dealers. I didn't think that was a good idea. I was extremely nervous, and I tried to walk in front or trail behind him by ten paces. I didn't want anyone to know that we were together.

"Craig," I said, as I slammed my gate and established a barrier between us, "you really must be careful when you go home. There are dangerous people out there."

He said, in essence, "Don't worry about this old broad. I can take care of myself. I know how to handle them."

With everything that he'd been through in his life, with the bars and the shows and the tough crowds, he probably could have taken on the Hell's Angels and come out kicking.

I went to the opening of *Too Outrageous* and watched Craig Russell accept the accolades of the crowd. He arrived in high heels and a pale-blue satin tuxedo with glittery lapels. He was on a high, but it was a hollow high. We both knew that the film was a bomb. I could see the loneliness out there on the stage as he kicked up his heels and camped it up.

Craig liked to say, "I'm a drag queen. I'm a transvestite. I'm a drug addict. I'm an alcoholic. I'm a homosexual. Other than that, I'm perfectly normal." Such people are bound to crash, somehow, some way.

I'm sorry that that brilliant, incredible man couldn't have lived longer and been properly understood. With him, I felt that I was seeing live theatre in my own home, better than any entertainment that I've ever witnessed: *théâtre vérité*, the real thing. I cried tears of laughter mixed with tears of respect.

Once, Craig came to my house with one of the fellows he was living with, a motorcycle and black leather kind of guy. Craig was poor, but he could do the most fantastic things. He could rifle a liquor closet and steal Scotch and rum in such a charming, hilarious way that you simply couldn't hold it against him. Sometimes, whether due to drugs or inebriation, he balanced and juggled rare objets d'art. Vases of flowers sprang from the mantelpiece, but he caught them in the nick of time.

On that particular day, he had arrived in a jacket, a pair of short shorts, a T-shirt, and bare feet. He left, higher than a kite, and leapt onto the back of his motorcycle, wearing his helmet like Nefertiti's crown – back on his head, bulging out like a bouffant hairdo. As he vanished into the sunset, he pulled two bottles of my Scotch from his jacket and waved them in a gesture of thanks. That was the last time I ever saw him. He died of a stroke resulting from AIDS not long afterwards.[*]

---

[*] Russell died on October 30, 1990, at the age of forty-two.

The Lost Dog

Going back to the time when I was seven or eight years old, the various branches of the Cranston clan (which originally sprang from the town of Arnprior, Ontario, in the Ottawa Valley) always had English setters.* English setters are bird dogs, quite the most beautiful members of the canine species, and when it came to choosing a dog for myself, no other breed would even have entered my head. I've had five English setters.

The finest dogs I've owned have always been bought sight unseen. They have arrived by airplane, and it has been love at first sight. My *most* favourite (but it's really a draw between two dogs) was Minkus, a dog with a unique personality and great smarts. But it's like *Sophie's Choice.* How can I decide which I prefer? The male dog, Minkus, or the female dog that I now own, Flora.

Minkus became impaled on a wire fence on the day that I got him as a puppy, so one of his eyes was a little bit crooked, which gave him a cocky, boyish *Little Rascals* look. That dog became a champion and was, among all the English setters that I've encountered, first among equals. Dog lovers occasionally hit the jackpot in that way.

In September 1986, I was having a fence built around my property to keep out the riffraff (the drug trade, the prostitutes, and sundry other lowlifes) on Pembroke Street in Toronto where I lived amidst brilliant trash and refined vulgarity. As the fence was being built, my back door was left open, and Minkus escaped.

Setters are wanderers by nature. That particular setter, however, was wandering around what amounted to the most dangerous, depraved area of Toronto. If I had lost him in a respectable

---

* Toller's grandparents raised his father in Arnprior. As a child, Toller spent summers at a lake cottage there.

neighbourhood, I wouldn't have worried as much. On Pembroke Street, I couldn't be certain that he hadn't been hit by a streetcar, abducted, eaten, or sold. There he was, the faithful companion who had slept rolled up like a doughnut on my bed every night, on the loose in the middle of a raunchy metropolitan area.

I knew many of the prostitutes who worked Pembroke Street, and they certainly knew Minkus, because we walked so much. I started out alone, not knowing where to go or what to do. I asked every street person, prostitute, drug addict, lowlife, alcoholic, and escapee from a mental institution, "Have you seen my dog?"

The search expanded in an unexpected way. A veritable army of neighbourhood recruits fanned out over the entire red-light district. There was a Danish prostitute with bad teeth but a good body who was over forty-five years old and teetered on the highest of stiletto heels. I told her about Minkus. I was flattered moments later when a john tried to pick her up, and she said, "I can't. I'm looking for a dog." Off she scampered down an alley in her stilettos.

That was not unusual. It is common knowledge that people who work the streets, and people who live in the streets, often have an enormous capacity for both passion and compassion.

Minkus became national and international news. I contacted the Toronto newspapers the *Star*, the *Globe*, and the *Sun*. They ran photos and printed articles about Toller Cranston's lost champion English setter. I went on every radio and television station. I begged people to give Minkus back or come forward with information. Something happened that was incredible and rather depressing. I had given out my private telephone number, and I had thirty calls from people who either claimed to have seen the dog or said, "Come over to my house. We have him. He's fine." The address would turn out to be an empty parking lot. I was in a rather terrible depression.

The Toronto police force got in on the act. So did the Royal Canadian Mounted Police. There were rewards. It became a national

issue. Eventually, I had a call from the police in Peterborough, Ontario, an hour and a half away from Toronto. Minkus had been found. Someone had, indeed, stolen him, but he had become too hot to keep. English setters are uniquely marked. Whoever had taken him had become nervous and had abandoned him, tied to a tree.

So Minkus came back. Of course, you're hoping that he will run into your arms and whimper and cry, which is what people would do, but the dog was more interested in what we were having for dinner. Still, I was happy to have him home. You don't know how important anything so dear to you is until you lose it.

That's not quite the end of the story. To show my appreciation, when the Pembroke Street house was absolutely at its rococo-gone-loco best, I had a cocktail party for all the people who had helped me: the drug addicts, the prostitutes, the pimps, and the mental patients from the streets. They all came. They behaved better than anyone could possibly have behaved in the presence of

Elizabeth II. They were imperial. They were perfection. They were so helpful. They were so "Can I pass this? Can I wash that?" Both the men and the women.

There were a gazillion objects in the house, yet not a thing was stolen. My guests appreciated the party, and they were like all the rest of us – people having a good time, having a nice little drink. They behaved, because the environment (which, after all, was like Versailles) dictated their behaviour, even though outside the door was the street where they picked up tricks. It was surreal, yet pleasant and thought-provoking.

The next day, when they were back on the street, many who had been kind and polite didn't want to know me. They didn't say, "Hi. How's your dog?" They went back to their profession, and I went back to my life. It was business as usual.

Sonja Henie's Prediction

Don Watson, the manager of Ice Capades, understood stardom. He had skated in Holiday on Ice as a principal and knew every old show poodle in the history of the world. What that kind of person always says is, "They don't make them the way they used to" and "There are no stars any more."

Don had enjoyed my participation in Ice Capades because he liked my attention to detail and my willingness to perform with as much passion as possible, even with three shows a day. He likened my approach to the obsessive-compulsiveness of Sonja Henie.

In his office, he had a photograph of her – a large, antique photograph, quite valuable. He gave it to me. I went home and signed it in swirling penmanship with elaborate flourishes:

> *To Dearest Toller,*
> *Only you will compete with my legend.*
> *Love, Sonja*

I dated it. Then I had it attractively framed and hung in the red bathroom at 64 Pembroke Street.

That photograph scored many points. JoJo Starbuck, one of the first to see it, asked, "How did she *know*? Tell me about her." I was aware that Sonja Henie had died in the late 1960s. I said that I'd been in L.A., had met her (which I hadn't), and had asked, "Could you please give me a photograph, and would you kindly sign something dramatic?" That was my story. JoJo was absolutely intoxicated with that photograph.

Brian Boitano blanched when he saw it. Caryn Kadavy did somersaults. They couldn't believe that Sonja Henie had predicted my future while I was still so young.

"There are people who know that sort of thing," I assured them.

If the crime was forging a signature, then it truly was a crime, but Sonja Henie is dead, and it *is* an original photograph. I think of it as an original fake. It gave such a thrill to so many people that I could rationalize the forgery. Brian Orser was quite taken with it, and Robin Cousins paled when he saw it and made no comment whatsoever.[*]

The Royal Family

In 1987, after the World Professional Figure Skating Championships in Landover, Maryland, produced by Dick Button, all the skaters were invited to do a television show in Lausanne, Switzerland, called *"Hommage à Dorothy Hamill."*[†]

Peter and Kitty Carruthers, Scott Hamilton, Robin Cousins, Norbert Schramm, Oleg and Ludmila Protopopov, Tiffany Chin,

---

[*] Robin later forced Toller to confess, then obtained a similar photograph and forged the more modest sentiments, *A joy to have met you. Much success always. Sonja.*

[†] The event was filmed by Home Box Office TV on December 16, 1987.

Rosalynn Sumners, Judy Blumberg, Michael Seibert, Barbara
Underhill, Paul Martini, and I flew to Europe in first class. We were
picked up at the airport and taken to the most sumptuous place in
hoteldom. To this day, I think that it is the most splendid hotel in
which I have ever stayed. The Beau-Rivage Palace has lawns and
gardens that stretch down to Lake Geneva. It is an imposing hotel,
grand belle époque. All the floors open onto a huge atrium.

I checked into my room – the most wonderful room. I could
have lived there for the rest of my life. It was a rhapsody of vanilla
shades: vanilla wall-to-wall carpeting, vanilla walls, vanilla bed-
spread. It was somewhat anemic in the daytime, but as dusk
descended and lights came on, the vanilla glowed like golden toffee.

There were crisp sheets and a panel of dials beside the bed.
One button made the blinds go up and down. Another fluttered
the shutters. The lovely marble bathtub in the white marble bathroom had dials for adjusting the television that overhung it. I was
quite in heaven about that. On the first day, I rarely left my vanilla-
toffee room.

I decided to send my laundry down to be washed. I phoned room service and up came the valet. Soon after he left, it dawned upon me that I could buy three times the number of new clothes for the price of the washing. I demanded that my dirty laundry come back. ("This is room 203. The dirty laundry that I sent down? Could you bring it back immediately, please?")

I then decided to order room service: a memorable meal by any standard. After the waiter brought it in, I jumped up and down and gave it a standing ovation. It was simple enough: a fresh salad with sprinkles of edible pink and violet Alpine wildflowers; lamb chops, cooked to euphoric perfection; and an apple tart with crisscross pastry and ice cream. That exquisite meal cost $135 American, and it was worth every penny. I wanted to do it all again.

Next came the interviews for the tribute. Dorothy, who had just won Landover and was very successful, was married at the time to someone whom I thought to be drippy. Although it wasn't his real name, I called him Ken Hamill.

I remember going into a grand suite with parquet floors and oriental rugs. We all had to sit in Louis Quatorze chairs and rhapsodize about Dorothy – while Ken presided. Only Scott Hamilton refused to go along. He was not fond of Ken either. When we presented Dorothy at the end of the ice show, he refused to come out until we had finished.

I have skated in many cold rinks, but the Patinoire de Malley in Lausanne has to be one of the coldest. It was an open, unheated rink, and although it was covered by a roof, the wind blew in through the sides. Dick Button's friend Dennis Grimaldi tried hard, but he did not have skating credentials, and nobody bought his choreography for the final number. I did something extremely mean. I don't think that Dennis Grimaldi has spoken to me since.

But we were all cold and irritable – irritable for two reasons. First, every time there was a practice, Ken Hamill arrived with

Hermès bags and presented Dorothy with a growing mountain of gifts. That did not impress us. We were working, we were freezing, and he was shopping. The Hermès bags piled up daily. We didn't really want to see what was in them, but we had to, because he kept showing us.

As Ken was procuring the Hermès bags, Dennis Grimaldi was attempting to choreograph the finale. Instead of getting it over with, Norbert Schramm, Scott Hamilton, Peter Carruthers, and I pretended that we didn't know the steps. Although we were getting colder and colder, poor Dennis Grimaldi was standing on the ice in street shoes. I'm surprised that his feet were not amputated after that session. We kept him there for hours to punish him for not knowing how to handle us.

The show came and went. We all rode on a bus from the Beau-Rivage to the airport. Then something happened that I really cannot forget. (It happened several other times.) We had done the show. We had gotten up early. We were tired, sore, and stiff. We were lining up at the Swissair counter to check in for our flight to Paris. Ken arrived and stomped to the front of the line. He announced, "*We* are the stars of the show, and *we're first!*" Peter Carruthers almost exploded. We had tried hard for Dorothy, but in that family, in that company, nobody is first over anybody. When Ken threw himself in the front of the line, perhaps we were too tired to react, but no one ever forgot.

We went on to Paris for an exhibition at the new Palais Omnisports Paris Bercy, that remarkable building half underground with grass growing up the sides. It was the first time we'd ever had elephants in the next dressing room. I don't know what the correct word for elephant smell is, but it's way beyond hircine.

So we practised in the rink next to the circus. Then something happened to me that all skaters fear. Where you skate in the program reflects your position in the skating world. All of a sudden, I saw that my name (the *Patineur du Siècle!*) was second on the bill. That had never happened to me before. It caught me unaware. I couldn't do it. My ego would not support it. I knew that if I allowed that to happen, it would be the beginning of the end. Dick Button really couldn't have cared a smidge about what skater and which skater. Nonetheless, I threw down the gauntlet and said, "If you dare put me in the second slot, I will leave immediately on the next plane" (even though – but Dick didn't know it – I had lost my return ticket).

Scott Hamilton came to the rescue. You know how you sort of owe somebody something? Scott said, "Toller, I'll be happy to skate second. You skate in my position." I suspect that he wasn't thrilled about being in Paris, about the Dorothy Hamill thing, or whatever it was, so I thanked him and skated in my accustomed place.

I wanted to be svelte for that particular show. It was being televised all over Europe. I spent the entire night eating Ex-Lax. I went to bed thinking that I was chubby, but I woke up pretty thin.

Dick Button absolutely refused to allow anyone who had skated in Landover to perform the same numbers in Paris. I hadn't arrived prepared, but I did what many skaters do. (I'm not sure if I invented it, but I definitely support it and recommend it in a jam.) I took a new piece of music and used the choreography from another number. Everyone loved my new program. Well, I did get a few boos, because I performed to "Ave Maria" (which may have been sacrilegious in France).

There is something else that I remember clearly from that show. On the surface, I project a bravura attitude and a certain kind of arrogance. It's all my little act. Everyone has one. In truth, I am always extremely nervous about skating. Oleg Protopopov said something in Paris that was just what I needed to hear. (Oleg is very sage, one of the few intellectuals in skating. Both he and his wife are wise. Anyone who knows them is lucky.) He grabbed me and said,

"Why are you nervous? Can't you just go out there and enjoy skating and love skating and drown in the pleasure of skating?"

I did drown in the pleasure of skating that night, thanks to Oleg. I had forgotten how you can go out and love it. I've tried to impart that to others since then.

The evening ended, and we were all taken to that splendid restaurant where I had dined with Artur Rubinstein, the Élysée Matignon. We had the most wonderful meal. I could not get enough of the delicious hors d'oeuvre. After the third helping, I had to ask what it was. The answer was sweetbreads. I didn't have a fourth helping. We ended the meal with a pineapple *bombe* dessert.

That was one of the rare nights when the royal family of skating was all in attendance, and everyone had a jolly old time. It was about being in Paris, being an ice star. That was the way things were supposed to be.

I'm afraid that I was extremely rude to Dick Button's associate Jirina Ribbens before we left, because I was terribly worried about my lost ticket. Somehow I managed to get on the plane, though I had to come home by a circuitous route. Still, those were the wrinkles, textures, fibres, and designs that made up the fabric of membership in the royal family of skating in 1987. I was so happy to be a part of it.

The Duchesnays in Prague

If the Bob McAvoy incident was the most dramatic thing that I ever saw as a competitor, the Duchesnay performance at the 1988 Europeans in Prague, Czechoslovakia, was a country mile ahead of anything I had seen as a commentator.

Going to Prague was exciting, because Prague, and before it Budapest, were cities on the brink of bringing down the régimes that had governed and oppressed them for decades. Revolution was in the offing.

Prague has celebrated more than one thousand birthdays, and its medieval past has been preserved. It was a city that I knew and looked forward to visiting. The CBC contingent stayed at the Inter-Continental, a grand hotel on the Vltava River. Being the frugal man that he was, Bob Moir, the CBC's executive producer of television sports programming, never took a taxi to the rink. We took street-cars and mingled with the people of Prague.

I had skated in the building many times. The layout was extra-ordinary: the seats rose from ice level, almost vertically, to the ceiling. Many famous performances had been played out there, notably Donald Jackson's in 1962 when he achieved the first official triple Lutz.

As a commentator, I ensconced myself on a rather lofty perch. I could see the competition, meet and talk with judges and members of the International Skating Union, and also fraternize and kibitz with the competitors themselves. When it all ended, that was what I missed most.[*]

The competition that year was rather forgettable except for one incident: the revolution in ice dance caused by Paul and Isabelle Duchesnay. The Duchesnays, Canadians by domicile, had been more or less rejected by the Canadian Figure Skating Association. They had gone to Europe to skate for France, but trained in Oberstdorf, West Germany, with a Czechoslovakian coach. It was the competition in Prague that was to catapult them to renown, serious money, and world and Olympic medals. Before Prague, no one had taken them seriously.

The Russian school of ice dance – that had begun its reign with Ludmila Pakhomova/Alexander Gorshkov, passed to Irina Moiseeva/Andrei Minenkov, then continued with Natalia Linichuk/Gennadi

---

[*] Toller provided colour commentary on major CBC skating telecasts between 1982 and early 1991.

Karponosov, and the list goes on – was characterized by a flamboy-
ant, melodramatic, over-the-top, overly choreographed style that the
Soviets did well and nobody else could manage. Jayne Torvill and
Christopher Dean were the first to present an alternative, but what
the Duchesnays offered at Prague was the complete antithesis of the
Russian style.

The favourites of the moment, who subsequently became the
1988 Olympic champions, were Natalia Bestemianova and Andrei
Bukin. They presented their Olympic program in costumes that, if
not the emperor's new suit, were akin to the emperor wearing very
new, very gauche, and very gaudy clothes. They had gone so far off
the deep end that Andrei wore a kind of tunic skirt and Natalia wore
the pants – more precisely, the bloomers.

The Duchesnays skated what was to be probably their most
memorable, although not technically their best, performance, a
number to which I refer (indeed, I guess the world does) as the
jungle dance. As brother and sister, they had to avoid any suggestion of romance. So while others came out in gold lamé, black
velvet, and rhinestones, they came out in leather tatters and rags,
almost non-costumes: again, the complete antithesis of what the
Soviets offered.

The music was almost non-music, with a preponderance of
drums. It was like an Amazonian brother and sister hunting a wild
beast: primal, ritualistic, and intense. They paid absolutely no attention to the audience, or even to the environment in which they were
performing. It was an out-of-body experience for them as well as for
anyone looking on.

Whether it was the rhythm, whether it was the complete alternative to ice dancing as we knew it, or whether it was the drums
beating on the hearts of the Czechoslovakian people who were soon
to rid themselves of the Soviet yoke, nobody knows. But with that
four-minute performance, the Duchesnays pressed a button in the
audience that triggered a revolution – a revolution that not only

changed the face of skating and offered an alternative to what we had known, but also one that potentially preyed upon the inclinations of the Czechs to revolt against tyranny.

That performance, as all great performances do, became secondary to the personal feelings of the voyeur. It triggered an emotional response within each spectator that had little to do with skating. It made each one feel something about himself or his state of being. The audience became so passionate that it bordered on the dangerous. There could have been an incident. The Czechoslovakian revolution might have started in an ice rink. It was possible.

The Duchesnays were a threat to Soviet medals, and the Soviet bloc had a glorified mafia holding up the top three teams in the Olympic year.[*] The Polish judge, I'm sure, got caught. She did what she was supposed to do, while her colleagues jumped ship. The

---

[*] Bestemianova/Bukin, Annenko/Sretenski, and Usova/Zhulin finished 1-2-3 in the original set pattern dance. The Duchesnays placed fifth for compulsory dances and fourth in the OSP. As a result of their free dance, they won the bronze medal.

Polish judge gave the Duchesnays 4.7 and 4.8, while the others, who had probably planned to give 4.8s too, decided that they had better give 5.8s if they were going to get out of that building alive.

The Polish judge blanched and later had to be physically escorted from the building by security guards. She had been going along with the old régime, and she was caught with her pants down. She later tried to recant by saying that she'd accidentally pushed 4.7 and 4.8 instead of 5.7 and 5.8, but whether that was true or not, it did not change the temperature of the building or the reaction that the Duchesnays had provoked.

' 12 '

The Electric Chair

*S*ometimes in one's life, one has absolutely no indication, no sense, no premonition, that an innocent-seeming request could actually be the equivalent of agreeing to one's death sentence. Such was the case with Christopher Bowman, a U.S. men's champion and world silver medallist in decline.

Shortly before he skated the long program at the Goodwill Games in Seattle during the summer of 1990, Christopher asked me to teach him if he came to Toronto.

I was moderately interested in teaching. The one thing that every teacher knows is that it's not really a question of how brilliant a teacher you are, but whom you teach, that makes your name. Christopher Bowman was a very large fish in the skating pond.

He had a legendary controversial background. Many stories about him circulated in the skating world. As a Canadian without firsthand information, I had no way of knowing whether the stories were exaggerated, true, or false, so I paid no attention to them. Silly me. I agreed to take him on but didn't expect to hear from him again.

A week and a half later, my doorbell rang. Seven suitcases were on my doorstep, accompanied by Christopher Bowman. Certainly I remembered our conversation, but I was in no way prepared for his arrival. Still, deep down inside, I was rather thrilled. That was how much I knew.

Christopher said that he was hungry. I had another skater staying in my house at 64 Pembroke Street, a French-Canadian boy who suggested that we go out for a bite to eat. The French-Canadian boy, I think, was somewhat awed by the presence of the great Christopher Bowman on our doorstep. He happily agreed to drive to Greek town, which had the only restaurants we knew to be open on a rainy Sunday night. No sooner did we arrive in Greek town than we had a traffic accident. The French-Canadian boy's car was severely damaged.

Christopher took it in stride. He told the French-Canadian boy, "Look, you just stay here and deal with the police. We'll go and have souvlaki in the Greek restaurant." If that was an omen, why, oh why, couldn't I have understood it?

I might add that at another time our entourage was pulled over by the police because the hapless French-Canadian boy had a fake European licence plate on his car. Somehow, the police and Christopher Bowman were drawn to each other like two magnets.

The Orphean Descent

The next day, Christopher made his inauspicious début at the Cricket Club. I was shocked at the level his skating had slipped to. He could do no more than a waltz jump and a sit spin. I tried hard, knowing that he had problems, knowing that it was all going to be a new beginning for him, to coax him, for what I believe was hours a day, into the most modest manoeuvres such as an Axel, and did he think that maybe he could give birth to a double Salchow?

I had to leave Toronto to honour a previous commitment. When I woke up in the morning, quite prepared to leave Christopher and the French-Canadian boy home alone, I walked into my living room to find Christopher naked on the floor – with a female skater I knew (not his girlfriend) lying naked beside him. That was not exactly what I had in mind.

I ran outside and phoned Ellen Burka from a pay phone. She suggested that I pitch a pail of ice water on them, but I declined on the grounds that I was rather fond of a valuable oriental rug beneath them.

Early on in the stay, Christopher's girlfriend hit the scene and became a major distraction. She was pregnant, and what could *we* do about that? A legal abortion had to be arranged.

There were rumours that Christopher had a problem with drugs, but I, too, had taken drugs now and then, and somehow I felt that I could be his saviour. Again, silly me.

By midway into Christopher's stay at 64 Pembroke Street, just before the U.S. national championships, drug dealers buzzed the front doorbell morning, noon, and night. Prostitutes invaded my house from the street. Christopher sometimes announced that he was going out for a carton of milk and didn't return for three days.

Ellen and I both taught Christopher, but in many ways that wasn't fair. The real responsibility of living with him, of being accountable for his appearance at the ice rink, was on my shoulders. When Ellen lost her sister and had to go to the Netherlands, I called her and cried on the telephone, not knowing what to do. Ellen howled with laughter on the other end of the line.* Truly,

---

* Ellen denies "howling" with laughter.

she – a good friend and confidante – did not understand what was happening.

Before I went to the European championships as a commentator, I begged Christopher, who was going to be staying at my house alone, "Please, you don't have to skate, you don't have to work, you don't have to do anything, but *do not* have that girl here while I'm away."

As I was flying out of the Toronto airport, his girlfriend was landing, I later found out. She moved into my house. Objects were sold, I believe to buy drugs: crack cocaine, to be precise. Christopher and his paramour apparently hoped that, in my museum, I wouldn't notice that things were missing.

Christopher (he thought it was very funny) many times brought hookers from the area where I lived into the Cricket Club, something that I could not condone.

He had no conscience. Often money was stolen from my skate bag. When confronted, Christopher would admit to stealing it, yet he could not be insulted or be made to feel guilty. His mother (who came to stay) would say, "Oh, did he do it again? Don't worry. I'll pay you."

That wasn't the point.

Christopher Bowman was responsible for a major change in my life, but I do not blame him. Nor do I blame his mother, Joyce, who came from California for a time to act as the guardian pit bull. The fact that I could no longer enjoy my house, the fact that I had given up my own skating career, the fact that I was so depressed and frustrated that I could not paint and did not paint for nine months, was my own fault. The torture that I went through was perceived by those who knew us both as extremely comical. For me, it was like living in an electric chair. The depth of my frustration cannot be articulated.

Why didn't I just send him away? I had passed the point of no return. I had given up my life. I had given up my art. I had given up my skating. I had nothing. I had to go through to the bitter end, because that was all I had. In the Aries way, I could not give up – just as, in my skating, I could never take no for an answer. I couldn't accept failure.

Clothes Make the Man . . . or Whatever

Living with Christopher Bowman was destructive and painful, but amusing things invariably happened. Truly, he had huge charisma, tremendous personality, and a wonderful sense of humour. He could be kind and generous as well. One incident struck him as especially funny.

Mikey was a drunken, anorexic, toothless, middle-aged street person I knew who had been a bartender at the Granite Club for many years, until he was thrown out for drinking the profits. He often did things around my house. He looked after my yard. He was supremely meticulous.

I asked him if he would mind cleaning out my basement (which, in the five-thousand-square-foot house, was large). Like everybody's basement, it was full of things that I had casually stashed there because I didn't need them or didn't want them or wasn't using them. I asked Mikey, without giving him precise instructions, to generally tidy up and throw in the garbage anything that he thought was unimportant.

At about seven o'clock that evening, I arrived home via Dundas Street. (My house was almost at the corner of Pembroke and Dundas.) I immediately sensed that something was up. There was tremendous action outside my gate. There was energy in the air. I thought that it was a street party, which struck me as strange, because it was in front of my house, but I wasn't there. Suddenly, the truth dawned upon me.

As I began to whimper in the back seat of the cab, Christopher started to roar. What little Mikey had done was clean out the basement the way a piranha might clean the flesh off a cow crossing the Amazon. It was to the bone. He had pitched my life into the street.

Countless cardboard closets had been thrown out, and all the drug addicts, all the pimps, all the street people, and all the prostitutes were having a wonderful time trying on my skating costumes, of which, without exaggeration, there must have been fifty. My 1973 Worlds costume was being paraded around by a buxom platinum-blonde prostitute in red stilettos who couldn't quite manage to do up the front zipper.

Those costumes were, in their own way, sacred. They had played their role in special moments. They were also rather expensive. And there were *fifty* of them, strutting up and down Dundas and Pembroke.

An even more grave and horrendous loss than my costumes were the scores of scrapbooks that I had kept from childhood, the memorabilia, and the many letters (including one from Pierre Elliott

Trudeau, and a telegram from Princess Diana) that were literally lying in the gutter. I went into shock.

Christopher thought that it was quite the funniest thing ever. Indeed, if one can step out of one's skin, the scene was unlike anything that Toronto had ever witnessed. The costumes were androgynous, heavily encrusted with beads, feathers, and rhinestones. Both men and women were dashing around in them, like a swarm of locusts – Las Vegas locusts. I did not know quite what to do.

As I was walking through my gate, making my way past the grasping, clutching, half-dressed, frenzied hordes, I somehow struck up a conversation with a pimp – a sensitive pimp.

He said, "Look, guy, you don't need all this shit. These people are having the time of their lives. They need it more than you do."

I realized that he was right. I would never again wear those *outré*, jewel-studded costumes. Even then, they were of an era that had run its course. I went into the house, had a glass of strong liquor (which I don't usually drink), and shared a laugh with Christopher. He and I were in harmony for once.

For months afterward, I saw fragments of my glittery, star-studded life popping into johns' cars and trolling the streets in high heels. Perhaps it was the ultimate, sad proof of how far off the track my life had somehow gone.

Off with His Head

During the time when I was teaching Christopher Bowman, it is true that, as a commentator, I started to become somewhat drunk with my own power. Christopher, because of his talent and charisma, was a genuine threat to any competitor in the world, but particularly to Kurt Browning, the reigning two-time world champion.[*] Because

---

[*] Browning went on to earn a third world title a month later. He won his fourth and final championship in 1993.

Christopher was cause for alarm in the Browning camp and within the CFSA, and because the CFSA objected to me teaching him, the CBC in February 1991 found itself between a rock and a hard place.

The CBC knew, certainly, that I had a reputation for being precise, somewhat caustic, and cruelly truthful. In one sense, the CBC liked that. In another sense, and particularly in the upper executive stratosphere, the network was not at all comfortable with me. There must have been, I am certain, much discussion, way before the final showdown, of how to get rid of me, but how can you get rid of a journalist for being precise? It was a difficult situation, untenable, uncomfortable, and one to which I was oblivious.

As accurate as I was as a mediator of truth and righteousness, I recognize in hindsight that I could have said things differently. I was not a diplomat. When the February 21 phone call came from Bob Moir, my mentor and friend for what amounted to two decades, informing me that the top brass of the CBC wanted to haul me into headquarters to peel off a few stripes, I felt that, in effect, I was being invited to my own execution. In a voice as cold as steel, Bob summoned me to the office of the head of CBC Sports, Alan Clark, to be reprimanded for my honesty.

What was truly devastating was that someone who had been so close a friend, someone who had dined at my house, someone who came to the Cricket Club to watch the skaters because of me, could, after the years of loyalty and friendship, become the bearer of the order to banish me. That sent me into somersaults. I started to doubt the human race.

It was during that phone call that Bob quoted to me from letters that had been faxed by David Dore, director general of the CFSA, and by William Ostapchuk, president of the CFSA, to the minister of sport and to the head of the CBC, charging that I was against Canada and detrimental to skating at large.[*] The words are indelibly etched in my mind. I could have had them tattooed on my biceps. I had rhinoceros hide, but an elephant gun could not have wounded me more than those words. I had thought of myself as a friend to all skaters. Because I had been victimized by international judges from many different countries, I wanted to be the one person to whom skaters could point and say, "Well, *there* is one man who will speak out on our behalf." I was accused of treason.

I was naïve. I didn't know about the corridors of power. I thought my job was secure. When the phone call came, I went into shock. I was bewildered. I certainly felt that the CFSA and the CBC were ganging up on me. I assumed from Bob's tone of voice that the guillotine was waiting in the CBC offices, and I chose not to go to the meeting to find out if my assumption was correct.

I admit that I did say to Bob, "I cannot go. I will have to resign rather than go." When he repeated those words to the CBC brass, it was music to their ears. Bob phoned me on a Thursday. By about 7:00 P.M. on Friday, the CBC had hired new commentators.

I phoned my agent, Jay Ogden, and told him what had happened. He said, in essence, "Look, don't be ridiculous. I will fax them and tell them that you are ready, willing, and able to go to work at the world championships and that you have a signed contract."

---

[*] Dore wrote about "growing concern among our members and our World Skating Team athletes regarding the negative viewpoint of your commentator, Toller Cranston. Reading recent media articles (as attached) there appears to be a concerted effort to negate the efforts of Canadian skaters, in particular, two-time World Champion Kurt Browning." Ostapchuk wrote, "I would be remiss if I did not express my concern regarding Toller Cranston's recent comments and promotion of his coaching skills, especially promoting Christopher Bowman and his 'exceptional' talents and to some extent talking down our Kurt Browning. . . . I question his objectivity, and his aims, regardless of what he says."

By some fluke, the contract that had floated for a couple of months had been signed several weeks previously, so the CBC and I had a contract, yet my good friend had heard and repeated, "I will have to resign."

The White Cobra

Ice dance had hit its all-time height of weirdness. Isabelle Duchesnay had competed in the Europeans at Sofia, Bulgaria, wearing a man's suit, and Marina Klimova had skated one of the weirdest programs ever seen, wearing green make-up and red eye shadow. Although I taught a team that was not at all comparable technically, mine was equally weird, mysterious, and interesting.

When Mark Janoschak and Jacqueline Petr skated at Canadians in Saskatoon, I had watched with my trained eye and could not understand why every judge had put them second by a country mile – second to good friends of mine but lesser skaters, Martin Smith and Michelle McDonald. The CFSA judges then told me to scrap their number completely and go back to the previous year's. Barely more than a week before the world championships in Munich, that demand added pressure and increased my vulnerability.

On the night after Bob Moir's phone call, I had to report to the Cricket Club to work with Petr and Janoschak. In attendance was a particular world-class skating judge (whose name I prefer not to mention) who didn't like me and didn't like what I represented. When I went to the rink that Friday night, hurting but trying to put on a good face, I wanted to tell anybody who would listen what had happened to me. I told that judge that I had been fired by the CBC, and I described the circumstances.

When I saw the face of that wizened woman, it reminded me of *The Jungle Book* movie when Mowgli was shown to the treasure chamber of the King's city. Out sprang the old White Cobra with tiny, beady red eyes, threatening to bite him if he dared to take any of the treasure. It seemed to me that I was looking into the face of that cobra.

As I told that judge more and more about my predicament, her eyes began to twinkle and the corners of her lips curled upward. What she does not know (what nobody knows) is that it was because of those twinkling eyes and the upturned corners of that mouth that, under great duress, I dug very deep and, from that second, decided to go to war with the CBC, no matter what it took. That twinkle was the spark to the tiny puddle of gasoline that I had left.

Throughout the three years that I fought the CBC, I had one little hope. When I won (because I was either going to win or commit suicide, and that is not a joke), I was going to send the White Cobra with the twinkling eyes an enormous bouquet of flowers with the message, "Many thanks for your help. Best Wishes, Toller Cranston."

I am certain that the note and bouquet would have been entirely baffling to her. I actually hoped that they would drive her insane.

The Tiger Waits to Pounce

I'm not a businessman. I'm not a scientist. I'm not clever with numbers. But I have an ability to understand situations more quickly than many people. I knew exactly what had happened.

Imagine that, in some village in India, a tiger is on the loose, eating a lot of farm animals. The tiger is an ominous and unpleasant influence. The head of the village says, "We have to go out and hunt down that tiger." The villagers plan to capture the tiger by running it into a huge pit. They go out with their weapons, but just before they enter the jungle, the tiger emerges. He does not see them. To get out of the sun, he goes into the pit of his own volition.

The villagers can't believe it. They have caught the tiger without coming to blows. They look down at that sleeping tiger, but the tiger wakes up, sees them, and jumps out. What they had forgotten to do was put the net over the top. What the CBC had forgotten was to get my signature on a letter of resignation. They jumped the gun. They fired too fast. They thought they had me.

Had Bob Moir come over to talk to me in person, had he gotten that piece of paper – just at that vulnerable moment – the fight would have been over. I couldn't have sued. But they forgot to put the net over the pit. I invented the analogy, and I understood what had happened. I was that tiger, and I was still on the loose, and I still could take a nasty bite.

San Miguel

In 1990, I had gone to San Miguel de Allende, Mexico, and had fallen under its spell. By the time Christopher Bowman arrived on the scene and I filed the CBC lawsuit, I had rented a house and started my search for property to buy. It was immensely hot, hotter than I've ever known San Miguel since, and I was living on a street travelled by many buses, so the air was rather contaminated. All of a sudden, San Miguel wasn't quite as pleasant as I had thought it was. I felt like a parched scorpion in the desert. It was so hot that I couldn't breathe. I didn't think that I liked it, but I couldn't go back to Toronto, where things were hitting an all-time low.

My house on Pembroke Street had been destroyed for me because of the connotations and feelings associated with Christopher and Mrs. Bowman. My old friend Thom Hayim was also living in the house, but I was no longer comfortable. I could no longer be the patriarch of the clan. I had no more juice to give. Those people (and it was not their fault – I was too weak to resist) almost took over 64 Pembroke Street. I would, more often than not, take a taxi to Ellen Burka's and sleep there.

In May 1991, three months after the CBC episode, I found the Mexican property that I wanted, a sixteenth-century tannery that had been a residential school before its transformation into a private estate. After viewing some sixty properties, I stood on the cobblestones of calle Sollano in front of an open gate (with the town park behind me). I took one look at the two-and-a-half-acre Garden of Eden and said, "There it is!" The parcel included a large house; three *casitas*, one of which would serve well as a studio; a swimming pool; and the finest gardens in San Miguel. I was ready to give up skating, give up everything, and start life anew in Mexico. The difficulty was finding a way to pay for it.

Museum or Bordello?

My four-storey house on Pembroke Street was definitely equal to one of Ludwig II's castles: so magical, so obsessive, so over-the-top, so greedy, so enchanted, so off-the-wall, so artistic, so grotesque (all at the same time) that there has never been an interior like it, certainly never in Canada. Perhaps somewhere in New York, people live like that, but most of them aren't artists who can do the work themselves. It wasn't just collecting; it was creating.

For years, I had visited Waddington's auction house at 189 Queen Street East to sort of buy love. It was an addiction: I had to get my regular fix. Near the end, I added literally two or three or ten things to my house every day, so that there were thousands (if not hundreds of thousands) of objects designed to overwhelm, flabbergast, *im*press, and *de*press people. It was an astounding environment. It served as a weapon. I didn't care that it was located in the most dreadful area of Toronto, because I was getting more footage for the dollar than I could have anywhere else, so I could fit in more things.

That house perhaps should have been featured in *Architectural Digest*. I had drawn on my experience as a colour expert. The walls in the sixty-foot living room were of a deep forest-green lacquer that looked almost black. There was also a medium shade of green: moss grey-green. The floor was black lacquer. The twelve- or fourteen-foot ceiling was lacquer as well, the shade of dark ruby-red claret.

Every square inch of the ceiling and the mouldings was painted in minute detail with wild, tangled gardens, transparent flowers and bushes, apple orchards, and butterflies. I would paint various flora. Then my friend Chris Williams would paint realistic ten-foot fish and birds in the trees and bushes. Finally, the ceiling was encrusted with thousands upon thousands of cut-glass stones purchased from a stained-glass shop. The whole canopy twinkled. It had a luminescence, a magical fairy-tale quality. You couldn't be certain that you weren't going to levitate and float to the ceiling.

That is a modest description. The sum of the parts was something that you couldn't imagine in your wildest dreams. Even people like Chita Rivera, Rita Moreno, Donna McKechnie, and Danny LaRue, a well-known London female impersonator, had never seen anything like it. When Zandra Rhodes, an avant-garde English designer, saw that house, she said, "No one in London has anything like this. You make me feel conservative." And she had fluorescent-pink hair!

I had a vast collection of contemporary art, much of it kitsch: sincerely tasteless objects, wonderful in their own way. There were serious, huge paintings that only my house could take. *Obsessive* took on a new dimension. I was an artificial fantasy figure who floated around in that environment with perfumed water, candles, and incense in every room. You had to announce your arrival an hour in advance, because it took me three quarters of an hour to get the lighting dimmed and the special effects going: the smells, the fountains, and the flowers.

No one ever said they were appalled by it. Probably some people were. Certainly many guests said, "Very interesting, but I could never live here." Yet nobody ever really told me the truth about that environment, because I don't think anyone ever told me the truth about anything. I was allowed to reign in my artificial Louis XIV nightclub. I became conspicuously eccentric.

It all had to go.

The Glorious Divestiture

One day, Bill Kime from Waddington's dropped in, and I said, "You know, I think that maybe I should sell a few things."

He said, "Why don't you just get rid of everything?"

In one second, without batting an eyelash, I said, "Get rid of it *all*."

It was my first major attempt to reinvent myself, part of the stripping off of layers of my hide. I had to reveal the honesty underneath. I think that it might have been among the more courageous things I've ever done. If not courageous, then it was my most unconsciously brilliant move.

The Sale of the Century followed a well-established pattern. I wasn't at all sure why I was doing what I was doing, but something propelled me to do it. As with, say, continuing to skate as an amateur for so long or buying the house in San Miguel, I almost felt that the decision had been made *for* me. I was somewhat reluctant, yet I was coerced by powers beyond my control.

I gave Bill Kime the key to the house, and the Waddington's trucks rolled in. Everything had to be itemized, of course, which took a month. It all had to be packed and set up for the sale. That generated a tremendous amount of interest. Many people thought that I was dying of AIDS. Others thought that I was bankrupt. Those were just two of the rumours.

Of course, I did have to sell some things to finance the house in Mexico, but the real reason was that I had to punish myself for being a bad boy, a wicked, evil creature, and for buying so many things. I had to punish myself for Christopher Bowman. I had to punish myself for the impending CBC lawsuit. I had to deny myself all the things that I really liked and cared about. I had to purge myself. I had to become a Spartan mouse, living in emptiness, to pay for the terrible, excessive existence, the fantasy, the bubble. When the bubble broke, I had to pay for it.

I went to San Miguel and waited for Waddington's to send me the auction catalogue. I had done special drawings for it, and I had dedicated it to my good friend Bob Moir. Not only did I want the cause-and-effect relationship between the firing and the sale recorded for posterity, but I also wanted to document it as a reason for the court to award personal damages in my lawsuit. I planned to say, "Look! I even dedicated the sale of my household to Bob Moir because he hurt me so badly."

Bob actually called to thank me. I didn't get the call, but he left a message.

Many newspapers and radio stations and television people phoned me in Mexico about the sale. There were hilarious articles about it. One called the house a cross between a Greek Orthodox church and a bordello. The situation did have humorous aspects; yet, deep down below the surface, there was a certain bitterness. It wasn't all that funny.

I had just read *Under the Volcano* by Malcolm Lowry, who ended up an old alcoholic, thrown in the ditch in Mexico with dogs eating at him. I was thinking, "Is this what's going to become of me?" I could picture it happening.

Meanwhile, for a month, I thought that I had a brain tumour. I had a blinding migraine headache twenty-four hours a day. I wolfed down tons and tons of Advil, ten in one gulp. Afterwards, I realized that the headache had been caused by pressure and tension.

I flew back to Toronto at the end of June, feeling sensitive, empty, and lonely (although dressed well, in first class, because I figured that the big sale would pay for the tickets). It was a Canadian Airlines flight, and I was on the front page of every newspaper on board. All of a sudden, I was reading about myself. Some of it was amusing. Much of it included colour photographs.

I realized that I had a great deal of work to do. I had to be the one to orchestrate, design, and promote the sale. I had to do interviews. I couldn't just say, "Take it and sell it."

With all of the thousands of objects, I had to turn the rather dreary three-room auction house into my house. I set up living spaces, the way things had been in the house on Pembroke Street. I bought tons of candles and oceans of flowers to make a dazzling display.

With the exception of maybe six things, I wanted it all gone. Only a few items had reserve bids. With the rest, I just didn't care. Perhaps that was stupid, because a $10,000 rug may have been sold for $1,500, but that $1,500 still helped to pay for the property in San Miguel.

By then, Christopher Bowman had vacated my house under a cloud, leaving behind his prize from the Trophée Lalique competition. I had one of my own, given to me at an AIDS benefit in New York. They were a matched pair. Both mine and Christopher's hit the block. They were worth $2,500 each. I don't know how much they went for – probably a couple of hundred. They had to go.

Stampedes of people came to the preview. Then, after everything had been set up, I was allowed one night to invite my friends for a drink, one final farewell.

Ellen Burka, who had been part of my collecting, never went to the sale. I don't know why. There were thousands upon thousands of souvenirs. Once, she suggested that we sneak downtown. I could hide in the back of the car and peek through the window. I didn't want any part of it. My sister went and bought a number of things. My mother and father did not, nor did either of my brothers.

It was interesting to observe that sale from a distance. Each day, there was more press. There were fights and disputes. People came like curious vultures to see what I had. They were not disappointed.

It was the most eclectic mixture that has ever been assembled in Canada. Good, bad, and ugly, it was all there. There was a small group of seven paintings that might have gone for $25,000. On the other end of the spectrum, I had once bought at auction somebody's size-seventeen boots, because who in the world has ever heard of

size seventeen? I hung them from my ceiling like the Jolly Green
Giant's shoes. People could only imagine what I had *done* with all
those things.

I had a green Murano glass fountain that lit up, played music,
spewed perfumed water, and changed colour. Madness, but the best
in madness. I had nine-foot-long Mexican Christ figures from the
eighteenth century flying in the air. I had jewelled boxes; anything
that would illuminate itself; marble columns that lit up; secret,
strange things; magical things; wonderful things; terrible things;
practically hideous things; exquisite things. The sale began on
June 24 and went on non-stop, day and night. It was the only show
in town. Waddington's had never had a sale like it. It did not
make record amounts of money, because we were in the worst of
economic times, but it received the most publicity. It earned
Waddington's a national name. To this day, I might be in Vancouver
and someone will say, "I saw your sale."

After I had rid myself of all of it, I still had not come up with
enough money for the house in Mexico. At auctions, you're expected
to pay for your purchases by the next day, but there are people who
still have not settled up.

I never bought anything again, from that day until today. That's
not quite true, because I have bought one or two things here and
there, but from that day on, the GST, that unpleasant 7% tax,
ruined any real desire that I had to shop seriously. Moreover, I still
had to do penance. I had to live in solitude and emptiness. I didn't
even keep a bed in the house: I put a mattress on the floor to
punish myself. Virtually everything that I had ever owned in my
life went out the door. I kept some large modern paintings that I
knew wouldn't sell. I kept my clothes, yet I sold stupendous things
such as an extremely elaborate belt collection. I sold the fantasy
stuff. I sold the baroque, the rococo, the over-the-top, the "Oh, my
God, where did you *get* that?" kind of stuff. I could not attract

attention to myself any more. I had to wear sackcloth and smear myself with ashes.

My taste had changed, and I had changed. I started to appreciate modern design: the designs of the future, not the designs of the past. All of the objects and accessories that I had lived with had sucked the creativity out of me. I had been living in a creative stew. I had to clear my mind.

After the sale, I avoided 90 per cent of the stores that I used to haunt, because it was like seeing my life in the shop windows. Every dealer in the city had bought things at my sale. For years I would see objects that I had owned displayed in stores for vast amounts of money, always with the provenance "from the collection of Toller Cranston."

I had never fully appreciated until after the fact that all the objects I had collected were intensely personal. I was vulnerable to anyone in Canada who had seen what I had owned. The residue from that sale set in like mould over time. Instead of the new broom sweeping clean, there was the shock of giving up one's life, giving up one's possessions, giving up one's environment in a single crack.

In yet another respect, my troubles weren't over. I wanted to get rid of the house at 64 Pembroke Street, but it just wouldn't sell. Living in that empty shell, in that seedy neighbourhood, was the very worst thing that I could do. I knew that if I could get out, I might be able to save myself, but the timing was disastrous. I had the house on the market for three years. I would practically have given it away. It started out at $925,000 and was eventually sold for $310,000. I was luckier with the Waddington's sale. Had I waited one week longer, I wouldn't have made half the money. It was the start of the summer, and most of the potential buyers would have left for their cottages. The Canadian dollar was fragile, but in the next week, the next month, it dropped to the bottom.

Many people had come to see the set-up of the sale, to see the preview of the preview. A rather precious, shrivelled-up, possessive type who had collected ecclesiastical things for a long time (and I had a lot of those things) said to me, "Oh, I could never give up any of these things from my collection. How can you do this?"

I took a step out of my body, and I said to him (in my mind), "Oh, thank you so much for coming. You are the ghost of Christmas to come. You are what I could have been if I had continued collecting, and you are exactly what I don't want to be: a lonely, brittle, precious, insular, shrivelled-up, possessive, greedy little man."

I told him, "Thank you for showing me what I never want to become." I don't think he understood.

The Final Travesty

That October, Christopher Bowman competed at Skate America in Oakland – brilliantly, I was told. (I refused to go because of an incident that I dare not mention.) No sooner had he returned to Toronto than he made international news. He was beaten up so badly in a drug deal gone wrong that he cancelled his plans to take part in the 1991 Lalique competition. As far as I remember, he did not hit the ice for six or seven weeks.

During that brawl on Sherbourne Street at four o'clock in the morning, there had certainly been a chance that he could have been murdered. I guess he was lucky to be alive. I did feel sorry for him. I had never seen anyone with such black eyes and a face that had trebled in size.

Even though I was just a spectator to Christopher's antics, every time something happened, another little chip, another stab, another pin stuck me. There were many times during that period when I simply did not know what to do. I would leave my house, whatever the weather, and walk the streets for hours. The clincher came (as it must) at Robert McCall's funeral in November.

Christopher attended the funeral with orange peroxided hair. Many important skaters were there. Nobody thought that it was funny. We went back to Brian Orser's house. Every friend that Rob McCall had ever had in the skating world was there. Christopher arrived at the wake. Because of the sadness of the day, I simply could not address him, and I simply could not comment on his orange peroxided hair. I left early and went home with a headache.

What happened next was the *coup de grâce*. Brian Orser, Christopher Bowman, and Doug Haw, the lead coach of the Toronto Cricket Club, drank and chatted well into the night. Christopher said that he was too inebriated to go home. Although Brian was flying to Sun Valley the next morning, he said that Christopher could sleep on the couch. Doug Haw also chose not to drive home. Everyone went to bed.

In the middle of the night, apparently, Christopher got up, stole money from Brian, and stole Doug's car. He then went to a seedy part of the city that was probably quite familiar to him. When Brian left in the morning, Christopher was not to be seen – nor was Doug's car.

The doorbell rang at Brian Orser's house. Doug Haw got out of bed and answered it. It was Christopher at the door, held at knife-point by three transvestites, including a black cross-dresser in a blond wig. They were demanding money for drugs that had been consumed but not paid for.

When I heard that story, I realized that telling Christopher to stretch his little leg and point his little toe was somewhat ridiculous. I phoned Mrs. Bowman at work in California and told her that she must come and get her son. Joyce Bowman was certainly well-meaning, and why she's still alive in spite of the torment she suffered, I don't know. She said, "I can't come this week, but I can come next week."

I said, "Joyce, you are coming today. *Right now*."

The final farewell was played out at the Cricket Club bar. Ellen and I explained to Mrs. Bowman that we could no longer teach her son and that she had to take him home. Once again, Christopher listened while others talked about him as though it were someone else. He showed not the tiniest bit of remorse.

I am kind of a softy in many respects, and if someone dropped to his knees and begged forgiveness, I would be inclined to offer it. That was not the case.

Christopher left for California with his mother, and I never saw him again.

Choking on Eels

That's not the end of the story.

To say that I was running on empty is to say nothing. There's a strange story in the Günter Grass book *The Tin Drum*. A woman who's out in the river with an eel fisherman is so horrified by the eels and how they're caught that she vomits in the boat, but the end of the story is that she dies from eating too many eels.

When Christopher Bowman left my house, I became a cocaine addict.

I'm not quite sure how that admission is going to play, but I'm over the hump. I'm not running on empty now. That kind of problem does not right itself overnight, but I got my life together.

At that time, I felt like a table with the veneer ripped off. My emotions were too close to the surface. The smallest thing could push me into the deep end. With my inability to sell the house that had been ruined for me, with more than a year of living in absolute torment, with a lawsuit pending against the CBC, with the complete loss of identity, with the loss of skating, with financial stress, it just was too much. I had no family life. I had disappointment on every front.

Up until that time, I had been driven, ambitious, and disciplined, on the go all the time. That changed. Because of the addiction, I began to despise myself for what I had become, for how low I had allowed myself to sink.

Christopher Bowman had sucked the life out of me, and I was unable to cope. Alcohol, drugs, or religion can freeze the pain for a moment. Under their influence, particularly cocaine's, you reach a point where you don't give a good goddamn about anything. Then you do it to punish yourself. It's all quite understandable. You know it's so wrong; you know it's so bad; you know that you could die; you know a whole lot of things, but you don't give a fuck. And if you die, good for you, because that's really what you want and what you deserve.

It's very important to me not to blame Christopher Bowman or the CFSA. It was a result of my own situation. Like so many (me being so strong, me being so tough), I crumbled. I went past my limit, and I had neither close friends nor family. I had no one to turn to. No one understood. And, on every front, I had been taken advantage of.

I was always the one who helped people, who gave, who was the shoulder to cry on. All of a sudden, I was out there on my own, and my suppressed anxiety and torment threw me into the abyss. There was an extremely black time in my life, and it was not months. It was years.

It was like drowning in a swamp surrounded by quicksand surrounded by beach surrounded by earth surrounded by rock. Sometimes I reached the beach, only to slip back into the quicksand, back into the swamp.

But now, if I can be candid – because I *am* being rather horrifyingly candid – I'm much closer to rock than I've been in a long time. I'm convinced that this problem had little to do with the drug itself. It had to do with the reasons for taking it.

Incidentally, I am not a bad person. Perhaps, at the time, I had created a persona that was too far out, and I had to crash. I had to get real. I had to grow up. I had to start playing the game of life like other people in the world, not live in a fantasy.

I crashed. I crashed so badly. I am a mixture of strength and terrible weakness. That's true of many people you least expect it of. Maybe it's part of being human.

My mistake during that dreadful period – and this was my biggest mistake – was thinking that my turbulent, tortured, textured life was really the life of an artist. I fooled myself into thinking that was what people like me did: people such as Jim Morrison and Kurt Cobain, drug abusers who died tragic deaths. Only geniuses and artists did that. The myth was that to be a great artist, you had to live a tortured life.

Well, if that's true, and if that's what it takes, I don't want it. I would today, right now, prefer to be normal and not be tortured than to be a tortured artist who ends in a terrible way. Maybe that's not true, because another voice is saying, "Don't be such an asshole." But I have worn that artist's mask for a long time, and I've lived that life, and I don't want it any more.

· 13 ·

Reaching for Dry Land

At the end of 1991, drugs and drug-related problems loomed large. I lived from day to day. I didn't even know if I'd be able to eat. I was flying by the seat of my pants, chronically depressed. If I was having a nervous breakdown, I was too much of a chameleon to let anyone see how desperate, how out of control I was. Rather than tell someone (at the time, I didn't feel that I had the sort of friends whom I could tell), I chose to cover it up.

I might go for a week or two without showing up at the Cricket Club. Then I would rally. People would ask, "What have you been doing?" I'd say, well, you know, I'm working on this or that. In truth, I was drowning, suffocating, dying, screaming for help, incinerating myself. It dawned upon me that nobody really liked me. Things had to change, but I was too weak to change.

I had agreed to buy the property in San Miguel although we were in a recession, thinking that I would continue to live the life that I was living. All of a sudden, I lost Christopher Bowman, I lost Petr and Janoschak, I lost my job at the CBC, and I hadn't painted in nine months. I was in serious trouble – and short $50,000 of the purchase price.

I had invited Ellen Burka to Mexico. She and her younger daughter, Astra, stayed in my house for the entire month of December. I flew down with Petra, the 1965 world champion, on the day before Christmas. I arrived at the house feeling sensitive and under great pressure, the kind of pressure that I had never experienced before. I am sure that I wasn't exactly Mr. Cheerful Host.

Ellen is one of those people with vast amounts of energy who is easily bored and has to be up to something – which explains why she is such a great coach. She is intense, a steamroller, a diesel truck in the energy department, tough, artistic, highly opinionated, intelligent, amusing, and slightly paranoid about what people think.

Ellen, her daughters, and I went out for Christmas Eve dinner with a San Miguel neighbour at the Villa Santa Monica across the park. Sometimes the tiniest remark becomes a blade stabbed into the heart, although the one who makes the remark may never know it. At the end of the dinner, Ellen said something that devastated me. At a time when I needed a family, support, and somebody to care about me (even though maybe I was unlovable), she said, "I'll pay for my two daughters' Christmas Eve dinners. You pay for yours and your friend's."* That hurt me. I felt so alone. I walked back to the house and went to bed.

---

* According to Ellen Burka, she objected, for personal reasons, to dining with Toller's San Miguel neighbour. When Toller insisted, she felt that he should pay for his friend's dinner.

I got up on Christmas morning, already beaten up emotionally. I was depressed. I had a severe headache. I remember having a headache for a very long time.

There was a certain tension in the air. There was a chilly "Good morning. Merry Christmas." I started painting. Whenever I had problems, I turned to work. That was the panacea for all my ills.

And then, at nine o'clock on Christmas morning, a chance remark caused us to air some deeply felt grievances. Ellen threw down my house keys and marched out with her two daughters following her. I went into shock. I don't know what psychiatrists would call it, but I was paralysed – mentally, physically, and spiritually. The *Titanic* was going down, yet somehow I froze on the deck. I didn't try to save myself, to rectify the situation. I couldn't.

I went down to my studio and started to cry – the dramatic tears that one hates to waste on the air. I cried as I worked. I painted a number of gouaches, all very fine and passionate. There was a whole collection of tear-stained drawings that I eventually sold – among my finest work, I might add. For two days, I sat on that rather deserted estate and cried.

Then, when I was dry-eyed and had a bit more energy, I made a list three pages long. The gist was, I have to grow up. I started making little notes, maybe twenty-five altogether, including: I must go to the dentist; I must start skating again; I must phone IMG to get into Stars on Ice. Little things. Big things. A primitive little tear-stained list.

It was also a social housecleaning. Who took everything from me and didn't give anything back? Those people were countless. Almost everyone I knew had to go. They didn't fit into the new chapter.

It might have been the pent-up anxiety from Christopher Bowman and the lawsuit, but I was at a point that went beyond suicide. Suicide wasn't even an option. Lifting a pencil, lifting – however one was going to do it – would have been unthinkable, because I just didn't have the energy. Suicide, at least if it is done in a heroic way, is a passionate act. You know you're doing it. You're ready. You're brave. I mean, you can't do it if you are a piece of wet newspaper.

So I was sobbing, not for a stupid thing like thrown keys, but for twenty-some years of mistaken existence. The rug had been pulled out from under me. I had no handle on my life. Rather than defend myself, I acknowledged: Okay, I'm a phony. Okay, I'm a this. Okay, I'm a that. I must be real. I must not exaggerate. I must dress simply. I must lose weight. *Anything* that I could possibly think of to make myself a better person.

I came back to Toronto and started to make good on all my resolutions, particularly to start skating again. When I saw Ellen at the rink, at first we were like two moose meeting each other. She had known me long enough to know that, had she spoken a word, I would have strangled her. I went for three months without speaking to her.

But I was frozen. I was bruised. Also – which maybe was the beginning of something positive – I didn't trust anybody at all. I had to go to zero.

I've always known that, in a pinch, if things are really bad (stupendously, suicidally bad), skating is the best medicine. If I can just drag myself out of my little world, just take that half-hour taxi ride to the rink, even once, I'm already 50 per cent better. So, I started.

Four Angels

I've always thought of myself as unlucky. I've changed my tune about that in the last year and a half. I have been helped so many times. Angels have flown out of the floorboards.

The creative reservoir that I'd always drawn on had dried up, because there wasn't any more feeling left in me. I walked the streets. I might have gone to a movie, just to hide in the dark. One day I did go to the movies, and an angel was waiting for me outside the theatre: the Canadian dance choreographer Robert Desrosiers.

I don't know anyone more brilliant. I think that he's even more creative than I am. I said, "Robert, I'm in trouble. I have to go into Stars on Ice in April, and I don't know what to skate to. I don't know what to do. I need help."

He told his girlfriend (a lovely, swanlike creature named Robin) to go on into the movie with her friends, and he went off with me. He started picking me up and driving me to the rink. He inspired me. He choreographed me. He got me on track – I don't know how. I never told him how bad things were, but maybe he knew. He saved me. With Robert, I got onto dry land for a while before I slid back into the swamp.

Stars on Ice 1992 went across Canada in a ten-city tour that featured Paul Martini and Barbara Underhill, Ekaterina Gordeeva and Sergei Grinkov, Katarina Witt, Brian Orser, and Kurt Browning. It was a major show with major skaters. The *Toronto Star* called me the hit of the show. That was thanks to Robert.

I was still short $50,000.

The people who have been closest to me in life, my best friends, the people I have allowed to steer the ship of my destiny, have always been women. I never had any intense male friendships. Yet, three more male angels came out of the woodwork. One was Paul LaPointe, my art manager, who was not in a position to help me financially but helped in a spiritual, emotional way.

The second was Clive Caldwell, whom I've known for many years, a member of the Cricket Club and a friend of my family. I'm the godfather of his son Dylan. One day, knowing that I was in trouble, he said, "Look, how much money do you need?" I said, "Even to close the deal on the San Miguel property and pay the legal fees, I need $20,000 American." He wrote out a cheque that afternoon.

Then there was Haig Oundjian, my oldest friend. I said, "I'm under so much tension." (I would never have told him about drugs. I always tried to keep up a front.) He said, "I'm not going to let you sink. How much do you need?"

I said, "I need $50,000 American." He wrote out a cheque. He even flew to Mexico for one day, just to meet with the lawyer. So, all of a sudden, the possibility that I would lose my investment of about $500,000 American flew out the window.*

The Wrong Miss USA

During those Dark Ages of depression, drugs, economic penury, and loneliness, to name but a few of the ingredients, the thought of doing anything professional – even answering a phone call from my agent – was out of the question. I spent much more time licking my emotional wounds. In the midst of that bleak period, an unusual invitation landed on my doorstep. Although my life didn't change dramatically as a result, it was an early indication that the climate was about to improve.

I was asked to judge the 1992 Miss USA Pageant in Wichita, Kansas. I had a great aversion to Wichita. The worst performance of my career occurred there with Stars on Ice. (My skates were defective, but the audience didn't know that, and I disgraced myself as never before with several single Salchows in one program.) The thought of returning to the scene of the crime did not delight me, nor do I believe that there was any financial incentive.

However, it was a chance to step out of my life, to escape 64 Pembroke Street, and to get away from the raging bonfires that threatened to consume me. I agreed.

On my previous visit to Wichita, I had stayed in one of the most lugubrious hotels in the history of the world, a motel/hotel with a swimming pool in the atrium. Even the sheets smelled of chlorine.

---

* The value of the property has since more than doubled.

I had demanded on that particular occasion that the okra and mustard paintings be removed from my room because I simply couldn't spend the weekend with them. That was probably unprecedented in the annals of hoteldom. I wasn't thrilled at the prospect of having to do that again, so I arrived at the Wichita airport with a certain trepidation.

A chauffeur in a white suit with gold buttons grabbed my luggage, threw me into quite the largest white limousine I'd ever seen, and off we drove. My heart skipped a beat when we neared the chlorinated okra hotel, but the driver just stepped on the gas. We continued on to a grand hotel where a special floor was reserved for the A group. When the elevator doors slid open, we stepped into a huge lounge where hors d'oeuvres and champagne were being served at eleven in the morning.

The woman staging the event greeted me with open arms and told me how thrilled everyone was to have me. I began to cheer up. At the back of my mind, a voice said, "Maybe this is not going to be as dreary and as laborious as one might have imagined." As it turned out, the experience was supreme. Wichita, as I soon found out, is the seat of stupendous wealth. We judges were entertained by the social élite of Wichita three times a day, which meant changing one's clothes six times a day. We were expected to be exponents of glamour; aesthetic masters dressed to kill.

The Miss USA pageant is watched by an incalculable number of people. It is a major event, way beyond Miss America, because the winner goes on to the Miss Universe contest. Miss America is more about nice American girls next door. Maybe you're not really that stunning, but you play the piano well. Miss USA is about length of leg, texture of hair, and perfection of teeth. I quickly realized that I was in the middle of a major tornado.

The judges were a diverse group. There was a country and western singer who told filthy but hilarious jokes; a very nice fellow, a Mexican from L.A., the number-one designer of floral floats for the

Rose Bowl parade; a putter-togetherer of photographic shoots whose claim to fame was the Demi Moore pregnant nude *Vanity Fair* cover; a totally gorgeous black woman who had been on a sitcom; another black woman who was sort of a news person – so sickeningly attractive that she should have been competing; a pro football quarterback; a writer from *People* magazine, and me.[*] Never before in the history of Miss USA had there been a Canadian judge.

The competition itself was arduous and complicated. The contestants, under threat of disqualification, were forbidden to lay eyes on a judge until the event itself to ensure against influence or predisposition. We were herded around like secret armies in holding compounds. Before the contestants were due to go by, we'd be let out of our compounds and led down secret passages patrolled by security guards.

Round one was the interview phase, a surreal event that took place in a huge gymnasium. Each judge sat at a table far from the others. As if in a prison, each girl appeared and stood in front of one of us. They were not allowed to address us, but they knew that they were being judged and making an impression. A girl slithered in my direction each time a bell rang. I stood up. We shook hands. I then had exactly five minutes to interview her on any subject I wished.

I have never seen such beauty in one room. Those girls were, with few exceptions, stunning beyond one's wildest dreams. They had a particular way of showing their wares without being too obvious. They had a way of sitting down, extending a hand, and tossing, in a single, fluid motion, the glistening hair that cascaded over their shoulders. Then they stared at us with their jade-green, black, blue, or turquoise eyes. Each five minutes was a professional exercise in devastating us with their gorgeousness.

---

[*] The judges were: Toller, Chantal Cloutier, Steve DeBerg, Mickey Gilley, Laura Herring, Paula McClure, David Marlow, Raul Rodriguez, and Kimberly Russell.

Their attire for those interviews consisted of glamorous cocktail suits in extravagant colours, often with sequins, beads, and jewels. For interviews as early as 9:30 in the morning, it was *un peu de trop*, but that's what they wore. Cocktail suits.

Being the arrogant son of a bitch that I am, I wanted to find out how bright they were. In truth, they had to find out how bright *I* was. That was one of my hang-ups. As it turned out, my desire to be brilliant cost an aspiring Miss USA her crown.

At the time, the William Kennedy Smith and Mike Tyson rape cases and the Clarence Thomas sexual harassment allegations were in the news. My opening question to the first contestant was, "If you had been the judge, how would you have sentenced Mike Tyson?" The girl had a complete breakdown. She cried her eyes out. I tried to comfort her, although I didn't quite know what button I'd pushed. Then we had an intense conversation about rape. She had been a victim, and the question had brought back memories. I did a lot of borrowing Kleenexes and mopping her eyes instead of demonstrating how brilliant I was.

I continued on the same tack with every one of the contestants. Many were disturbed about the whole phenomenon of rape. Three had breakdowns. I would estimate that at least ten had been rape victims.

We also discussed relationships. Those beautiful women, many of them university students, the finest that America can produce, frequently admitted that they didn't have boyfriends. Their attractiveness intimidated men. Of such boyfriends as there were, every second one didn't want the contestant to win the competition because he was afraid that he would lose her. He wanted her to be barefoot, pregnant, and baking apple pie. The truth about those young women ran completely counter to their appearance, which suggested anything that Hollywood could muster up.

Another question that I posed was, "Now that you're here competing in Miss USA, what beauty secrets have you learned that you

didn't know before you came?" That lanced a cosmetic abscess. The
number-one trick was the taping of breasts with masking tape to
push them as high as they could go. Even women who didn't have
any looked like wenches in *Tom Jones*.

The answers to some questions were most peculiar. One girl,
Miss New York, whom I would have expected to be the most urbane
of the group, was definitely not a Manhattan girl. She said that her
main interest in life was opera. That was fine with me. I asked, "Do
you get to the Met often?"

"Well, no, not really. I've never been to the Met."

"Oh. Well, what is your favourite opera?"

"*The Phantom of the Opera*."

I said, "My dear, don't even think about going to *La Traviata*.
You would hate it."

I learned something about the business of Miss USA. A lot
depends on what state you're from. If you're from Texas (and Miss
USA has been won by Texans many times), it's serious stuff. After
you win Miss Texas, you go into training. The make-over can
include breast implants, nose jobs, capped teeth, cosmetic surgery,
anything to make you as perfect as possible. If you come from
Alaska or Iowa, there isn't the budget. What you see is what you get.
The wealthy states win.

The questions went on over a period of two days. We rated the
contestants from one to one hundred. There were a number of girls
in the high eighties, more in the nineties, and few in the sixties.
Their charm and ingenuousness were quite startling.

Many of the other judges asked lightweight questions such as,
"What do you think of Harry Connick, Jr.?" One said, "What's your
favourite song? Sing it to me." I took an intellectual tack. I heard
later on that I was the hardest judge.

One girl stood out among all the others. Miss Georgia was a
feline, leggy, sickeningly attractive southern belle who, to me, was a

star among the stars. On pain of death, none of the judges was ever to discuss either the contestants or their own preferences. What I found to be great and pathetic at the same time was that, just as in skating, we were all weasels and snakes. We never *stopped* discussing the contestants, and then we started to campaign for them. Lobbying, corruption, and influence were the order of the day, with me as one of the main lobbyists on behalf of Miss Georgia. The black judges leaned towards the Latinos or blacks. The Caucasian, blue-eyed blondes weren't scoring many points with them, so there was a power struggle. How was I to get Miss Georgia onto the throne?

The days were becoming exhausting because of the number of luncheons, receptions, and cocktail parties in the Wichita palaces. The owner of Pizza Hut had a swimming pool that we enjoyed. Full orchestras constantly serenaded us.

The evening gown event was to be our television début. Some of the judges declined coiffed hair and television make-up, but I pounced on the make-up artist. Instead of looking tanned, I again opted for the pale and interesting look. A man had been flown in from New York to do the hair. To this day, mine has never looked so full.

We all sat together with buttons to push. The first contestant came out in a dress that had apparently been designed by Bob Mackie, the kind of dress that you have to be sewn into. It was gold lamé with gold bugle beads in lines that accentuated the contours of her hourglass figure. You had something like twenty seconds to make up your mind. I was so smitten by her golden aura that I forgot to judge. When her score came up, it was minus a mark, and of course it was total points that counted. I started to be more attentive.

I wouldn't say that it was *difficult* to judge, but you might have liked the girl and not the dress, or you might have liked the dress and not the girl. A certain group was bunched together between eighty-five and one hundred. There was much muttering under

one's breath, glancing over at other judges and excoriating them for
giving the wrong marks. We punched the marks in on our personal
television screens, and you could glance over and reprimand
someone just in time for him or her to change a mark before it went
up on the big board.

Miss Georgia seemed to be leading the group. She wore an off-
the-shoulder white Grecian dress. She had cascading honey locks, a
Julia Roberts larger-than-life mouth, a "too tired to be truly beautiful" attitude, and the longest legs that I had ever seen. Those became
more visible when the bathing suit competition commenced.

From the doldrums of 64 Pembroke Street, all of a sudden, for
the first time in a long time, I was having fun. I was laughing. I was
mixing with people who were interesting and up to things. I caught
fire again and made friends. There wasn't one of the judges that I
didn't like. You bond, because you're all thrown together. I was more
partial to the set director of the Rose Parade than I was to the pro
quarterback, but we all got along, and we all had fun.

Certain contestants were pulling ahead. There was a group
within the fifty – maybe eight girls – who topped the list. On the
final night, the girls were culled down to eleven semi-finalists.[*]
Then, after they were asked questions by the host, the field was narrowed to six. Meanwhile, steam and smoke started to pour from the
judges, because we were going in for the kill. We were not at all
unanimous. It came down to Miss Georgia, but of course; a black
girl from one of the southern states, a willowy creature who was
more graceful than beautiful; and a gorgeous but short-legged Grace
Kelly type from California. Those are the three that I remember.[†]

---

[*] Miss Texas, Miss Georgia, Miss Kentucky, Miss Kansas, Miss South Carolina,
Miss Alabama, Miss Virginia, Miss North Carolina, Miss Louisiana, Miss
Arizona, and Miss California, in descending order of scores.

[†] The six semi-finalists were Miss Alabama, Miss Kansas, Miss Kentucky, Miss
California, Miss Georgia, and Miss South Carolina.

Each of the six semi-finalists had to pull a number from a fish bowl. The number indicated the judge who was to ask her a question. All of the questions had been pre-arranged by the organization, and I suspect that the girls had been prepped on the kinds of questions they would be asked. Wouldn't you know it? Miss Georgia drew my number, number six.

I posed my question on live television while 200 million people watched. Miss Georgia struck a pose and pursed her lips, ready to astound us with her charm and wit. My question was, "Do you think women can have it all?" I thought, "What a ridiculous and stupid question. Of course we know the answer, because what person who is going to be crowned Miss USA says that women *can't* have it all?" What were those 200 million people going to think of me? How stupid is that Canadian figure skater? How could he ask that inane question? So I changed it in midstream. With a loquaciousness and a mellifluousness that would have thrilled anybody, I asked, "Whom do you believe to be the most influential woman of this century, and why?"

With that, the pose and the pursed lips disintegrated. I guess that they hadn't told her about that one backstage. She gasped, she choked, she muttered, and she spewed. She completely lost her composure.

The host said, "I'm sorry, but you have to answer."

Out of the mouth of Miss Georgia came a very lame "Well, Barbara Bush."

The judges and the audience let out a collective groan, because she'd blown it. I remember the judge beside me saying, "Barbara Bush? The fact that she cleaned the vomit off George Bush at that state dinner in Japan does not make her one of the great women of the twentieth century."

Miss Georgia, the one who had been destined to win (and actually did make movies in Hollywood), came a strong last among the semi-finalists. She had crumbled, crashed, and burned on my question. She should have been Miss USA. It was not to be.

It took me weeks to figure out that my clever question was impossible to answer. You cannot respond to it by saying who is more important, because there are so many spheres of influence. You cannot compare, say, Barbra Streisand to Margaret Thatcher. I also had not defined influence. Positive or negative? It could have been Elena Ceausescu, or it could have been Betty Ford, Indira Gandhi, or Golda Meir. The more I thought about it, the more impossible it became. I should have said, "Could you tell me *one* of the most influential women," not "*the* most influential," which threw her into a tailspin.

Miss Kansas, the hometown girl, and Miss Kentucky also failed to make the cut. We were down to the top three. Miss USA was about to be crowned. It was between the graceful black creature from the southern state, another southern girl, and Miss California, the Grace Kelly with short legs.

What happened then was so incredible, so fantastic, that no one has ever dared reveal it. For the final question, the women were herded into a glass cubicle so that they couldn't hear each other's answers, but the 200 million viewers could watch them. They were all asked the same question – and it was topical, because President Clinton had just been subjected to the Gennifer Flowers scandal: "Is it relevant to you whether or not the President of the United States has extra-marital affairs?"

After everyone had answered, we were to give each contestant a mark of one, two, or three. One meant that you were placing her first, two meant that you were placing her second, and three meant that you were placing her third. A mistake occurred that split the panel. Some judges thought that giving a three meant the most points and hence the most weight. There was confusion. The person who should have ended up in the middle, the gorgeous, short-legged Miss California, won over the ones we all thought we had voted for. As it turned out, Miss California, Shannon Marketic, was the most intelligent, and facially the most beautiful, creature. She lived with her father and had put herself through university. Just about as nice, as lovely a Miss USA as you could get.

But we realized, at the Miss USA ball that we were commanded to attend afterwards, that my ego had cost Miss Georgia her title. I might have figured, "I lost the Olympics, so she can lose Miss USA." Well, I didn't really feel that way at all. It affected me so badly that I fled early, like Cinderella from the ballroom, and scurried back to the hotel by myself on our private bus.

It was just as well that I left, because apparently there were some unpleasant incidents. The mother of one of the contestants actually attacked a judge and chased her around the ballroom. Back in my hotel room with a severe headache, I took solace in the Scotch from my minibar.

At four o'clock in the morning, I heard a chorus of voices outside my door. They were singing "Georgia on My Mind." The other judges demanded that I come out, and we had a drink and a good laugh. We embraced and promised that we would see one

another in the not-too-distant future. I sort of believed it for the
moment, but I never saw any of them again.

I went home recharged and inspired. I'd met my own kind of
creative, interesting people, the kind of people that I had lost touch
with in Toronto. Since then, no other Canadian, to my knowledge,
has been asked to judge Miss USA – nor is that likely to happen in
the future.

The Bodyguards

If you look back on your life and wonder what went wrong (if I had
only won the Olympics, or if I had just squeaked through with a
legit world title), sometimes the pendulum swings in the other
direction, and you're given something that's better than medals.
You're so lucky to have done it, and you know that it's a one-of-a-
kind experience. Such was the case with IMG's Stars on Ice conquest
of São Paulo, Brazil, in November 1992.

Olympic- and world-calibre skating is virtually unknown in
South America. The Amazonian tribes are always elated when
Holiday on Ice drags its fifth-rate companies through the jungle,
but, in truth, South Americans did not, and largely do not, get to see
top-quality figure skating.

My trip to São Paulo got off to a nasty start. For some complicated, incomprehensible reason, my air mileage was denied by
Varig, whereas Christine Hough's, Doug Ladret's, and Brian Orser's
were accepted. All the champagne, caviar, and foie gras in the world
could not assuage my irritation at losing 17,000 air miles. Many
skaters, particularly Lea Ann Miller, Rosalynn Sumners, and Paul
Wylie, virtually live for the air-mile totals they accrue. I am sure that
few actually use them up, because the thought of diminishing the
total would be too tragic. There's grave competition within the hierarchy of skating.

When one goes to destinations unknown, every minute of the
experience, even in boredom, is new and different. The first thing

that happened in São Paulo was certainly new. A charming fellow named Fulvio introduced us to an army of armed bodyguards. None of us could understand why, but we were to find out soon.

The morning ride from the Rio airport to São Paulo was not unlike E.T.'s discovery of Earth. The terrain, the landscape, the silhouettes of the buildings were unlike anything I had ever seen. São Paulo is the largest city in South America. No one can determine the exact population of the extended metropolitan area. It is in the tens of millions, second only to Mexico City. Because of the size of the population, land is very valuable. Stalagmites of skyscrapers rose up from the landscape, sharply pointed apartment needles, very close together, with exteriors so badly weathered that they looked leprous.

On one side of the bus we could see a slow-moving, if not entirely stagnant, river filled with garbage, cans, and bottles. As I later found out, it was hardly a river. It was raw sewage, perhaps seventy-five feet wide. People who say that you can't walk on water, trust me: in São Paulo you can, and you don't need a halo.

We arrived at our hotel called the something d'Oro at about one o'clock in the afternoon. After travelling for almost eighteen hours, we all went to bed. The bodyguards marched us to our rooms. One of them took up guard duty in front of each skater's door.

Those bodyguards were by no means unattractive, and all the women (and a few of the men) developed instant crushes. It was interesting to have the object of one's romantic fascination just millimetres outside one's door twenty-four hours a day, but that was hardly a topic for open discussion.

The hotel was first class and had a certain old-fashioned whiff. Breakfast and lunch were served on the lowest level, which opened onto a garden filled with semi-tropical plants and a lovely oval swimming pool with a waterfall.

On the first evening, unbeknownst to me, everyone was summoned and given instructions. We were absolutely forbidden on pain of death – or, as it turned out, on pain of rape and murder –

to venture out of the hotel. Nobody told *me*. I decided to go out and get the lay of the land. I walked around the area and returned in due time, oblivious of the trauma that I had provoked among the ranks of the bodyguards. If something had happened to me, they all would have been fired on the spot. The something that could have happened was very real. Bands of thugs roam the streets of São Paulo, poverty is rampant, and thefts and muggings are the order of the day. Anyone with serious money has his own private army. People of moderate means have guarded gates.

The Beatles on Ice

I couldn't liken São Paulo to any city that I had seen. There were streets with huge mansions in a peculiar architectural hybrid, neither Spanish, French, Italian, nor North American. It was extreme glamour in the L.A. movie-star mode.

The first night, tired as we were from our flight, we were summoned to a genuine nightclub with action, entertainment, and food. I suspect that Paul Wylie and Kristi Yamaguchi were invited to dine with the top brass. I took solace in the company of Peter and Kitty Carruthers, Lea Ann Miller, and Bill Fauver.

Brazil is renowned for meat. We had steaks so enormous that they almost had to be veiled for fear that someone would see what we were eating. I am partial to dessert, but I believe that I hit my all-time record that night with seven in a row – desserts that I can't really put a name to: strange custards and sweet and sour fruits, each more delicious than the last.

The next day our bodyguards took us to an enormous arena. The ice itself was *très* my cup of tea, even smaller than Holiday on Ice size. A wealthy São Paulo resident, a rock promoter, had taken a chance on us – we were the very first skating show of that calibre in South America.

Holiday on Ice had played the week before, and many of those skaters were there to rehearse their next show. One had a certain pleasure (at least I did) in performing for a captive audience of South American chorus skaters who had never seen our kind of skating.

The first show came and went. Business was poor, but that show was locally televised. Television is such a powerful force. For whatever reason – the novelty of skating, the rhythms, the costumes, the virtuosity, the athleticism, or the artistry – that itsy-bitsy television show ignited a keg of dynamite in São Paulo. The next night, and the three nights to follow, there was standing room only.

We were part of a medium that captured the imagination of thousands, if not millions, of people. I do not believe that the Beatles' entry into America was any more spectacular than the impact of our small collection of skaters. We thought of ourselves as the Beatles on Ice. Several times, we became nervous when the assembled hordes rocked our bus. There were moments when we truly feared that it might turn upside down. The experience was wonderful in its uniqueness. We belonged to something that was far beyond the sum of our parts.

Paul Wylie and the Groupie

On the second evening, we went to a nightclub/discothèque. Its door was like an airplane hatch that had to be slammed shut to seal in the noise. We had a splendid meal, and money was of no consequence. Whatever we wanted, we ordered. It was all paid for by our promoter (who was feeling a lot better now that 23,000 people were attending the performance nightly).

Paul Wylie was the principal male star of the show. He was skating very well, and many of the little Holiday on Ice maidens became quite entranced by him. Being the friendly guy that he is, Paul had announced to a number of those young women where we would be eating and suggested that we might go dancing afterwards. I'm sure that they were at the restaurant hours before we were. After dinner, one particularly ardent admirer affixed herself to him. I went home early because I didn't wish to be sealed into an airtight disco, but Paul and a few others much younger than I decided to stay.

I cannot speak for Paul Wylie, because I do not know exactly what he thought, but as to the girl, he was the man of her dreams, and she would never let him go, no matter what. I do know that she spent the night at the hotel. The entire company of Stars on Ice was thrilled that Paul had found a lady love at last, but, by the look on his face the next morning, we sensed that it hadn't been a night of abandoned euphoria. We surmised that the consummation of the affair, however hungry the admirer, had not occurred.

The Bodyguards Gain New Respect

We felt somewhat constrained by the fact that we could not walk anywhere without one or more bodyguards five steps behind us. I was particularly uncomfortable, because I've always liked to explore cities by myself.

One night Peter Carruthers, Brian Orser, and others were involved in a nasty incident. The story was that several armed thugs had shot at the tires of their cars in order to rob the occupants. The only way that their drivers could protect everyone in the cars was to run over the perpetrators, which they attempted to do. The bodyguards, after that incident, took on a new importance in our lives.[*]

---

[*] According to Brian, three cars of skaters, with two security guards each, were returning from a shopping trip when the youthful thugs appeared. "They weren't actually shooting, but they did have guns which were quite visible. I was in the front car. It was chaos. The drivers swerved and went aggressively at the kids. When the kids took off, all the cars stopped, and the security people told us to crouch down in the back seats. Then they got out and pulled out their guns. When everything calmed down, they got back in the cars, and off we went. It was exciting, but it was pretty scary at the same time. Toller wasn't with us. I can just imagine if he had been!"

Tarzan

The glamour of skating in São Paulo cannot be overstated. Our dressing rooms had been specially appointed with additional lighting, hair dryers, perfumed soaps, upholstered sofas, chairs, and a non-stop kitchen that served anything we wanted. Our ethics prevented us from imbibing the champagne that had been provided for us to drink during the show, but the liveried waiters couldn't understand why and were somewhat miffed.

There were several touching events that affected me profoundly. Brazil is one of the world's most enormous countries, yet word that we were coming to São Paulo must have spread. Several people we met had actually lived in a bus for days in order to see our performances. There was one fellow, a Brazilian Tarzan, who was the most handsome man on earth. I don't know how South America managed to provide skates for him. Who has ever heard of size-eighteen skates? He was a giant.

Tarzan didn't speak English; but he had journeyed by bus for three days to see the show. There was the tiniest little sprinkling of skaters in São Paulo, and they all skated at a minuscule rink in a shopping centre. How it came to pass, I don't know, but as the rest of the cast went rushing out to buy cheap shoes, perfume, and souvenirs, I gave a lesson to those skaters, including Tarzan.

Our host had kindly given me a chauffeur-driven car. The skaters were prepared to pay for a taxi, but I'm so glad that I had the car, because the taxi would have cost them a year's salary. What country we eventually ended up in, I don't know, but it was miles from the hotel. I was aching and stiff. Skating at all after the final show was the last thing that I needed, yet I felt that to go, as the skater that I was, to the strange little rink in the farthest reaches of São Paulo was an experience not to be missed.

The rink was in the bowels of a fancy shopping centre, as lavish as any mall in North America. It had that horrid, chalklike, squeaky tropical ice and was flooded just once a day. It was virtually unskateable, but for those skaters, ice was ice. They had never before come into contact with anyone who knew anything about skating. Whatever they had learned, from a peculiar double Salchow to a cheated double toe loop, they learned by watching films over and over again.

Tarzan tried so hard to please. Those skaters all knew that they would have only an hour with me. They sweated so much that there were puddles of perspiration on the ice. Had we continued, they could have flooded the ice with their sweat. Their technique was so primitive and archaic that to give them pointers was next to impossible. Everything was totally wrong.

Yet they were so earnest that I had to give them every ounce of my energy: to help, inspire, and encourage them, and maybe, best of all, to equip them to audition for one of the lowly touring companies. If only they could affix themselves to a professional show until they got to Europe, then they might really learn how to skate.

I left the building with the various skaters and said my goodbyes. Although it had been no big deal for me, I knew that I had had the opportunity, without much effort, to give pleasure and memories that might never be forgotten, to give something that would be talked about and even told to grandchildren. My boredom and aching muscles were incidental compared to the euphoria that was frozen onto those skaters' faces.

I never did hear from any of the others, but Tarzan once dropped me a note in broken English, inquiring if I could possibly come up with Rosalynn Sumners's address.

Goodbye, Bodyguards; Bye bye, Brazil

The final day of our visit to São Paulo was dramatic and exciting. After our last performance, we were to be wined and dined at the mansion of the contented promoter. Several of the skaters, for whatever reason, had booked early flights and missed the party. What happened to them in the car en route to the airport cannot be mentioned in precise terms, because I do not wish to destroy relationships or marriages. I like those young women far too much to disclose any indiscretions that may have occurred. A great deal would have centred on those last few desperate moments with the very attractive bodyguards they were never going to see again.

I went to the party, a grand, glittering, fun party. The host and the hostess gravitated towards me, for reasons that I do not know, and pulled me into a part of the house that no one else entered. We had an intense conversation about myriad matters. I sensed that they liked me, wanted to see me again, and were already plotting next year's Stars on Ice tour in Rio de Janeiro and Buenos Aires, but it was never to be.

We left for the airport. I was flying to Mexico City to do publicity for yet another adventure that lay in front of us all, while others headed temporarily to their own destinations. The bodyguards were almost teary-eyed that we were leaving. They liked us. We liked them. They walked us into the airport. Mine walked me right to the plane.

Flying over São Paulo, seeing that strange, enormous city twinkling under me, I had the distinct feeling that I had been standing upside down during my entire stay there. It was so different from any place that I had ever been. I look forward to returning to South America, but I don't see myself going as a skater.

· 14 ·

Trial and Error

Nearly three years had passed since I was fired by the CBC. I had lost all sense of myself. Because of my difficult, drug-induced state – sometimes okay, sometimes not, sometimes skating, sometimes suicidal, a bleak, grey period – the bloom of youth truly was ebbing away. I knew it, and I couldn't do anything to prevent it. Sometimes I'd look in the mirror and try to pull myself out of it, but if I did, the reprieve lasted only a day, at most a week.

Many people have gone through periods like that. Tai Babilonia is one of them. We discussed it at the Special Olympics in Strasbourg. She had had a problem with pills and alcohol, had lost face, and had been through a rocky time. I grilled her about her own black period. What she didn't know was that I was fishing for answers for myself. If she got out of it, how did she get out of it?

Tai was very sage. She said something that, although it didn't help me to get better, did help me to understand: you can't cite one particular instance as the root of that kind of problem. It's cumulative. She reckoned that she would have reached a crisis sooner or later, because certain things had to be exorcised. She had too much emotional baggage.

Tai had crashed and had pulled herself up. I was about to fall off the same cliff, and I was wondering, if I did fall off the cliff, how much was it going to hurt, and was I ever going to get back up again?

The worst thing of all, the unbearable strain, was within the royal family of skaters. That would have included tours with Stars on Ice and trips to world championships. In my own estimation, I had lost my title. If I had been a count, I had become a commoner. Since the other skaters weren't aware that I'd lost my credentials, I had to pretend that I still belonged in the group.

I maintained a public façade and appeared confident, yet I could return to my house on Pembroke Street and self-destruct in a second. Sometimes I wouldn't be seen for days. I often hoped that somebody would notice what was happening, but nobody, it seems to me, ever figured it out. I was allowed to live a duplicitous life without anyone (as far as I know) suspecting that I was some sort of werewolf or vampire – good in the daytime, bad at night.

Discovery

There was a discovery before the trial. I recounted what I believed happened and Bob Moir told what he believed happened. Discovery can be painful, and the opposing lawyer can be ruthless. I kept waiting for the baby questions and the smooth talk to lead me down the garden path to a land mine. When the discovery ended, there had been no land mine.

When the transcript is set in print, you must go to court with it. Those are the facts. You cannot say one thing in discovery and change it in the courtroom. Bob had taught me about precision in journalism, about integrity, about articulateness: everything that I put to good use. He was a great teacher but a dreadful performer. When he opened his mouth (because he had not really thought about his testimony and had not really understood its importance), he self-destructed.

On the Docket

I went to Mexico a few months before the trial date with my own and Bob Moir's discovery transcripts, and I studied them as though they were notes for a final exam at Harvard. I could almost recite them. I could do Sir Laurence Olivier. I grilled myself. I knew my act. I knew my strategy.

I went to Dick Button's Landover professional competition in December 1993 knowing that, on the day after I returned home, I was finally going to court. As I was happily judging the Paul Wylies and the Brian Orsers, I had my transcript in front of me. It was do or die. I couldn't lose. If I did, the original accusations would hold up in the press. I would be seen as a traitor to Canada. I also would have to pay all my litigation costs plus the CBC's, which could have amounted to $100,000. I was wondering where the next peanut butter and jam sandwich was going to come from. How was I ever going to find that much money?

When I got back to Toronto, I was supposed to meet my lawyer, David Harris, an expert in wrongful dismissal, for a Sunday-night cram course in how to behave in court. I went to his office at the appointed time, but he was not there. Another lawyer informed me that the CBC lawyer's father had either died or was very ill, and it wasn't certain that the lawyer would be able to go to court.[*]

---

[*] There was more to it than that. According to David Harris, "We had agreed to the adjournment at request of counsel for the CBC due to the fact that the expert who had agreed to give testimony for us had backed out at the last minute."

Once again, God or the angels had given me a chance. By postponing the trial, the CBC lawyer had given me another month to work with David Harris.[*] I saw it as a fortuitous omen, a break in the clouds.

I went to San Miguel at Christmas and consulted a white witch, a mystical woman, a clairvoyant. I did not ask what was going to happen to me. I asked how the planets were aligned and if there was harmony around me. If there wasn't, then forewarned is forearmed.

She read her tarot cards. She could see no discord, only harmony. That confirmed what I had already sensed. I believed that there would have been discord had I gone to trial on December 13, but the year had changed, the numbers had changed, and the planets had changed.

By that time, I was close to what must have been a nervous breakdown. As I haven't had one, I don't know exactly what they are. It's not as though you go downstairs and there's a nervous breakdown that has been left by the milkman on your doorstep.

The Final Showdown

Two days before the trial, Paul LaPointe, my art agent, made a helpful gesture. I was under so much pressure that I could easily have gone on such a drug binge that I would never have made it to court. Paul offered me a free weekend in a swanky hotel that he and his wife had won but couldn't use. I went to that hotel, stayed in the room, and studied my script.

I felt that my appearance in court was important. I couldn't come across as flamboyant and flashy. I had to be earnest. For me, earnest meant a black suit, black shoes, black socks, and a black cashmere round-necked sweater with a tiny white starched collar at

---

[*] The case was heard in the Ontario Court of Justice (General Division) on January 24 to 27, 1994.

the top: a little boy going to choir school. I thought, and it was deliberate, that priestly attire was correct.

I also knew that my behaviour in court, because with every single word that you say, you are being studied, would be critical. I suspected that the CBC wanted to present me as theatrical, impetuous, volatile, erratic, and subject to mood swings. I made an absolute Olivier attempt to convey the exact opposite: that I was intelligent, soft-spoken, earnest, credible, and sincere, and that I had been victimized by the CBC in their unseemly haste to get rid of me.

I dressed in my clerical clothes and walked from my loft at Bathurst and Queen to David Harris's office at Richmond and Yonge, a healthy twenty-five-minute walk in freezing weather.[*] I wanted the elements to punish me. It was like wearing a hair shirt. If going to court meant committing suicide at the end of the week, that brutal walk was good training. We discussed how the day was going to play out. Then I walked in the arctic cold to a part of Toronto that was new to me: Queen's Park.

David Harris had assured me that cases such as mine rarely get to court. Seconds before we walked in the door, the CBC would settle. I believed that was going to happen. When we marched into court and there was no settlement, I was surprised.

I went to court by myself. It was like competing in the Olympics without a coach and teammates. I was going to kill myself if I didn't win, and I had to go alone, without one friend to support me.

Ellen Burka, who knew some very important details, the good old friend that she was, refused to go to court on my behalf and had to be subpoenaed – forced to appear and tell the truth. I don't believe that her reasons were malevolent, but she was so selfish, and

---

[*] After Toller sold the Pembroke Street house and moved to Mexico, he used a studio as his Toronto *pied-à-terre*: first on King Street, then on Queen Street West.

she did not understand that she could have saved me. Instead, she had to be forced at gunpoint – my friend of twenty-five years.

Joyce Foster, an honorary member and grande dame of the Toronto Cricket Club, was subpoenaed by the CBC to testify against me, although she proclaimed herself an unwilling witness. She was another good friend who was there but couldn't help me, through no fault of her own.

The CBC arrived with three different lawyers plus three law students, a total of six. I arrived with David Harris.

Only people who have been there can understand what's at stake in a court case like this. You can be sentenced to life imprisonment, or you can be playing golf when the trial is over. My life was in limbo.

The judge's name was Ferrier. He was about fifty-eight and earnest, with dark hair and an intellectual face. He showed neither charm nor emotion. Perhaps judges are supposed to be like that. Throughout the trial, he rarely looked at anyone, yet I had the sense that he was taking everything in. He made copious notes.

The CBC lawyer tried to provoke me. He supposed that I had hit the roof, as I believe he put it, when Bob Moir told me that I had been accused of being against Canada and detrimental to skating.

I replied that his supposition was entirely inaccurate. The information came to me like a stab. Instead of hitting the roof, I fell unconscious to the floor, because it was a devastating wound. It was not about emotion. It had nothing to do with anger and hysteria. It stunned me.

He had tried to show the judge that I was volatile. What he didn't know was that, whatever I was or wasn't, I was going to be as cool as a cucumber, clerical, intellectual, and solemn in the courtroom. I never raised my voice. I never became too passionate. For that particular four-day sojourn, I was a Bay Street stockbroker.

The days came and went. I kept waiting for some terrible bullet to whiz out of their gun. I had to fight the desire to be too brilliant, too quick. The inclination to be sarcastic had to be suppressed at all cost. I could not reveal the arrogance that is, in essence, my nature. I could not squish the opposing lawyers on the pavement with the heel of my shoe, even though it seemed to me that it would have been easy to do.

Bob Moir had made a fatal mistake. Whereas I had been study-ing in the hotel all weekend, he had just flown into Toronto the day before the trial. He could have been in court to hear my testimony, but he wasn't. As a result, when he sat down in the witness seat at about a quarter to four on a Wednesday afternoon, within two and a half seconds (I exaggerate slightly) he had shot himself in the foot ten times.[*]

The CBC lawyer made a motion for recess at five past four. Would your honour mind? There isn't much time. We'd better end it here. The judge's expression was sardonically inquisitive, as though he had quickly gotten the picture that Bob Moir's testimony

---

[*] Justice Ferrier found, "Mr. Moir testified that he did not relay to Mr. Cranston the contents of the letters from the C.F.S.A. since he did not see them until the following week. In my view, Mr. Moir's recollection is faulty in this respect. . . . I am reinforced in this finding by the fact that the following day, the plaintiff's witness, Ellen Burka, was told by Mr. Cranston of the nature of the allegations in the letters. The only way that Mr. Cranston could have been aware of [them] was that Mr. Moir had told him. . . . In cross-examina-tion Mr. Moir acknowledged that in one of the calls Mr. Cranston had said something like 'I don't want to be forced to come in and sing the National Anthem' – which I take to be the expression of Mr. Cranston's upset at the challenge to his integrity and loyalty to his country. This acknowledgement by Moir buttresses my finding that Mr. Moir's recollection is faulty concerning the information that he conveyed to Mr. Cranston about the reason for the meeting with Clark." Reasons for Judgment, *Cranston v. Canadian Broadcasting Corporation*, Judgment March 29, 1994.

was inconsistent with what he had said in discovery. He agreed to the recess.

Whether he was or whether he wasn't, it seemed to me that Bob came across in that courtroom as a man without compassion. In fact, the image he presented jibed precisely with what I had told the judge. The judge asked him, did he not think that after a twelve-year relationship, he perhaps should have gone to see me personally since his office was just minutes away? Bob simply said no.

Ellen Burka took the stand. She was pristinely honest and completely substantiated what I had said.

The head of CBC Sports, Alan Clark, arrived in court wearing a pair of jeans and running shoes. I thought it was fantastic, actually. It said everything.

During the trial, I spent my nights alone in my Queen Street loft. To protect myself, to create a positive environment, to purify the air, and perhaps to discourage drug dealers, with the small dribs and drabs of money that I had, I would go across the street and buy as many potted spring flowers as I possibly could. By the time I was done, the door opened onto maybe a hundred and fifty pots of hyacinths and daffodils, a floating garden. People who stopped by thought, "Oh, how lovely." They didn't know that nature and fresh smells were the only armour that I had.

Playing the Passion Card

On the morning of the last day of the trial, I lay in bed trying to understand the big picture. I analysed what had been the clincher in the Clarence Thomas hearings in the U.S. David Harris had been meticulous, but no one in this battle was yet clearly the winner. No one had played the "high-tech lynching" card that got Thomas confirmed to the Supreme Court. I had to figure out how to tip the scales in my favour. I figured it out. I got it. I suddenly saw the winning move.

I also had a moment of private revelation just before I slithered into my clerical clothes. I was in the shower, plotting my strategy, when I realized that I had lost my youth, that I was middle-aged. It was over. I was into another period.

I walked to David Harris's office in the freezing cold. He was at his computer. I said, "Sit down in that chair and don't say anything. Your argument has been perfect. You're a nice guy, but you have missed one thing: you do not know who I am. You have not played the passion card.

"I am a passionate Canadian. I am a renowned Canadian. I am a member of the Order of Canada. I am an Olympic medallist. I am exactly the kind of Canadian who would inspire other Canadians. Is the CBC's treatment of me reasonable? I could have been an underling in a secretarial position the way they treated me. Is that how you treat a legend in Canada? You have not asked what is fair and reasonable for somebody like me."

He agreed. He was a Virgo, an unfortunate sign for a lawyer. Leo, Scorpio, or Aries would have been much better, but he did play the passion card. I was his theatrical coach. I juiced him up.

Several times Judge Ferrier spoke directly to the CBC lawyers (all six of them) and said, more or less, "I really would recommend that this particular case be settled out of court, if you catch the drift."

They would go into a room to deliberate, and then the head CBC lawyer would say, in essence, "No. We're not giving Toller Cranston one penny." David found that extraordinary. He couldn't understand it. I couldn't understand it. All I wanted was *out*. All I wanted was to save face. All I wanted was, "Well, I won."

At the end, I expected the knockout punch. What happened instead was that the boxers stopped the match and went home. The trial didn't reach a climax. When everything had been said, it fizzled into nothing.

David Harris and I walked out. There was a certain relief, the relief that one feels when the most awful thing in one's life, when it is actually played out, isn't really as awful as expected. The ramifications are huge, but the act itself isn't horrible.

The Verdict

I went home and stocked up on a few more hyacinths and daffodils. An extremely difficult period ensued. I had to wait. I had been expecting the judge to say, "After consideration, I find . . ." but that did not happen. I went through an arduous and stressful time, what amounted to eight and a half weeks, unprecedented for that type of case. Every time the telephone rang, I almost fainted. It was like sonic acupuncture. I would try to say hello in an aggressive, positive way. I always expected David Harris to be on the phone, announcing either my death sentence or my liberation, one or the other, because that is what it amounted to.

I had already planned several different ways of committing suicide, none of them spectacular (because, at that point, that hardly *was* the point). I was trying to figure out a painless way of doing it. I wanted to disappear like a sick dog or cat that goes into the forest and is never found. That was my plan. But as the days went on, my life went on. The sky hadn't fallen, and Chicken Little wasn't dead. I went to the same restaurants as before. I started skating again. At the time, I was revving up for Stars on Ice. Yet I was holding back, because I couldn't plan for Stars on Ice if my suicide was going to precede it. That would have been such a waste of energy and practice time.

Some time before, I had met Muki Held, an attractive New Yorker of Czechoslovakian extraction who had been a skater. She had informed me, at one of those little restaurants where you go for something to eat after a show, "Gee, Toller, you should do something with your art in New York and make it a big event."

With lawsuits, Christopher Bowmans, and no end of disasters around me, I had dismissed it and said, "Yes, I really should. See you later. Maybe we'll get in touch."

Muki managed the Dyansen Gallery in Trump Tower, and she proposed to have an exhibition. I agreed to it, but it all seemed rather nebulous. Nevertheless, she said, "Send slides, send photographs, send c.v.s, send this, send that." There were many phone calls back and forth. Finally the green light was flashed, and it was going to become a big deal. Muki flew to Toronto and visited my studio. Though she was supportive, she was not a Harvard art scholar, and the Dyansen Gallery was a commercial gallery, listed on the stock exchange. But who cared? It was a New York gallery and hey, I was a Canadian, and gee, wouldn't it be nice to exhibit in New York?

The pot started to boil. Then came the point when I pretended not to realize that something wasn't quite right. Muki told me to bring two framed prints when I came to skate at the Rockefeller Center rink in a little production with the Ice Theatre of New York. At the end of the performance, with New York's great unwashed in attendance, she grabbed the microphone and waved the prints at the assembled mob: "This is to launch the Toller Cranston exhibition at the Dyansen Gallery on May 3, 1994."

I think that I spent the night in New York. Then I crept home and walked to my loft from the Toronto Island airport. I was having a huge exhibition at Trump Tower, but I couldn't afford a taxi. I reached the door of my studio. All the flowers had peaked and had become a field of *nature morte*. They didn't smell right. They certainly weren't doing, at that point, what they had been intended to do: protect me and purify my air. Quite the opposite. I put down my bags and went into my messy, dreary studio. Then my eye alighted upon my answering machine. Ninety-three messages. Nine-three. I had never had ninety-three messages in my life.[*]

---

[*] The number of messages grows larger with each telling.

I pushed the button. There were messages from friends and well-wishers all over the country. Each one congratulated me on winning the lawsuit. I heard the verdict on my answering machine.

I am not a crybaby. Tears are not really part of my repertoire, but as I listened to those messages, tears dripped down the coiled cord and flowed in a spiral onto the telephone. I was fascinated that tears could drip in that way. Not sobbing tears. Not even tears of relief. Just a lot of tears that should have been shed over the last three years and finally were able to gush forth.

So then I knew that I had won, and my life had changed again.[*] I was not going to have to commit suicide (at least not right away). I had an exhibition coming up in New York. I had Stars on Ice to go into, and I'd better start practising. I had a rush of energy. Once again, I had luck, I had a chance to start over, and it wasn't too late. I could make a success of the next part of my life, and there was just enough time to do it.

There was no pleasure, really, in winning. I don't think there ever is in a lawsuit. Lawsuits are so unpleasant. Win or lose, live or die, just being a part of it takes a tremendous toll on you.

I never did send flowers to the White Cobra. I had slipped into middle age in the shower, and a middle-aged mind does not behave in such a way. It was time to move on. It certainly was not time to be vindictive.

I saw Bob Moir at the world championships in Edmonton in 1996. I was enjoying Edmonton, having fun, feeling my oats. I started to castigate him: "You taught me about integrity, and I taught you how to lie. Think about it." He stood there and took it. And then I did something that is one of those strange things that humans

---

[*] Toller was awarded $40,000, the sum still owed him under the contract, plus prejudgement interest and $20,000 in damages for loss of publicity.

can do. After three years of financial ruin and emotional destruction, I said, "Forget it" and gave him a hug. I cleared the air.

Things Begin to Look Up

Maybe the clouds were parting. Maybe I was on a roll. I was going to exhibit in New York, skate in Stars on Ice and Skate the Nation, and maybe then I could retire to Mexico. Wouldn't that be a good way to bridge the gap, to step over to the painting side of my life?

Stars on Ice rehearsed and débuted in Halifax, featuring the likes of Katarina Witt, Kristi Yamaguchi, Kurt Browning, Brian Orser, Ekaterina Gordeeva, Sergei Grinkov, Paul Martini, and Barbara Underhill. I was feeling rather happy. I was going to fly from Vancouver to New York, attend my exhibition, then join the Skate the Nation tour in Kamloops, British Columbia.

Send in the Clowns

Trump Tower was abuzz. The thing that I didn't immediately comprehend was that the exhibition wasn't in a gallery in Trump Tower; it was in *the entire Trump Tower*. Paul LaPointe and I had sent forty-five paintings, some of them larger than six feet by six. When people left the stores, we were going to have exactly an hour and a half before the exhibition opened to hang those paintings.[*]

I had decided that the exhibition was my middle-aged début. Wouldn't it be nice if all my old friends could come and be part of it? I had in mind a reprise of my thirtieth birthday in Paris. They came from all over the country and the world. It might have been naïve of me to think that I was the sole draw, because Donald and Marla were more important to them than I was, but never mind. We

---

[*] According to Held, paintings were hung in the Dyansen Gallery itself during the day, then around the balconies on all four levels of the atrium. Easels scattered throughout the main floor displayed the biggest works.

were all going to be there together. People came from Mexico, Paris, London, Vancouver, and California – one's life reunion.

On top of that, Tom Collins's tour just happened to be in New York, so every Olympic and world champion (with the exception of Nancy Kerrigan, who simply could not face the public at large, probably for good reason) came to pay homage. After all, I *was* the Skater of the Century. Maia Usova and Alexander Zhulin, Ekaterina Gordeeva and Sergei Grinkov, Oksana Baiul, Viktor Petrenko, Brian Boitano, Elvis Stojko, Scott Davis, and Michelle Kwan were but a few that I recall.[*]

I had submitted to a make-over, with special make-up and hair people and photographers. When the photographs were developed, I didn't recognize myself.

I am not exactly wet behind the ears in the painting department, but a meeting I attended of the people who were going to sell the work was something of a revelation. They were: groovy, aggressive, overly made-up, glittery women (in a hip, sort of attractive, kind of seedy way); single New York men who obviously had other lives; and the head honcho, who had flown in from the Dyansen Gallery in Beverly Hills to instruct the sellers. I sat, as a fly on the wall, and listened to the sales pitch. The head honcho began to describe my work. He emphasized key words such as "harlequinesque." Then he went into a soliloquy on the harlequin figure in the history of art. There was not one single person there who I thought knew a smidge about art. They were hot sellers. But hey, it was New York! And hey, it was a successful gallery, and I was going to be rich!

---

[*] Others were Aja Zanova, Dick Button, JoJo Starbuck, Ken Shelley, Elaine Zayak, Gary Beacom, Isabelle and Paul Duchesnay, Isabelle Brasseur, Lloyd Eisler, Elizabeth Punsalan, Jerod Swallow, Marina Klimova, Sergei Ponomarenko, Natalia Mishkutenok, Artur Dmitriev, Tracy Wilson, and director of ABC Sports Doug Wilson.

Starry, Starry Night

The number of people who were invited had gone from 500 to 600; had been coaxed up to 700; had been bumped to 900; had surpassed 1,200; and had topped out at 1,500. Now, that's not a bad turnout for a Broadway show, but for an artist's exhibition, it was unprecedented. It was to be the event of the season. With the guest list climbing and climbing, it was as though we were operating a phone-sex business. Calls of every description came in from far-flung locales. Someone asked if Marla would be wearing a tiara. Another caller wondered what hors d'oeuvres would be served, and was lobster one of them? Some inquired how many glasses of champagne they would be allowed. Others wanted to know if Michael Jackson would be there and, if so, would he be recognizable? The list went on. It was out of control. Part of me tried to be excited, but part of me sensed that something was gravely amiss. I chose not to acknowledge the pessimist in me.

Trump Tower was transformed. Paintings were hung on every level. Oceans of flowers hit the floor. Bars opened. Caterers poured in. It was a big production. Even my father, who was so ill that he should have been dead, insisted upon coming with my mother. He arrived in a wheelchair, quite thrilled to be there. Marietta de Aubrey, my estate manager, flew in from Mexico. Olympic champions dripped from the ceiling, and old friends decorated the four levels.

Robert Desrosiers came with me as my guest, which provoked amazement and unwarranted speculation on the part of the many who chose to think that there was more to it than met the eye, but we were friends. Would you like to come? Sure, why not.

I walked in fairly early. Then the Mongolian hordes stormed the barricades. There were fifteen hundred people scrambling up and down the escalators, all talking and shrieking at the same time. Someone asked me where Michael Jackson was, and did I think that Lisa Marie Presley had shown up? Where was Marla? Was she wearing the diamond?

The Anti-Climax

It took me about ten minutes to realize that it was a catastrophe. My début in New York was little more than a free-for-all and a hide-and-seek game with Donald Trump. Donald, incidentally (who has been very kind to me over the years), did make an appearance. Mrs. Trump was upstairs, ostensibly not feeling well – but it wasn't her health that was the problem. It was Michael Jackson having a breakdown over the child-molestation accusations. He was hiding upstairs.

There was a major *frisson* in the middle of the show, because many people thought that they'd sighted Mick Jagger. I'm not at all sure that anyone ever saw a painting. I suspect not. The hot sellers, who were going to ram harlequinesque motifs down people's throats, were eclipsed by the horde, never to be seen.

A frozen smile decorated my face. My head was pounding, and I was having little chats with God about what exactly he was trying to teach me and what it was that I had done wrong yet again. I was summoned down the escalator for the speeches. Donald Trump was

the first to speak. In Trump Tower, there is a waterfall that cascades down three floors, and someone had forgotten to turn it off. We had to shriek like opera singers, not only to the assembled mass on the *rez-de-chaussée* but upward to four levels. When my turn came to speak, I tried to rev up my voice to play to the upper balconies, but to no avail. The waterfall drowned out everything.

The whole thing became living torture. Every remark that came out of my mouth – polite, crisp, and precise – was like a hypodermic needle. I tried to hold my head up and behave with dignity (which I suspect I did), but near the end, as things were winding down, I slipped out onto Fifth Avenue. Some dear friends of mine (Clive Caldwell; my godson, Dylan; Paul LaPointe and his wife, Joanne; and Robert Desrosiers) strolled with me up Fifth Avenue and along Fifty-seventh Street to the Russian Tea Room. Even that had lost a certain allure. It had changed since I had lived across the street. The people I had known there had changed. I wasn't the least bit hungry.

JoJo Starbuck and Karen Kresge were there with their new *beaux*, and we had a good old chat – not about art, not about Marla failing to show up, and was it true that Mick Jagger was there? We just discussed old skating experiences. It healed the wounds and, at least for that moment, there was a dollop of friendship and warmth and a sense of family.

I went back to my hotel on Fifty-fourth Street, a fabulous hotel, the Élysée. I fell into bed like a petrified zombie and lay there until it was time to get up and scurry back to the ice. I took a limousine to LaGuardia and flew to Toronto; waited for three hours to fly to Winnipeg; waited another hour, then went to Saskatoon; waited yet another hour before flying to British Columbia. By then, I didn't know what time it was, and I was not at all sure what day it was. I crawled into a taxi, checked into a hotel, and resumed my petrified zombie act. The next day, I revved into Skate the Nation and pretended that it had all been a terrible mistake.

· 15 ·

Lessons Learned

At the end of 1994, I started to become a victim of what I call the Elaine Zayak Syndrome. I had accused IMG of creating a problem for Elaine, as they did for others, because, for whatever reason, her gigs were few and far between. Everyone criticized Elaine's weight, but I told them, "Don't you understand? It's because she's not performing that she's overweight." When you don't have any reason to train, you get fat, bored, and depressed. That's the problem IMG was creating for me.

One of the little bones they flung my way was the opportunity to skate in the three shows that they produce every year in Vail, Colorado, just before Christmas. I hadn't been skating much, and I was breaking in a new pair of boots. At that time of the year, you have to fly from Toronto to Chicago to Denver. Then it's a two-and-a-half-hour ride into the mountains. I had a hell of a trip. When I arrived, however, being the trusty old warhorse that I was, I thought, "Gee, the first show's tomorrow. Maybe I'd better rehearse." Then I told myself, "Gee, maybe I should wear these new boots."

I went out and practised. My boots were stiff. I pitched forward, but the boots didn't, and there was a *crunch*. I limped off the ice and said to Renee Roca and Gorsha Sur, "Something is definitely not quite right here."

"Well, maybe you sprained something. It will be better tomorrow. You should probably just go home and rest."

"No, I think that I'd better go to the medical clinic."

It was just across the way, so I limped over. You have to line up with all the mutilated skiers. My foot was definitely not feeling good. It was fortunate that I had removed my skate. Otherwise I would have lived the rest of my life with that skate on my swollen foot. So there I was on the assembly line, feeling quite a lot of pain.

Finally, a doctor looked at my X-rays and announced, "You've broken your leg."

"What?!"

I was surprised, because I had made one of my cheap deals with God. I truly had not wanted to skate at high altitude in new boots. In fact, I hadn't wanted to skate at all. My first reaction was, "Goody, I got my wish." But I hadn't wanted God to break my leg.

Pass the Percodan

I had no idea of the gravity of the situation. The doctor put my leg in a removable cast, a decision with which I heartily disagree. Go for the good old plaster every time. The thing about a removable cast is that you can remove it – to go swimming, for example, which I did.

Then I said through clenched teeth, "Do you have a painkiller?"

"No, we don't keep them here. It's too dangerous."

"Well, I have to have one *fast*."

I hobbled to the phone on my crutches and called Deb Nast of IMG, who picked me up and took me to a drugstore. The pharmacist asked, "What is it that you wish? You can have Aspirin. You can have Tylenol. You can have Percodan. . . ."

Bingo! I said, "Percodan will be just perfect." (Percodan is sometimes prescribed when wisdom teeth are removed.) I started to gobble it like gumdrops. I think that I swallowed five or six of the little yellow tablets. One would have done nicely. Five or six can send you to the outer limits.

I went back to the hotel, and an unpleasant reality of the skating world kicked in. I was friendly with Ekaterina Gordeeva and Sergei Grinkov, Scott Hamilton, Paul Wylie, Rosalynn Sumners, Lea Ann Miller, and whoever else was on the bill, but not one person came to see me as I lay in bed with a broken leg, flying out of my gourd on Percodan.

I looked at myself once in the bathroom mirror. My eyes were crossing, so I knew that I was feeling no pain – but I wasn't really feeling too good. The next day I left in a great deal of agony and flew straight to Mexico. That flight was my first encounter with being irregular in society. People look at you differently. I can understand now how those with a disability must feel.

On Christmas Day in Mexico, I received not one call from any skater. It hurt my feelings, but I remembered that when Brian Orser was removed from Stars on Ice, and the next year's show was being planned in Toronto, not one of his good old buddies and friends phoned him, although they were in the same town. It is survival of the fittest. If you're on board, fine. If you're not, nobody wants to know.

Paul Duchesnay had a serious accident, and there was a possibility that he would never skate again.[*] When I phoned Isabelle, I asked her how many skaters had called to see how they were doing. Not one.

---

[*] In the spring of 1997, Paul's medical condition forced the Duchesnays to announce their retirement from skating.

The severity of the broken leg had an enormous negative impact. I had to cancel my farewell tour. Then I remembered something that Chita Rivera told me when she was run over by a car: the reality kicks in that you may never be the same again. I thought, like Isadora Duncan being strangled by her scarf, "Is this my history? Is this the end of me?"

It wasn't. In the words of a Toronto physiotherapist, "You have done everything that is humanly possible to ensure that you will never walk again, but the injury has healed perfectly."

The first time I skated in public after the accident was at the 100th Anniversary of the Cricket Club. I had a horror of performing with a leg that didn't work too well, but I did it. My real comeback, as it turned out, was skating in a Katarina Witt movie in Berlin during the summer of 1995. Katarina helped me to regain my confidence, and I must say that I was more brilliant than I had ever been in my life.

Lu Chen

I am the skating world's greatest living colour expert. When I did Lu Chen's costumes for the 1994-95 season, I set out, in a very precise and conscious way, to design the winning dress – and did.* I meekly confess that, although her skating was brilliant in the 1996 Worlds long program, and I wouldn't wish harm to any skater who had worked as hard as she had, I was quite thrilled that she came second to Michelle Kwan. It had to do with the dress.

I had seen Lu Chen for many years and had commentated about her when she first hit the scene at Junior Worlds in Budapest. Then I particularly noticed her as the most brilliant and undermarked skater at Worlds in Munich, where she pulled out a triple flip at the last second. I kept her in the back of my mind.

---

* "Chen Lu" is the correct Chinese word order. The name is westernized as "Lu Chen." Lu is her given name, Chen her surname.

She has one of those thoroughbred bodies with thoroughbred legs.

IMG, who had cajoled her into their stable, realized that, for three years in a row, she had come third.* She'd gone from choreographer to choreographer, but (for whatever reason) nothing seemed to tip the scales. Yuki Saegusa, her IMG agent, contacted me during the spring of 1994 and asked, "Can you fix her?"

Humbly I said, "Yes, of course I can fix her. I can fix anyone."

"Well, how would you like to go to New Orleans to make the introduction?"

I went to New Orleans and saw the Tom Collins tour. I didn't speak to Lu Chen that night, but we had a very formal breakfast the next morning. We got a Chinese restaurateur to interpret. Every word was chosen with great diplomacy for fear that it would be misinterpreted.

I told her, "Look, I can make you win, if that is what you wish. I know how to do it. It is on the second mark. It is by your total impression."

Fine. We shook hands. I'll see you after the tour.

Apparently, Lu Chen has had perennial foot or ankle trouble, so when the great moment came, and I was expecting to hear from her and her coach, I didn't hear a word. The whole thing was forgotten. Then, in late September, I got a phone call. They were back, and they wanted my help.

I chose Lu Chen's 1995 Worlds music in Mexico. Because Lea Ann Miller was involved, I was asked if I could fly to New York to cut it. I was becoming a gofer. Nonetheless, I went. I did the cuts. Then I went home. Two days later, I flew to L.A. to play the music for Lu Chen and her coach in a room in an apartment/hotel beside the Burbank ice rink. There was no reaction. I thought, "Oh well, wait until we go to the rink."

---

* Chen was third at Worlds in 1992 and 1993; third at the Olympics in 1994; and withdrew, injured, from the 1994 Worlds.

No sooner had I arrived the next morning than coach Li Mingzhu asked the entire rink, "Does anyone have any ideas for music?" I tried so hard to be as gracious, encouraging, and complimentary as I could, but I found that there were two eyes on my back every time I made the smallest move. I was told that it couldn't work, it wouldn't work, it wasn't right, it was the wrong direction. I went back to my little room and collapsed into bed in exhaustion at 6:30 P.M.

It started again the next day. The long and the short was that I blew my top. I said to the coach, "Don't say anything. Just give me two days. I know what I'm doing. If you don't like it, it's only two days of your life, but I can't work this way. Otherwise, I'm going home."

In the middle of a public session, with every skater known to man playing Bon Jovi and Talking Heads, I had to come up with the program that would win Worlds. I set the short program in one morning and the long program in one day. Then we went over to dear, sweet Cindy Stuart's, Lea Ann Miller and I, and we all told each other, "Well, they don't like the music. Maybe we can recut it."

Then I said, "Let me just hear the music that I cut once more."

I listened.

"I don't care what they say. That's it. That's the best, and that will do it. Either they take it or they leave it."

I went back to the rink. Lu Chen did the program. Not a word of thanks.

Having a Fit

Lu Chen and I had an exhibition in Montreal. We flew together, and I felt that we bonded. I don't speak Chinese, and she hardly speaks English, but we had animated conversations. We discussed everything from religion to politics to boyfriends. I don't know how, but it was fine. I was flung into first class, because we flew Air Canada and they knew me, so that made a certain impression. The captain invited us into the cockpit.

I was supposed to fly Lu Chen from Montreal to Toronto to get her measured for costumes. The coach couldn't go along, and she was absolutely terrified to be separated from her student, so she said, "Just do the designs, and we'll have them made in China."

I said, "No, you don't understand. They have to be done by the Canadian National Ballet. I have to be there." So we flew out at five o'clock in the morning and got the costumes measured. Bleary-eyed, I did the designs. I knew exactly what I wanted.

Some months later, I was opening Rockefeller Center and Lu Chen was the special guest. That was the perfect chance to get up early in the morning again, go to Newark (which was farther than all the other airports), catch the first flight out to Toronto to take her for a second fitting, then drive her back to the airport, at which point I was totally wiped out. That was going far beyond the call of duty.

The costumes were made. They were then shipped off to Lake Placid, and Yuki Saegusa's Japanese husband took them on a business trip to Tokyo, just in time for Lu Chen to wear them at the NHK Trophy competition. I then got calls from Isabelle Duchesnay in France, Daniel Weiss in Germany, and a British journalist who wanted an interview. Everyone asked *what* had happened to Lu Chen. It was a complete and total make-over. She had beaten Bonaly, she had won hands down, and they just couldn't believe the change – until I explained it. In March, Lu Chen went to Worlds and won again (and, let's face it, winning Worlds is pretty bloody hard).

No one mentioned my name. Not a "Gee, Toller, thank you" or a "Toller Cranston helped me." Usually with top performances now, they say, "This was choreographed by" or "This was designed by." Canada made quite a lot of fuss about my role, but the American network, NBC, didn't mention me – because there was some professional jealousy involved, I suspect.

The Twenty-eight-dollar Motel

Lu Chen, as the world champion, was going on the Tom Collins tour. I was asked if I could just fly to L.A. via Chicago and Dallas (because that was the cheapest flight they could find) to help with her show program. After flying that circuitous route, I went out for dinner with her entourage. Still, never a thank you.

Meanwhile, I had broken my leg in Vail and hadn't laced on skates since the injury. At the time, I also had skates that didn't fit, and I was in excruciating pain from the second I arrived.

I had cut music for three exhibition programs. After five hours of working in the Burbank rink, Lu Chen's camp told me, "We're sorry. We don't like the music. We don't think your choreography is musical. We're going to skate to the Whitney Houston number that Cindy Stuart did."

I said, "You know, I think that's a really good idea."

I walked back to the twenty-eight-dollar-a-night motel that they had put me in and sat in the tiny little hole of a room with cardboard blankets and sheets, and I thought, "You know, something isn't right here."

The Boomerang

The next morning, I went straight to the American Airlines counter and said, "Here's my ticket to Toronto. Can I go to Mexico on it?"

"Sure, no problem."

I went to San Miguel, and I crashed. Then I phoned IMG and said, "That little trip from Toronto to Chicago to Dallas to the twenty-eight-dollar-per-night motel room to the five hours of work to the 'Gee, I don't think that your choreography is right' – that cost them $5,000." The next thing I knew, Lu Chen was working with Sandra Bezic – and came second at Worlds.

When I later met her group at various exhibitions, I was terrifyingly polite and distant. Then one day, as I was walking down the ramp into an arena, coach Li Mingzhu came along, with her sweetest little smile, and said, "Did you design Meno and Sand's long program costumes?"

"Yes."

"Those are the most incredible costumes that I've ever seen. I love them. Would you do Lu Chen's next year?"

I said, "What happened to *this* year?" Then I turned and walked away.

Lea Ann Miller and Bill Fauver did a Christmas special with the Colorado Symphony. They skated to something about snow. The costume I designed for that number was one that you would wear to skate with a symphony under lights: a pure-white dress that faded into pale, icy blue. Bill wore black, and Lea Ann looked like a snowflake. Because Lu Chen had horrible clothes, Lea Ann gave her that dress to wear during the 1995 Tom Collins tour.

After the little episode with me, Lu Chen had that dress copied in grey. Grey never wins anything. Grey is the kiss of death, and white and grey, probably next to okra and lime green, is the worst combination that you can wear under television lights. So Lu Chen wore the copy of Lea Ann's dress for the 1996 short program.

The very last thing that Yuki Saegusa did at the hotel in Edmonton was have Lu Chen try on all the clothes that she had brought with her. Yuki said, "Well, this will be fine, and that'll be fine, but absolutely do not wear *this*." That is what she wore. The dress that I designed for Lea Ann, the dress that Lu Chen had copied, was almost, in some strange way, responsible for her demise. It wasn't an aggressive dress, and you have to be aggressive and convincing in the short program. You have to have a colour that punches and takes over the building. She did the opposite. In a way, I felt that I had contributed to her loss.

There are very few choreographers or "putter-togetherers" in the skating world. They must be respected. You can't use them like Kleenex and discard them. As I was sitting in my twenty-eight-dollar-per-night motel room, I thought, "You help to tip the scales [and I believe that I did], but you get kicked in the teeth. This can't be the way it's supposed to be." Other teachers should know and protect themselves.

Whether or not I understand it all, I'm over it. The fact remains that with me Lu Chen won, and without me she lost.

The Star Trip

David Liu, a wonderful artistic skater, an American who represented Taiwan, was staying at my loft in Toronto when the invitation came, in the late spring of 1995, to skate a week of exhibitions in Hong Kong. Because I was teaching David, I was included in the invitation. In tandem with the skating performances, a rather serious painting exhibition had been arranged. Once again, I was wielding the double-edged sword, heading straight for Asia.

David had a strong connection to Ted Wilson, the linchpin of the Asian skating world. A businessman and a great supporter of artistic skating, he will go down in history for, among other reasons, bringing top skaters to Asia.

Hong Kong was a place that I had never seen and knew little about. I decided that the only way truly to take it by storm was in the clothes department. There is a place in Toronto that I frequent on such occasions: Tom's Place in Kensington Market. I felt that blazers and jackets in violent shades of yellow, orange, purple, red, green, and chartreuse would be just the thing for summer in Hong Kong. Armani and Versace were prominently featured.

What one was offered in exchange for skating in Hong Kong was something much better than money: a first-class trip, a first-class hotel, with all meals on the house. My art dealer and friend, Paul LaPointe, who is a dreamer but not an extravagant one, had been coaxed (in a second) into going to Hong Kong with David and me.

The trip got off to a great start. We flew first to Vancouver. I had been insisting to David that I really was quite famous. Like a scene from a movie, every third person we passed on the street recognized me. David was not only impressed, but he also thought the whole thing was pretty funny.

The long trip from Vancouver to Hong Kong seemed short, because Paul and I engaged in an extremely competitive chess marathon. The more inebriated I became, the worse my chess got. Paul rode a winning streak. The one thing that he could not understand was why the steward believed me when I insisted that I had won every game.

Hong Kong seen from the air took my breath away. Movies such as *Blade Runner* crossed my mind. We seemed to be hovering over the twenty-first century. I had imagined a teeming city of dirty streets, outdoor markets, and end-to-end sampans and junks in the harbour. On the contrary, the most splendid, avant-garde, sinfully expensive buildings on the planet stood like soldiers along the harbour on both the Hong Kong and Kowloon sides. The city was far smaller than I had expected, yet the concentration of people was incalculable. I'm convinced that the wings of the plane banked in order to slip between skyscrapers.

Hong Kong commands awe. Its energy pulsates twenty-four hours a day, and money seems to flow through the streets. Yet, as I was soon to conclude, it has not one speck of charm, no visible history.

I landed in Hong Kong wearing a sapphire-blue silk jacket and a lemon-yellow silk shirt with a white collar, just in case the greeting party didn't recognize my face when I sauntered out of the arrivals lounge. Ted Wilson was waiting in a Rolls-Royce. We headed off towards the Conrad Hotel, high on the upper reaches of the Hong Kong side.

When the Rolls careened under the *porte-cochère*, I was gratified to discover a retinue of staff lined up to meet us: four managers, at least six bellhops, a cook, and the executive president of the hotel. I shook hands with every one of them in a chilly, starry way. Checking in was quite unimportant. Filling out forms was beneath the dignity of visiting potentates. The entire retinue jammed into two elevators, and up we went to the seventy-ninth floor.

We walked to the end of the hall and entered a sumptuous suite. Fans I hadn't met yet had sent a profusion of oriental flowers. I remained suitably aloof and inspected my quarters. There was a large living room that overlooked the harbour. I was especially delighted that, from that vantage point, one could look down on flying planes. My bedroom, at the back of the hotel, faced a verdant mountainside where one or two villas floated on a sea of greenery.

The hotel had provided a bucket of champagne and a lovely jewel box loaded with chocolates – very my cup of tea. I stood gazing around, not believing my good fortune, while pretending it was exactly what I had expected. When my door finally closed and I was left alone, I jumped up and down like a jackrabbit.

My painting exhibition was held in the hotel ballroom. Portable walls with special lighting had been erected in the middle of the room. The paintings and drawings were hung during our first afternoon there. The next morning the exhibition opened. Champagne flowed like water, hors d'oeuvres appeared by the platterful, and floral offerings continued to arrive. The attendance was healthy, and there were quite a few sales. The American Shepherd Clark, who was on the skating bill with me, bought a rather large painting.

My brightly coloured clothes, as I found out, were highly irregular in Hong Kong, yet they created exactly the sensation that I hoped for. A woefully oversized Chinese fellow named Gary was always at the door to greet me by name and comment on the latest jacket. A point came when I didn't know what to do next. My sartorial palette was running dry, but I didn't want to disappoint Gary.

Ted Wilson's Rink

The Hong Kong rink run by Ted Wilson is in a shopping centre perhaps fifteen minutes from the hotel. It's a small rink surrounded by a gallery: from all reports, the most successful ice rink in the world. No tickets were sold for the exhibitions. The shopping centre provided a found audience, and every performance was full.

I asked if I could conduct movement or theatre classes. I enjoyed working with the children as much as anything I did in Hong Kong, even though it was always after the performances, sometimes as late as midnight or one o'clock in the morning. Children all over the world, and particularly skaters, are the same. There's a bond, a common denominator that goes beyond language and culture. A skater is a skater.

The Shirt Shop

Custom-made shirts are among the great bargains of Hong Kong. One day I discovered a better than average shop in the Grand Hyatt hotel. I went in on a free afternoon and started to choose material. There was such a huge selection that it was almost impossible to decide on one. As a result, I ordered about twenty shirts of different colours. The young proprietor kept trying to tell me that red, emerald-green, royal blue, and lavender silk shirts were not what most men chose. I said, "That is exactly what I know, but these are the colours that *this* man is choosing."

As I sat on a stool, selecting the fabrics, a strange couple wandered in. My back was turned to them most of the time, but I confess that I eavesdropped. One man, I imagine, was about sixty-five, with grey hair. The other, considerably younger, had a platinum toupee à la Andy Warhol. There was much discussion of the pair of pants that the elder was buying for the younger. I became convinced that their entire conversation was for my benefit. The afternoon climaxed when the younger man tapped me on the shoulder and asked me point-blank how I liked his pants. I slowly and deliberately turned on my stool and said, "The pants are great, but the wig's got to go." He shrivelled and was not heard from again.

Just Desserts

David Liu crashed at my Queen Street loft for quite some time. A born-again Christian, he had a sense of humour but was sensitive on some points. There is a restaurant known only to the Chinese in Toronto that offers a twelve-dollar buffet. There is no Chinese food in the world that is not available there. One day, David and I ate at that restaurant.

There was a 500-pound woman in the dessert section, balancing a plate heaped with twenty different offerings. I said to David,

"Look at that woman. That is a disgrace. I am going to go right over there and snap that food away from her."

David's mouth dropped open.

As I marched across the floor, the woman looked up and recognized me. She said, "Toller Cranston? Can I have an autograph?"

"Yes," I said pleasantly, "but you'll have to put down those desserts."

David didn't know about the autograph. Assuming that I had done what I threatened, he ran out of the restaurant in shock. To this day, he believes that I took away that woman's desserts. She performed to perfection, creating exactly the illusion that I had hoped for.

· 16 ·

The Great Unknowns

Many extraordinary performers, although they offer the skating world something original, rare, or profound, can only be called great unknowns. They have never been given proper credit, because their one crime is that, for whatever reason (it could have been money, nerves, an inability to execute certain difficult jumps, the era in which they competed, or myriad other factors), they did not achieve the sort of credentials that guarantee widespread recognition. To be fair – which is important to me – there are numbers of people who can lay claim to membership in this group.

Gary Beacom

One cannot talk about the greatest of the great unknowns. They all have achieved greatness in their own right. Yet one is first among equals: Gary Beacom, the king of the great unknowns.

Like so many of the most creative skaters of the twentieth century, Gary was spawned by the Cricket Club. His contribution to skating has been enormous: he invented a new language of movement.

Gary seems to me to have large reservoirs of bitterness and perhaps insecurity. As van Gogh did, Gary knows who and what he is and has a vast knowledge of his field, yet that has never been enough to tip the scales in his direction where official approval has been concerned.[*]

The proof of the pudding with contributors such as Gary goes far beyond specific abilities. There is a uniqueness of personality, an originality of spirit, and a conceptual approach to skating that sets them apart from all the others. Although guided, for the most part, by rather unimaginative teachers, he was privy to the creativity of all the interesting Cricket Club skaters. I put myself at the top of the list, but there were many more.

Gary borrowed from another great unknown, Allen Schramm. What sometimes happens is that the impostor becomes the original. Gary took Allen's vocabulary and, in a creative and individual way, made it far more than Allen, his mentor, could have imagined.

Allen Schramm

Allen Schramm is an American original who skated at the time of Robert Wagenhoffer and David Santee. He was conspicuously sexual, yet he would never have known that he was. He did not work the floor in that department. He had a tremendously beaked nose, penetrating eyes, and an almost deathly pallor, like rock stars who never see the light of day. His great head of hair worked well for him, and he was an athlete.

Allen had an ability to flow around the ice. He was outrageous. The first time I encountered him was at Superskates in New York,

---

[*] Beacom was number two in Canada in 1983 and 1984. He finished tenth at the 1984 Worlds before retiring from amateur competition.

where he performed his "Black Widow" number. He made me feel extremely old-fashioned. I had never seen anything like it, and I became his instant and ardent fan.

I was responsible, I believe, for his timing in turning professional. He was cast as the second lead in my first television special. Both "Strawberry Ice" and Allen were historical: the choreographic plan, as the television cameras recorded, was never precise. Almost all of that precedent-setting production was *ad lib*. Among that brilliant cast, Allen was *numero uno*. His first improvisational attempt was always slammed into the can. He just couldn't have gotten any better.

The curse of so many of the great unknowns is the burden of multiple talents. Allen was torn for a number of years between skating and becoming a rock musician and composer. He went on to become a rather major star in Holiday on Ice in Europe.

Angela Greenhow

Angela, a British girl, is another remarkable yet forgotten skater. Angela was an artistic instrument. She was a drama queen. She had perhaps too much energy, too much passion, too much music in her body. When she skated as an amateur, people might have perceived her as slightly off the wall. She was equal to any top Broadway performer. The fact that she skated was almost secondary to her personality and complete lack of inhibition.

Allen and Angela became man and wife while skating with Holiday on Ice. They now have two children. Who knows what sort of creation *they're* going to produce. I can't imagine joining up those two bloodlines without something extraordinary popping out.

The Three Graces

Three princesses have to be discussed *à trois*. Each is unique, yet there's a shared refinement that sets them apart from all others. Cindy Stuart, Catarina Lindgren, and Simone Grigorescu are women of artistic bent, special among their peers. All three took skating seriously as competitors, but each, however good she was as an amateur, struck out in the nerves department. They were sensitive creators and artists. The wicked world of the amateur arena was simply not for them. They achieved greatness as performers.

Cindy Stuart, a California girl with a sensual figure, is unique in the world. Her skating has a casual sophistication. She has an ability to happily hop into the fourth dimension simply by affixing herself to the music. She performs seemingly without effort. Only trained eyes can fully appreciate her brilliance. I have seen Robin Cousins partner Cindy in duets when she has not been one smidge beneath Robin in ability or impact. One is a great unknown and the other is a legit thoroughbred Olympic gold medallist, but, as far as I am concerned, they were equal in those performances. I would be remiss not to mention the choreographic genius behind Cindy Stuart: Jamie Isely, another great unknown.

Catarina Lindgren, of Swedish extraction, is the quintessential instrument of Sarah Kawahara. She may not be a Hollywood beauty queen, but she has an ability to step on the ice and become quite the most beautiful creature God has ever created. She has a splendid body, a splendid sensitivity, and, in comparison to the others, is the upper end of refinement, more highbrow – a Stradivarius violin compared to Cindy Stuart's fine guitar.

I have studied Catarina and Cindy, and they have taught me one of the most important things about choreography and performing: the ability to become intriguing, beautiful, exciting, and profound without doing one jump or spin.

Simone Grigorescu, of Romanian extraction, was by far the most athletic of the three in her amateur competitive heyday. People would have thought that she had it all. She was attractive. She had a beautiful body. She was artistic. She was flexible. She was a good jumper – but I believe that her nerves prevented her from ever becoming a top world competitor. She was too refined to sink so low.

Simone has an immense versatility – they all do, to be honest – and I think that her ability to present herself as a thoroughbred has something to do (as is true of Catarina) with being from Europe. She has an extra level of comprehension of art, music, and culture that rarely is seen on North American soil.

Without being movie-star beautiful up close, all three have an ability to transform into swans on the ice, whereas many better-known skaters could not carry the hems of their robes. They are far beyond triple toe loops. They are among the apprentices who have helped to hone the big iceberg of figure skating into a multi-faceted jewel, yet they were not able, for whatever reason, to achieve the same amateur credentials as other skaters who, in many ways, are less great.

Sarah Kawahara

Sarah is another of the golden guppies spawned by the Cricket Club, an artistic skater with an exceptional brain. Half Japanese, half Canadian, she is one of those fragile, sensitive Asians made of iron. She was a supremely important artistic skater in Ice Capades and used that as a launching pad to become one of the best choreographers in the world today.

Doug Mattis

Doug Mattis, in many ways, is a male version of Angela Greenhow. He has a personality that's larger than life and a thorough knowledge of technique, yet he could never, ever become the prince in *Swan Lake*. He isn't a noble skater. However, Doug is no less a character, a performer, and a multi-faceted personality than Scott Hamilton.

Christopher Nolan

Christopher, a Montreal boy with a legit theatrical sense, was a textbook example of a skater who could not fit into the amateur world. He was not meant to turn out eight triples in a long program. I saw him skate a gospel number during the 1992 Charles Schulz show in Santa Rosa, California. He had a chameleon's ability to transform himself into something quite fantastic, fascinating, and passionate. Night after night, as I watched him, I thought, "Very few people in the world can perform as well as that."

Stephanee Grosscup

Stephanee Grosscup is great for a number of reasons, but let's start with the skating. She is a beacon of art and culture who sprang up like a mushroom that never should have grown in Salt Lake City. She should have been the goddess of New York or the diva of L.A. Stephanee is a genuine artist with deep feeling, a sense of refinement, and a huge dollop of outrageousness. Her skating is secondary to a personality and a sense of humour that are unique on the planet. Why she has not been discovered and turned into a movie star or a great comedienne, I don't know. I have often tried to convince Brian Orser, another skater who appreciates Stephanee, to sponsor her as a lounge act. The state of Utah is so lucky to have her.

Linda Reynolds

Another great unknown, the kind of person to whom I can get down on my knees and thank on behalf of all the skaters in Canada, if not the world, is Linda Reynolds. She understands what skating is truly about. She has an extensive knowledge of music, an international perception of the world, of culture, and of art, yet her claim to fame is that she became the Martha Graham of Calgary without any stars to make her reputation. (She has subsequently flown the coop and now works in the United States.)

Linda became great as a choreographer, a conceptualizer, someone who inspired young children and gave the gift of the magic of skating to a level of skater who otherwise would never have encountered it. Linda Reynolds is one of the patron saints of figure skating.

Robert Wagenhoffer

It is so dangerous to talk about a skater whom you have never seen perform. If he walked through the door, I wouldn't recognize him, yet he has had such sterling endorsements from every skater on the planet that I would be remiss not to mention him.[*]

Robert was guilty of a crime that often has extremely bitter consequences. He was born with too much talent. He was a virtuoso to beat all virtuosos. It seems to me that America, when presented with virtuosos, often doesn't quite know what to do with them. America perhaps doesn't recognize that along with the talent goes a portfolio of special conditions that require special treatment. Rare instruments have to be coddled and appreciated. I suspect that Robert, as an amateur, became disheartened. He may have felt that no one really appreciated him, and threw in the towel prematurely.

Karen Kresge

Karen is a goddess, a long-legged girl whose ability to jump would probably not have exceeded a double Salchow in her heyday. She became a star of Ice Follies, particularly adept at contemporary music. I saw that blonde diva move and shake and bump and grind in an Earth, Wind & Fire number, and I thought that I was watching Tina Turner. Karen isn't just a showgirl. She has great theatricality, a sense of humour, sensuality, and a sense of rhythm that exceed those of her contemporaries.

---

[*] Wagenhoffer, Santee, and Hamilton were engaged in a three-way battle in the early 1980s for the status of American top dog. Wagenhoffer, although a highly gifted artistic skater, was among the pioneers of the triple Axel and quadruple toe loop.

Ann Pellegrino

Ann was a middle-class Italian who skated in Boston among the blue bloods. She was a long-legged thoroughbred colt. In a summer free-skating competition in the late 1960s, she decimated Petra Burka, the Canadian champion, the world silver medallist, the future world champion, on Petra's home turf. Ann had an ability to jump and to cover the ice with a bouncing, conspicuous joy in skating that was launched from a virtuosity that is rare. I saw her once, and I never forgot her.

Kitty Kelly

Kitty Kelly, another Cricket Clubber, was a redheaded Ice Capades skater who transformed relatively easy manoeuvres into a high art. Her mother was one of the truly great unknowns. Andrea McLaughlin was an apprentice and protégée of Sonja Henie who became a major star of Ice Follies. Her husband, the famous Canadian hockey player Red Kelly, fell in love with her in the 1950s: a hula dancer in a fifty-five-pound bugle-beaded Hawaiian grass skirt. Like her brother, an Olympic competitor, Kitty was trained in speed skating. She had a flow and a basic skating ability that no figure skater in the world, starting with Midori Ito, Yuka Sato, or Kristi Yamaguchi, could imagine.

Norman Proft

In the inside circles of skating, anyone who has seen Norman Proft, a splendid Canadian performer, rhapsodizes about him. He was a technically strong amateur skater who never quite made the world team. His real forte was a unique and special interpretive approach to skating. With a personality that eclipsed his technical ability, he was able to carve out his own niche in the skating world.

Norm teamed up with another unique skater, a temperamental, fiery French-Canadian redhead named Julie Brault. Julie cannot be compared to Cindy, Catarina, or Simone, yet her passion is intense. Perhaps because of her red hair and her French-Canadian blood, she has a special volatility on the ice.

Kathleen Schmelz

I performed with Kathleen in Stars on Ice until she was let go by IMG for lacking the gilt-edged credentials others had. She is memorable not for artistic pretension, but for a fresh and intense conviction that everyone could see and feel each time she skated. Fast and peppy, neither a thoroughbred nor an artist, she was special for sheer verve.

Daniel Weiss

Daniel Weiss was the beacon of artistry in all of Europe. An exceptional performer, he had no hint of inhibition in doing strange things: from skating masterfully as a drunk to mimicking a cat. His presentation had a certain refinement. He was quick in his movement and rhythm. His choreography was detailed. He could have been a world or Olympic medallist if only he had mastered a few more jumps. A German champion, he was a victim of the radical change in the sport after 1976, when the edict became, "Perform every triple jump or don't compete." He went on to skate in France in Isabelle and Paul Duchesnay's show and became the voice of skating for a German television network.

Suzanne Russell

Remarkable skaters are not produced by accident. In the case of Sarah Kawahara, the mentor, the guiding light, was a unique character who teaches at the Cricket Club, Osborne Colson. Sarah went on to international fame because of her choreography and her association with top skaters, but another girl who preceded her must be mentioned.

Suzanne Russell hit a height of sophistication, elegance, and musicality that the world has not seen since. She was Osborne's first protégée. If Sarah is the living knowledge carried from Osborne to other skaters, Suzanne *was* Osborne Colson – yet she plays no role in the skating world today.

Suzanne was from a wealthy Toronto steel family and was perhaps too spoiled because of her lifestyle ever to become a top world competitor. What she chose to do was become a great artist. She was one of those splendid Ice Follies stars who rounded out the show and gave it a particular flavour.

She was tall, statuesque, and had an almost lazy way of skating. She was conspicuously dramatic and absolutely and totally unin-hibited, because somehow she really didn't give a good goddamn about the Ice Follies. She was skating for her own pleasure. It was a self-indulgent performance every night. The limousines and the Russell steel fortune were waiting for her, so what did it really matter what she did on the ice? That gave her performance a reck-less elegance.

Suzanne seemed far too chic and cosmopolitan to end up in a tawdry ice show. She was like a private-school girl who had acci-dentally landed in vaudeville. You could see it from the second she stepped onto the ice. She was glamorous without a single sequin or rhinestone. Her aura was *haute couture*. In Ice Follies, she skated a Charlie Chaplin number as a man. Kirk Wyse, another great unknown, parlayed Chaplin into Olivier material in Holiday on Ice. Suzanne's interpretation, in its way, was no less memorable.

ˎ 17 ˏ

Three Funerals

*D*uring the 1980s, a number of male skaters of a certain renown became infected with HIV. I'm not sure that anyone talked about it openly, but it gave rise to an era of fear and shock and worry. None of the skaters, as far as I know, ever discussed their intimate sexual activities with anybody else, so when we would hear that X had been infected or that Y had been infected, they were close to us, yet we knew nothing of their personal lives. We also did not know if their personal lives had anything remotely to do with our own. Were we close to death, too, without realizing it? We really did not know much about AIDS in those days.

Perhaps the first shock to hit the Canadian skating world was news of the illness of an unusual, hilarious, immensely popular skater from Vancouver, Dennis Coi. He was a contemporary of Robert McCall and was the first of that group, to my knowledge, to be infected with HIV. Dennis was a theatrical skater who spent quite a lot of time in Toronto after my own amateur days there. He reached his heights under the tutelage of Ellen Burka.

I didn't know him well, but through Ellen I knew about him, and I don't think that (with the exception of me) there's another skater about whom more stories were bandied about: "You're never going to believe this" and "Did you hear that?" Anybody who knew him loved him. He should have been a paid professional partygoer. His behaviour was, in its own way, outrageously, spontaneously flamboyant. I was struggling for my own skin during my ice-show days, so perhaps what he did and how he behaved were not things that I particularly approved of.

Dennis Coi became ill, and he eventually died in Vancouver. One of the few things that I regret in my life is that although I had always meant to phone him or write him a letter, it never happened, and he died.

There was one slight whiff of poetic irony about his death. Near the end of his life, Dennis went home to his parents. He decided that he wanted to start every day by doing something that he'd never done. On the day of his death, the thing that he wanted to do was to play bingo. I'd like to believe that this is true, so, for me, it is true. The story is that he died the second that he won bingo. The line was, "Bingo, you're dead."*

I hated myself for not reaching out when I knew that, if I had just written a letter or made a phone call, it might have made his day a little bit brighter. I was determined, when I heard that Robert McCall was ill, that history would not repeat itself.

---

* According to an article in the *Calgary Herald*, "Coi died in his mother's arms while doing one of his favourite things – playing bingo. 'He missed a bingo by one number and said "Oh s—." Those were two of the last words he spoke before he went into an epileptic seizure.'" Coi died in 1987.

The Last Days of Robert McCall

When Robert was rehearsing for the Boitano show in Portland, Maine, in 1990, Stars on Ice was running concurrently. Robert was expecting to do a few Stars on Ice shows before rejoining the Boitano tour.[*] But he became terribly ill in Portland. I heard what happened through Brian Orser and Tracy Wilson, the partner with whom he had won a bronze medal in ice dance at the 1988 Olympics. Tracy, Robert, and Brian were The Three Musketeers.

Robert McCall came down with such severe pneumonia that he almost died in Portland. Brian and Tracy knew that something serious was up. As nothing was official, they could not speculate – but they kind of knew what the matter was. I think it poignant that Robert apparently waited two or three days to find out whether he was positive or negative for HIV. The Three Musketeers could not freely express their thoughts, because Robert was in a state of

---

[*] Skating II starred Brian Boitano and Katarina Witt.

paralysis. He was lying there, so frightened, like a rabbit facing foxes. He was waiting for his death sentence.

Stars on Ice was about to be staged in Calgary. That, in its own way, was historical because of Debi Thomas. It was a case of the victim returning to the scene of the crime. Debi had bombed so terribly in Calgary in the 1988 Olympics.[*] You don't ever get over performances like that. There's nobody you can make peace with. For her to skate in the Saddledome again was difficult, but at least the focus was diverted from Robert McCall.

In the middle of the opening, Tracy Wilson came out and got applause before she said a word. I was standing there, because all of us had been introduced: Scott Hamilton, Brian Orser, myself, Peter and Kitty Carruthers, Rosalynn Sumners perhaps. I remember it so clearly, because time stopped. She stood there under the spotlight in front of maybe 18,000 people and said, "Hi. I'm Tracy Wilson, and I have some bad news. My partner is sick in Portland with pneumonia, and he cannot be skating with me tonight."

We got off the ice, and everyone went scurrying into the dressing rooms. I stopped Jay Ogden, now vice-president of IMG, and said, "Jay, come here. Do you know what Tracy Wilson just said?" It had not dawned upon him, so I said, "Tracy Wilson just told the audience that Robert McCall has AIDS."

"What? What are you saying?"

"Look. *You* can have pneumonia, someone *else* can have pneumonia, but Robert McCall is the one sort of human who cannot have pneumonia."

He did have AIDS. Through some strange, ironic twist, I was the first to know (I thought) because of what Tracy had said.

---

[*] "Bombing" is relative. Like Cranston, Thomas won the bronze medal. Her sights had been set higher. After her first mistake, she skated an uncharacteristically dispirited long program.

Robert's fight with AIDS, like that of so many, was very valiant. I don't think that Sir Lancelot or King Arthur could have done much better in the courage department. He was kept afloat by a retinue of skaters and friends, and while he resided in a downtown Toronto hospital, there was almost never a time when his room was empty.

Because of Dennis Coi, I thought, "I must go and see Robert McCall." You obviously had to bring him something, and I didn't think that flowers or candy or a book was the right thing. I heard years later that he enjoyed what I chose: an extremely expensive kaleidoscope. He could sit in bed and watch designs.

When I went to see him, he was chirpy and cheery. He was in bed, hooked up to a Valium drip, with all sorts of things stuck into him, but he was his old jolly self. Brian Pockar was there. As I was the new guest and Brian the old, in my own rather inquisitive and perhaps insensitive way, I started to ask about the disease itself and what he knew about it, and was there any way he could pinpoint how he got it? Maybe I was even asking for myself, to find out, "If you got it this way, could I possibly have contracted it, too?"

I left to go to the bathroom, and Robert said to Brian, "Boy, Toller is really stupid. He doesn't know anything about this."

Brian shot him a remark that pierced to the core. He said, "Robert, until you got it, *you* didn't know anything about it."

What we did not know, what none of us knew, was that Brian Pockar had the disease, and knew that he had it, and was keeping it to himself.

Brian told me later that *he* had been the first person to know that Robert McCall had AIDS. He had known it even before Robert. Brian and Robert had gone to Mexico. Robert had done nothing but sleep and sweat. He was so tired that he couldn't move. Brian watched him, unconscious and sweating, knowing that Robert had AIDS but unable to tell him – because Brian himself had AIDS, and he didn't want anyone to know.

We said goodbye. I vowed to visit Robert again, and Brian drove me home. I was sitting in his little red sports car. I guess I was thinking about Robert McCall: "Oh my god, this is really it." Perhaps I was thinking out loud. Brian Pockar shot me another look that I thought was strange at the time, but it didn't click with me. He said, almost viciously, "Many people have crosses to bear."

Robert McCall was in and out of the hospital. There were tremendous fluctuations in his weight. At one time, he lost his hair. I believe that he was one of the guinea pigs when AZT was being dished out. The AZT was so liberally distributed that it practically ate him alive. Near the end of his fight, he decided that he could no longer stand the side effects and went off the AZT and the other drugs.

Robert was at centre stage with skaters of a different era than my own. I felt that, as long as he had company, and as long as he was just down the street, I could visit him when I wanted to. Often I decided not to. Months went by. When I saw him at the Cricket Club, he was always cheerful and chatty. He was also very brave about his appearance. Fat, thin, bald, or not bald, he never batted an eyelash. I think that I would have been very sensitive about it.

The CFSA, and particularly David Dore, was not at all close to the Brian Orsers and the Tracy Wilsons. I assume that the CFSA wanted to prove, somehow, some way, either to the world or to the skaters, that it was on the inside track. It was going to announce Robert McCall's death – and it jumped the gun.

Robert heard that the CFSA had issued a press release saying that he had died, and he listened to his obituary on the radio. Then he phoned the radio station and said, "This is Robert McCall. Rumours of my death are greatly exaggerated." (He also consulted with lawyers and was planning to sue.) That's an aside, but it's part of history – funny and macabre and somehow perfect for Robert McCall.

Tim Grech, a friend of Brian Orser and Robert McCall, was

working out at the rink one day, and he told me, "You know, Robert's really not doing very well."

I said, "I just have to see him. I think I'd better go."

"Well, I'm driving that way. Do you want to go with me?"

"Yes, I do, thanks."

"I don't know if Mrs. McCall will let you in."

"I'll go, and at least I'll show my good intentions."

I changed, and we drove down Avenue Road, where Robert was living. He was sort of hospitalized at home. We knocked on the door. Evelyn McCall was out walking her son's dog, so we went into the living room. The nurse who had treated Robert in Portland came downstairs and, without making much of a fuss, said, "Would you like to see Robert?"

I wanted to say no.

I went up to see him by myself. What I saw was no longer human. When I was eight or nine years old, my great-aunt took me to the Royal Ontario Museum. There was a mummy there, in fetal position, wrapped up in a straw mat. I looked at that mummy, not really able to believe that it was human, or that it ever had been human. I had the identical sensation with Robert McCall. The size of his head, in particular, seemed abnormally small. His hands had shrunken to almost the size of a baby's.

What I was seeing was neither life nor death. I believed (and as it turned out, it was true) that I was seeing him in the process of dying. I could have been looking at a television screen or viewing the event from miles away through binoculars. He was at peace, and his breathing was regular and easy. I saw him briefly, and I left. I am convinced that within one second or one minute or one hour of the time that I left, he was dead.[*]

I was the last skater, the last member of the royal family, to have

---

[*] McCall died on November 15, 1991, at 12:15 P.M., in the arms of his brother.

seen him alive. When I got home, there was a message from Tim Grech on my answering machine. Robert McCall was dead.

The First Funeral

Any members of the royal family who could possibly attend the funeral were summoned. It was *de rigueur*. It took place on a rich fall day, everything that autumn has to offer, yet the sky was overcast. There were white clouds, colour in the trees, and red and yellow oak leaves on the ground. The northern Toronto church was filled to the brim. I didn't go, really, with sadness – at least, I didn't think that I did. If anything, not being part of the immediate circle, I went with a sense of relief that it was finally over. He'd fought and fought and fought, and finally he'd lost.

There was a kind of pecking order as to who sat where, because there were so many major names in attendance: Katarina Witt, Tom Collins, Tracy Wilson, Paul Martini, Barbara Underhill, Kerry Leitch, Christine Hough, Doug Ladret, Shelley MacLeod – everyone Robert had ever known. It was like the skating protocol. Surprisingly, I got a seat in the fourth row, directly behind the immediate family. I regret that I had not paid enough attention to my appearance. I had changed at the Cricket Club after skating, so I looked rather scruffy.

One of the ushers and pallbearers was Brian Pockar. He shocked everyone, including many reporters, because, although it had not been announced, it appeared that he, too, might have full-blown AIDS. Brian was very aggressive, very brave, as he show-directed the proceedings.

When funerals start, it is often as though the deceased somehow is not quite dead yet. There's an element of life, or their spirit is still there, and they are surrounded by friends. There were many candles in the church. The atmosphere would have been much more appropriate to a Thanksgiving service. I don't think that there were pumpkins decorating the altar, but it was almost that kind of feeling. Turkey and cranberries were not served, but they could have been.

The service itself, which was neither sentimental nor dramatic, perhaps reflected Robert's skating style: *not* dramatic, not poignant, not poetic, but somewhat light. It was similar in mood to the music of Scott Joplin, to which Robert had skated. We could all have had a good cry (and many of us wanted to have a good cry), but no one ever pushed the sentimental buttons that would have opened the floodgates. There were whimperings and snifflings, but it wasn't a grief-stricken funeral.

Brian Pockar read a poem, the contents of which I don't remember, but his appearance obliterated anything that he said. He was gaunt, with sunken temples, and his wonderful mane of hair was diminished by half.

We left the church, and then it was helter-skelter. Everyone was going somewhere else. Shelly MacLeod, my partner at Radio City Music Hall and a great friend of Robert, was with me. We caught snatches of conversation and fleeting impressions, like Katarina Witt running to a car with coloured oak leaves blowing around her feet.

We all wanted to talk about Brian Pockar, but nobody could say the words: *Does Brian Pockar have AIDS?* The half-formed questions swirled in the air like the autumn leaves.

We went to Brian Orser's house, and although I can't remember every single person who was at the wake, it was mostly skating people on the inside track of Robert McCall's life. David Dore had not been invited.

Brian Orser hosted an immensely sumptuous buffet. I remember sushi and a pasta bar that I couldn't get enough of. I was ravenous. Christopher Bowman was crawling around with his peroxided orange hair, so I had to avoid him. I said hello to a few people and spoke with Mrs. McCall, but I left shortly thereafter and went home with a headache, a headache that was multi-pronged. Part of it was because of Robert McCall, part of it was the worry about Brian Pockar, and part of it was the horror of Christopher Bowman and his orange hair. That ended the funeral.

Perhaps Robert McCall's death only truly struck home at the end of the AIDS benefit in his memory a year later.* We were in pairs. I skated with Katarina Witt. At the end, we all formed a circle and looked in front of us with our hands extended. A spotlight swept to the middle of the circle, and then the light got smaller and smaller until it disappeared, and we were left in darkness. It was only then that his death kicked in with me, the fact that he was gone. It was a moment that, for the royal family of skating, stopped time.

Almost without exception, everyone skated very well that night.

The Last Days of Brian Pockar

Leanne Pockar, Brian's younger sister, lived at 64 Pembroke Street for almost two years. At Christmas 1991, when I was having sort of a gallery opening there, Brian came to visit. I have always envied people who are thin. When he came to say a Christmas hello, I thought, "How wonderful to be so thin. God, you must have worked hard in that show."

Rumours circulated. The most persistent was that Brian, whom many didn't often see, had a drug problem. Time moved on, and I was trying to put out my own fires. I received a phone call inviting me to attend Brian Pockar's farewell party. He was saying good-bye to his Toronto friends and moving back to Calgary, his family seat. The party was going to be held in the Jane Corkin Gallery, which was run by Patti Cook, a friend of both Robert McCall and Brian Pockar.

Although I was in a fragile state because of my own problems, I got myself together and went. The Robert McCall group was there (minus Robert, of course). Brian Pockar was there, cheerful but thin. I cornered Ricky O'Neil, a long-time friend, a Cricket Clubber,

---

* The tribute, Skate the Dream, took place on November 21, 1992, at Varsity Arena in Toronto.

and a member of the "Strawberry Ice" cast. I said, "What is going on? What is this party about? I *demand* that you tell me." I came on about as strong as I ever have in my life – but nobody told me a thing. The friends who knew for sure were sworn to secrecy. I had seen Brian Pockar skate at the Stampede Corral in Calgary when he was eleven years old. I had known him for years, had competed against him, had travelled with him, and had spent the 1988 Olympics at his house, but I was not allowed to know.

Brian returned to Calgary to die. He later told me that when he went down the escalator at the Calgary airport, he said to his mother, "Well, Mom, this is the end of the line. This is the last stop on the tour."

When I went to Calgary some months later to skate in an outdoor production that Moira North and the Ice Theatre of New York were putting on, I was met at the airport by Moira and Frank Nowosad. Frank was an eccentric, and probably more knowledge-able about skating history than anyone else in the world. He was a skating connoisseur with a bitter, caustic streak – caustic because, in his mind, there were very few people who understood the art of skating. (I think I just made it by a hair.) Again, I went into shock, because I noticed heavily made-up Kaposi's sarcoma on his nose and cheeks. I said nothing as I was led off to the Palliser hotel. As soon as I got to my room, I phoned Moira, but she couldn't say anything because Frank was there.

Brian Pockar came to the rink. He arrived in a coat that I had helped him buy in Munich years before, and *nobody knew who he was*. The kids knew who *I* was, but he was the hometown boy, a world bronze medallist, a Canadian champion – yet nobody recognized him. We vowed to meet that night in a restaurant called Mescalero, my favourite of its type in Calgary.

He picked me up at seven o'clock in his little red sports car. We drove to Mescalero, went into the restaurant/bar section, and sat down. Even before the waiter had asked for our drink order, I said, "So, Brian, why are you here? This is ridiculous. All your friends are in Toronto. You shouldn't be in Calgary. This isn't for you."

Brian looked me straight in the eyes from across the table and said, "Toller, I am very, very ill. I have AIDS. I have come here to die."

I forgot the spaghetti that I had planned to have. We immediately ordered Scotch. Then we talked. We talked as skater to skater, brother to brother, father to son, human to human, artist to artist. We had to talk, because there wasn't much time left. We talked without emotion. We talked about anything that had to be said. I told him things that went to the grave with him, and he told me certain things that I can never disclose to anyone. We traded notes and confidences. The next day I had to skate again in the freezing little rink, but we vowed to meet a second time. Three nights running, we met at the same restaurant, at the same table, had the same drinks, and talked.

I then realized that there was a certain onus on me. With Brian (unlike Dennis Coi and Robert McCall), I had to move into the inner sanctuary. I started phoning him often just to talk, just to find out how he was.

I think that many people with AIDS start to build fantastic ambitions, such as, "Gee, I want to come and visit you in Mexico."

I'd say, "Of course, and your mother can come."

"Well, I can't come this week, but maybe next month."

We started making long-term plans that scared me, because I guessed that they would never happen – and they never did.

The next month, I returned to Calgary. Brian, who was inclined to be private and secretive, requested that certain members of the Stars on Ice cast come to see him. I was asked to go, and so were Kitty and Peter Carruthers, Brian Orser, and Rosalynn Sumners – but no one else. We had a cup of coffee in the little house that he had bought. His mother was there. He was laughing. He was cheerful. He was so happy that we were there – happy and, I think, reassured. It was like the good old days, only something was terribly the matter.

I said, "Brian, I know you're weak, and you may not be able to, but I would love to see you come to the show tonight." He did. I told him, "Look, I've done this tango number, and I just want you to see it. It's especially for you." I was making light of it, trying to attract attention to me and not to him. I said, "I'm wild and outrageous. You've got to see me."

I did my little tango, but it wasn't really the tango that I wanted him to see; it was the second number, the number that I later skated at the AIDS benefit in Toronto, to a remarkable song by Stevie Wonder, "I Never Thought You'd Leave in Summer." That song was chosen for him.

When he came backstage, he said, "I know that the tango number wasn't for me. It was the second number." I said, "Yes, it was the second number." We sort of hugged, and we went back to the hotel briefly, and then there was that frozen-in-crystal, pathetically insignificant moment that you know is historically important: the I'm-never-going-to-see-you-again moment – yet that reality was never verbalized. So it was hug hug; keep in touch; maybe Mexico. I turned and didn't look back, because I knew that I never again would see him alive.

During one of our nights at Mescalero, Brian had reached out his hand to me and said, "If I ask you something, will you promise not to refuse me?"

"Yes."

"Will you come to my funeral?"

Of course I agreed.

Certainly all of us expected that it was going to come later as opposed to sooner. When I got back to Toronto, I touched base with Brian again. I phoned his house and someone staying there referred me to the hospital. He had suffered a relapse.

I called the hospital and Brian answered the phone.

"Brian, hi. It's Toller."

"Hi, Toller. How are you? I've got great news."

"Well, what is it?"

"I have a brain tumour."

"Oh, I'm so sorry to hear that."

"No, no. It's *good* news. The brain tumour's on the top of my skull. They can operate on it."

"Oh, that's very good news. Is your mother there, by any chance? Let me just say hello to Norma for a sec."

"Sure," he said in a cheerful, high-energy voice.

I said, "Norma, this is Toller. Please don't change the tone of your voice."

"Uh-huh."

"This is it, isn't it? This is the end."

"Uh-huh."

"What am I going to do? What should I do?"

"Uh-huh."

She never said anything but "uh-huh." She said it in a way that Pee-wee Herman might say it, bright and perky and fun, but I knew that inside she was dying – and I was dying. I hung up the phone, and within days, hours, minutes, Brian was dead.*

---

* Pockar died on April 28, 1992.

The Second Funeral

I was having my own problems. I also had no money. I phoned the airlines, and it was going to cost $1,200 to fly to Calgary. I didn't have it. Ricky O'Neil, Patti Cook, and I, along with another friend of Brian, managed to track down cheap fares. We flew to Calgary on an airline called Canada 3000 and paid $250. I recommend it in a pinch.

I believe that we were met at the airport by Leanne Pockar. I was asked by numbers of television stations to comment upon Brian, and I did. (I'd never really spoken about anyone dead before – at least not a friend.) I stayed at Brian's house, which had been bequeathed to Leanne. That night, there was a special service for friends. We went to the church, the same church where the funeral was to be held. I wouldn't say that it was like stepping out of my body, yet I didn't feel like myself. It was an unearthly feeling that came over me. I was a voyeur. I was almost physically distant from everything that was going on around me. Even as words came out of my mouth, I could hear them as though someone else were speaking them. Nothing seemed real.

Two members of the family, as I recall, stood up and spoke about Brian: his older sister, Serena, and his younger sister, Leanne. Leanne was perhaps closer to Brian than anyone else. They were almost like twins. They loved each other very much. It was emotional in the way that Robert McCall's funeral had not been. I found the girls' eulogies heart-wrenching. I had never heard such raw emotion expressed. I had never run into love that had been dragged across the coals. It was the very essence of love and loss, and it hit me right between the eyes.

There was another reason why I found it so disturbing: perhaps selfishly, it was because I had never experienced that kind of emotion, nor could I imagine it occurring in my own family. I could not picture any of my siblings standing up and speaking about me the way Brian's sisters had spoken about him.

The day of the funeral dawned. I was a pallbearer. I started to develop an excruciating headache. I also know that I looked particularly ugly on that day. I didn't feel good, and I didn't look good. I couldn't somehow throw myself together.

At a meeting before the funeral, horror struck me: there were only two Canadian skaters present. There was no one from the Canadian Figure Skating Association, none of Brian's dear, good, loyal friends – none. It wasn't at all like the Robert McCall funeral, where everyone and his uncle had turned out. He was alone with his family. It was oppressive; you couldn't breathe because of the grief. I didn't know that emotion. I didn't know about deep feeling, blood to blood, brother to sister, father to son.

I feel that it must be mentioned that Tai Babilonia and Randy Gardner managed to get to that funeral despite great difficulty. The Rodney King riots were taking place, and the L.A. airport was closed, but somehow they got there. Lisa-Marie Allen was there, and good old Michael Rosenberg, who's busy with his management agency, came too. If I sort of dropped dead, I'm not certain if IMG would be there. I wondered. But Michael Rosenberg supported his own.

Perhaps I had been more emotionally moved the day before, but at the funeral I was overwhelmed by a feeling of horror when the coffin came down the aisle, flanked by Mr. and Mrs. Pockar, their heads bent like two wilted tulips. They had no strength to hold them up. I watched, somehow thinking that it was a movie, but it wasn't. I was watching life at its most raw.

Everyone went to the grave site. The weather was that cruel, chilly spring weather. It was sunny, and the trees were just beginning to bud, yet the wind had a nasty sting. The cemetery road wove upward. Brown, lifeless plains stretched into the middle distance below an ugly, menacing, cloudless sky in a cruel shade of blue. There were graves in sombre rows as far as the eye could see.

We got out of the limousines and walked down a slope. The coffin was immensely heavy. The Province of Alberta insists that anybody who dies from AIDS be buried in a steel box. I was at the front, and it was almost heavier than I could carry. I nearly slipped into the grave.

The sun paled. Our hair and coats swirled around us. The coffin was lowered onto straps that extended across the pit. The priest said a few words. Then the coffin began to descend into the freshly dug grave. Mr. and Mrs. Pockar, in black, with their drooping tulip heads, held on tightly to Leanne, Serena, and Serena's husband and children.

What occurred then was among the most naturally dramatic things that I have ever seen. As the coffin was lugubriously lowered, Mr. Pockar, a shy man who suffers from Parkinson's disease, began to have convulsions and shake, the way a dog would shake a game bird in its jaws. Then, out of his mouth, came the words, "We love you, Brian. Our family loves you. You were the best son. We were so proud of you." At that, the coffin sank to the bottom of the pit.

As we climbed the hill to the limousines, there was a strange and horrible sound: the sound of earth being thrown on top of the steel coffin.

There was a lot of time to reflect, to compare my own situation. Could it have been me? If it had been me, who would have attended my funeral? Would any of my skating friends have come? Do I have any skating friends? Do I have a family?

The Pockars have a large, modern house where I had stayed for three weeks during the 1988 Olympics, but of course it wasn't the same after Brian's funeral. There were little lime-green and pink petits fours that brought to mind another memory of green and pink, a disastrous combination. Probably the worst skating performance ever in the history of the world was given by Joanne Conway in 1988. She wore an identical shade of acid pink and green. As I consumed as many of those petits fours as I could, I made a mental note never to dress anyone in lime green and pink.

The day ended with a memorable remark by a slightly tipsy Barbara Graham, who was no longer part of the CFSA. I said to Barbara, in a somewhat weighty and profound way, that no one in skating had ever been better looking than Brian Pockar.

"Yes," she responded in slurred syllables, "he was so much better looking than you were."

Two days later, we had to go home on our cheap Canada 3000 flight. The plane was due to leave at noon. All of sudden (this interested me greatly), there were rumours in the air concerning Brian's will. Brian was the most penurious skater in the history of the world. He never had any money for cigarettes. It was unthinkable, in my experience, that he would ever buy a dinner. In fact, he was stingy with his own pleasure. But stories started to circulate that Brian had left a proviso in his will allocating funds for certain people to do things that he'd always wanted to do but hadn't done.

At breakfast, it was suggested that someone was going to be sent to Egypt. I felt that I would be most suitable for that trip and could appreciate it as no other could, especially for him. Someone else was to have been given his car. I didn't really need one, but if I were given the red sports car, I could learn how to drive, and it would be very nice. Someone else was going to be sent on a hot-air balloon ride, which didn't thrill me. The Egyptian trip sounded better, but you take what you get.

As I was beginning to pack my bags, I went into the kitchen and told Mrs. Pockar and company that I was leaving for Toronto, not to return to Calgary, so that if there was anything that they really had to tell me, maybe they should tell me now. They kept saying, "Goodbye. So nice of you to come. Brian would really have appreciated it." I kept saying, "Well, I really will be going now. In five minutes the taxi will be here." I was fishing, but I caught no fish.

I was not mentioned in that will, but someone else was, and I feel that it is salient and poetic to bring it up now. David Dore was mentioned in the will. The executors of the will were to have sent him a bunch of dead roses with a message involving the F-word. The executors, with their perfect taste, elected not to do so. I'm reporting it now because I think that Brian would have wanted that.

I went home on my $250 flight, and the only thing that I can remember is feeling depressed – because of the tragedy, because of the stress, because of the grief of Brian Pockar's funeral. So often, it is the best and the brightest who die young.

The Third Funeral

Although he was not centre stage at main events in my life, it was my father who showed interest and initiated action where I was concerned. For example, my parents made a pilgrimage to the Broadway show in New York. They came to visit me in my unfurnished, twenty-five-room strawberry mansion in Bermuda. They came to my Parisian apartment and saw me in Holiday on Ice. Each of these excursions would have been out of my father's desire to see his son achieve things of note.

There were two important examples in recent years when my father should have been at an undertaker's parlour. First, he pulled himself together, at great emotional expense to my mother, and forged his way in a wheelchair to my painting exhibition at Trump Tower. Second, he had never been to the estate in Mexico, but he very much wanted to go. By hook or by crook, he was going to get there. Again, he should have been dead, but he went.

He never really left the property in San Miguel, but he did eat, go swimming, and sit in the garden. My dog, Flora, sat beside him, lashed to his patio chair, and I think that he was very happy. We didn't have last words with one another the way I did with Brian Pockar. My father was hard of hearing. However, he spent a week

with me, and, somehow, he and I were at peace and in harmony with one another in a way that we had never before been.

My mother brought him back to Ottawa, and the only thing that I heard about that trip was that it was among the worst experiences of her life. He had eye problems. He had heart problems. He had stroke problems. There were many, many things. His body was virtually falling apart.

I never saw my father again. I do not want to belabour the build-up to his funeral, because, in many ways, I played no role in it. I would have stayed in touch with my mother, but, because there was so much unrest within the family (particularly with regard to one of my brothers and my mother), even during that stressful period, it was difficult. Several times it was announced that he was going to breathe his last. However, my father, like a tortoise (slow and steady wins the race), was resilient and refused to die.

My mother worried about his decline and his resilience for a number of reasons. One was, "My God, what happens if he lives for another ten years and has to go to an old-age home? I don't think that I want that, and I certainly cannot put up with him in the house." Also, my mother had planned, the way Auntie Mame planned, to take one of her grandchildren on a major trip. She planned to take Ashley Cranston to London, England. The tickets had been purchased. The trip had been laid out. It had been much discussed and anticipated, and excitement ran high. However, my father was not dead, and you could not exactly go on that type of trip in light of his serious condition.

There were many reports. It's going to happen. It almost happened. Another week, another night, another day. I was involved in a television show called "Skate." It was hosted by Tracy Wilson, and I was the skating critic. There were three more shows that had to be done and, wouldn't you know it, they had to be done on the day after my father died.

The death was announced, in a rather cool and clinical way, on my answering machine: "Your father has died. The funeral will be at such and such a time, and [in essence] it would be nice if you showed up. Your mother."

Of course, I had to go, but I also had to do those television shows. I could not just cancel them. I made a habit of looking particularly dynamic on those shows. I always wore brightly coloured blazers, secretly trying to eclipse, in my two and a half minutes, the more than twenty-five minutes of Tracy Wilson's on-air presence. My final costume for that particular day was a blood-red cashmere jacket and a blood-red shirt. I looked pretty good. Everything went well.

I ran out of the studio, went to the Toronto Island airport, and flew to Ottawa to be picked up by my brother Goldie. It dawned upon me, riding to Arnprior on my way to the memorial service, that maybe blood red wasn't quite the colour to wear. My hair was meticulously coiffed, and I still had full make-up on, which made me look unnaturally natural.

I arrived just as the memorial service was about to start. It took place in the sleepy, little out-of-the-way Ontario town that had been the seat of the Cranston family for several generations. I wasn't certain how my arrival at the last second (in blood red) was going to go over with the rest of my family, but everyone was polite. There was not a spare pew to be had. Many people from my earliest past were there. It really was like going back to the family roots.

I had to speak at that service. Normally I'm quick on my feet, never at a loss for things to say, but I was struggling. I kept thinking, "I didn't know my father. He didn't know me. I'm not sure if I liked my father. Did he love me?"

The show – because it *was* kind of a show – was improperly mounted. My sister, who had been close in my father's final days (they lived twenty minutes apart), gave the first speech. Her name is Phillippa but her nickname is Flip, and I felt that she *was* a bit flip. It was sort of, "Good old Monte, he liked the Mills Brothers, he liked this, he liked that." Maybe anything that she really, deeply felt had been sapped and expended in the previous months. It was, "That's what happened. That's the way things are. He's dead. He's probably happy now."

When I got up to speak, I had no idea what was going to come out of my mouth. My sister had talked about Arnprior and the family cottage, the place that my father had loved so dearly. He had spent his boyhood years there, and we had spent summers at that cottage. He was going back to the place that he had loved.

Without being absolutely precise, what I said was, "How strange that I am wearing a blood-red jacket and a blood-red shirt to a funeral. However, blood is the reason that we are all here today. The blood relations have come, and it is blood that, whether we like each other or not, and whether or not we have problems or hostility or feuds, binds us together.

"My sister has rhapsodized about the Arnprior connection, the family seat of the Cranston clan. For me, it was the seat of every nightmare that I ever had. Prior to an Olympic Games, when anxiety runs high, I was forever being strangled and suffocated in the lake outside the cottage by seaweed that wrapped itself around my neck and pulled me down. My experience was the complete antithesis of Phillippa's.

"But although I had little in common with my father, in the latter part of his life – or maybe all along, and I didn't even know it – he *did* love me, and he *did* love his family, and all that he really wanted was for his family to function as a family. Now that he's dead, wouldn't it be nice if we could? Wouldn't it be the ultimate tribute? I wish it could. I don't know if it can."

From a friend of a friend of a friend, I did hear that my little speech riveted people. It became like Brian Pockar's sisters'. It was genuine emotion and genuine truth, whether one liked it or not.

My two brothers, I suspect, eclipsed what I said, because they were able to squeeze out genuine tears. They spoke about a man I didn't really know. Guy said that my father had been his hero. I had never known what he and Goldie thought until that moment.

The final speaker was my sister's husband, Dan Baran. Although well-intentioned, he really couldn't compete with the raw veracity of our feelings. He started to chit-chat about good old Monte, so the proceedings circled back to the vein in which my sister had begun them. The thing that was clear to me and to my brothers (who, at the time, although twins, did not speak to each other) was that it was blood that drew us together, and it was blood that allowed us to talk about our father in the way that we did.

I then spoke to my mother. We went back to her house, a house called Plum Crazy, in Pakenham. It was a temple to the frog – over 900 of them, I believe. She also collects nuns, of which there are more than 1,100. I think that she went through a camel period as well. Her house, compared to mine, even at its height, far outdid the genuine eccentricity of anything that I could ever have come up with.

There were rather unappetizing home-town salami sandwiches and cucumber sandwiches and perhaps homemade cookies. The air had a distinct chill because certain members of the family didn't talk to other members. I met some childhood friends. I certainly put up a good front. I was fighting my own demons and wars, but in my blood-red costume, no one would have suspected.

Epilogue: Lausanne

Circles are so often part of a skater's life: figure eights, spins, rotations, and choreographic circles. This book began, quite unexpectedly, when I met Martha Kimball, in a way that was ordained by our destinies, at the 1996 World Figure Skating Championships in Edmonton, Alberta. The book and the time spent doing it have exorcised many of my demons, secrets, and insecurities. As the stories unfolded, I unfolded, too, like a butterfly emerging from its cocoon. I experienced a catharsis.

Many tales remain to be told. Yet I sense, spiritually and emotionally, that like a spiral curving inexorably towards its starting point, the story came full circle at the 1997 championship in Lausanne, Switzerland.

The Lausanne adventure began with Carol Anne Letheren, head of the Canadian Olympic Association and member of the

International Olympic Committee (IOC), who suggested that I have a painting exhibition at the Olympic Museum to coincide with the figure skating championships. Piles of faxes crisscrossed the various levels of officialdom, all the way up to Juan Antonio Samaranch, the head of the IOC. The problem, as I found out, with any endeavour on an international stage is that there is so much red tape that one wonders how anything ever gets done.

It was difficult to get the green light, to find out who was going to pay for what and who was going to take responsibility – and to get it all in writing. As late as three days before the paintings were to be sent, I had a call from the curator of the museum saying that he was very sorry but all the works that I had painted during the past five months were too large. He had put a stop on the shipment. The paintings were in a crate so enormous that it had ripped off the outside door of my loft. What was I going to do?

I told the curator that if the paintings didn't go to Lausanne as they were, then I wasn't going either. He tap-danced and said, "We'll pay for the crate and accept the paintings, but don't expect all of them to be hung." I thought, "If I get the paintings and myself to Lausanne, there's a good chance that I can work something out."

How I got to Lausanne was dramatically different from the way I had gotten to Edmonton a year earlier. In Edmonton, I skated as a bat on plastic ice in the local opera company's production of *Die Fledermaus*. In Lausanne, I was an official guest. One-third of my expenses was paid by the Olympic Museum; a third was paid by the organizing committee of the competition; and, irony of ironies, a third of my expenses, and my accreditation, came from the International Skating Union, all the officials who, at least in my mind, had prevented me from winning a world championship. It was curious how the chessboard had been swept clean. New games had started. New players were in positions of power.

I flew first class on Air France (thank you, ISU), not to be met in Geneva by my art manager, Paul LaPointe, who was stuck in a traffic jam. I created the illusion of a miffed aristocrat, pretending to the welcoming committee at the airport that I was a personal guest of Samaranch, and I didn't understand (stamping my foot) why my limousine wasn't there waiting. After a transatlantic plane ride, my performance was not Academy Award-calibre, but while others took the train, I was ensconced in a huge black Mercedes limousine and whisked off to Lausanne.

I learned that I would have to bluff my way through the accreditation. Getting credentials at Worlds is like breaking into Fort Knox. Either your name is on the list or it isn't. IMG, the owner of the rights to the world championships and my long-time agency, was supposed to have acquired credentials for me, but that was not the case. Yet, the ISU – my enemies – came through with accreditation that gave me such stunning privileges that I was more fortunate than any competitor, coach, or team official.

For that fleeting moment, I was part of the ISU and could eat its shrimp and drink its champagne in the special tent reserved only for the Old Guard. Sitting in that tent, talking to people who had judged me and affected my fate, I saw them in a different light. For the first time, I saw most of them as all-too-human beings, not as evil sorcerers who cooked up magic potions and ladled them onto one's destiny.

Lausanne was a bend in the road where I could stop, rest, take stock, look back, and look forward. For once, I was not at Worlds as a competitor, coach, commentator, or fisherman trying to lure talent. Above and beyond being a guest of the Olympic Museum, I was there as an extremely professional spectator with no axe to grind. I was in the inner sanctuary, specifically in the very seats that the ISU had reserved for judges and officials, yet wasn't one of them. I felt equally estranged from the skaters on the ice. I sensed no

rapport with skating and only a distant and removed fascination for
it. I was no longer under its spell.

Worlds are like a convention. You touch base with people with
whom you've skated and shared years of experiences. The skating
world rarely changes. The cast just gets bigger. If the competitors
aren't the same, then the competitors become the teachers, the judges,
and members of the ISU. Circles, circles, circles. Interchanging roles.

The Unwelcome Guest

Somehow all the paintings that I had sent were hung and looked
rather good, but like Trump Tower, like Broadway, like Radio City,
my exhibition, which should have been so great, was a disappointment and a failure due to the curator's polite negativity. Probably his
reasons were valid. I think that I had been thrown at him. Yet I got
no pleasure out of the exhibition, knowing that I was an unwelcome
guest. The international press corps, three hundred strong, attended
the opening. In my naïveté, I thought that the journalists would be
interested in what I had to say, and maybe even in my paintings. As
it turned out, they were salivating only at the thought of the free
food on the table upstairs.

The O. J. Simpson Effect

The championships themselves, the high point of the skating year,
often struck a boring chord with me. My happiest moment as a
spectator was spent lying in bed in the Hôtel Royal-Savoy, eating a
hamburger and French fries, while I watched the absurdity of what
ice dancing has become. Unless the rules of ice dance change, allow-
ing it to be more creative and interesting, I plan in the future always
to watch it in a horizontal position in a fancy hotel. Thanks to the
sham and deception of the O. J. Simpson trial, which had a profound effect on global culture, what I wanted, what I think people
who were prepared to come to terms with their emotions wanted,

was reality, straight down the middle of the road. No artifice, no illusion, no smoke and mirrors, no superficiality. People wanted the real thing. That's what I wanted in Lausanne, and that's what I want for the next part of my life.

I watched Elvis Stojko win the men's event in a style that was foreign to me, alien to the vision I had in the 1970s, yet (perhaps in the way that John Curry won the Olympics) Elvis won on his own terms, making little or no compromise with the establishment. The artfulness of his skating is debatable, but the integrity, the meat and potatoes approach, can only command respect.

I watched little Tara Lipinski evolve from an unknown mouse who had alighted on my knee to have her photo taken in Edmonton to the youngest world champion in history.[*] Michelle Kwan, who might have thought after her brilliant performance in Edmonton that she was in for the long haul, was beaten by her fourteen-year-old teammate. In a much more tragic way, Lu Chen, who won in Birmingham in 1995, then nearly repeated in Edmonton, slid from almost first to an unprecedented twenty-fifth position, which prevented her from making the cut and skating the long program. That was history, too – a different kind of history. The players change; the game changes; the winners are the losers; the losers are the winners.

Poison Darts

One dart launched straight at the heart of the skating world, much discussed at the championships, was Scott Hamilton's testicular cancer diagnosis. Even in tragedy, the great entertainer had chosen the perfect moment for his announcement: just when all the skating world had congregated at Lausanne.

---

[*] Lipinski, an American, took the long-standing record from Norwegian Sonja Henie, who was thirty-two days older when she won her first of ten consecutive world titles.

Equally tragic was the death of Carlo Fassi, a world-famous coach, the teacher of Olympic champions John Curry, Peggy Fleming, Dorothy Hamill, and Robin Cousins. He had always been my enemy, a teacher of my competitors, a threat to my career. I thought that he never understood me. I wasn't at all sure that he liked me. I had no idea if he respected me. Yet in Lausanne, for the first time in twenty-five years, we had a man-to-man talk. Afterwards it seemed to me that he did know who I was, and vice versa. I suspected, with that score settled, that we probably would work together in the future. He died the next day of a massive heart attack.

Although Carlo Fassi was not part of my inner circle, I went to his memorial service because of my new respect for him. Whenever one of the great personalities of the skating world dies, it is only right, whatever side of the fence you're on, to pay homage. I had never before seen a funeral audience erupt into applause, galvanizing each speaker to top the last by being more clever, more amusing, and more slick. I will not name names.

The simple sincerity of Carlo's son Lorenzo completely eclipsed the slickness of some of the speakers. Thanks to him, the lasting image of Carlo Fassi is of a man who was loved by his wife and adored by his children. His family, as with every other normal man in the world, was more important than anything. Probably Carlo understood the meaning of life, yet I had never considered him as a father or a lover or a husband. To me, he had been that Italian operator who seemed to know how to get things done behind the scenes better than anyone else. Without him, a rare and special colour is gone from the great skating tapestry.

An Appointment with God

Near the end of my stay in Lausanne, I was granted an audience with Juan Antonio Samaranch, president of the International Olympic Committee. Many feel that his power equals the Pope's. I went without trepidation. If I've learned anything over the past twenty years, it's that men are men, and positions are, for the most part, conferred, not inherited by divine right. Although I sensed that he was a smart old fox who knew a lot of secrets, he was also a frail little man with a vulnerable side. Dick Pound, one of two Canadian IOC members, was very kind to escort me to Samaranch's office. I asked Dick how I would know when my fifteen minutes were up. He said, "You'll know." I did.

The audience concluded when Samaranch went into a closet and pulled out a box. I later found out that there is a hierarchy of presents that one might get from the Olympic Santa Claus, ranging from a museum brochure, an ashtray, a T-shirt, and a Swatch watch to, in my case, the top gift, a very fancy watch with so many dials that North American jewellers can't discern all its functions. I was proud to know that, at least for that moment, he liked me and had given me first prize. Besides, I needed a watch.

This Way to the Exit

When I was seven years old, my father – with whom I rarely did anything – took me through the fun house at the Canadian National Exhibition in Toronto. I remember it vividly: insane laughter, animal noises, secret pedals that sent a blast of cold air up your pant leg, horrible rubber tentacles that slapped against your face as you groped in the darkness. There were ink-black passages that narrowed until you found yourself wedged in a corner. There were cobwebs that hung on you, doors that slammed in your face, things that grabbed at you, screamed at you, or fell down and dripped on you; mirrors that made you look fat, thin, tall, or projected someone else's reflection next to yours. There was an omnipresent sense of being watched in the dark, but there were also times – which was disappointing – when it wasn't pitch-black and you could see how seedy and seamy and cheap the whole experience was. Whatever emotions one felt, the emotion upon exiting was the best.

My father went through that fun house with me. Yet, as it turned out, the real house of horrors was the twenty years that I experienced in the dark, alone, without him: twenty years of performing, travelling, exhibiting myself, creating and living out illusions. I paid the ten cents to get in. I had the thrills and the kicks and the emotional highs and lows. I can look back at those twenty years with respect, interest, curiosity, and a lot of good and bad memories. Artifice, fabrication, the creation of images are all wonderful to behold, but in the final analysis, facing up to the truth about oneself is what matters.

I have confronted the memories, the myths, and the horror of the illusions that life threw on my doorstep. Reality and truth are the prizes one gets at the end if one can face them. Now I know what is right for the next chapter of my life. By spilling nuggets of memories onto the floor, I was able to edge my way towards the exit. In Lausanne, the secret door swung open, and I left the house of horrors. I have no desire to go through the fun house again.

The Photographs

Page 1

Toller and Phillippa Cranston with their twin brothers, Guy (left) and Goldie.

Page 8

With Ellen Burka and Haig Oundjian.

Photo: Boris Spremo

Page 11

Winning his first Canadian championship: 1971, Winnipeg.

Page 13

Polar bears, 1958: Ronnie Shaver (left) and Toller (standing, centre).

Courtesy Ron Shaver

Page 37

The Palace Theatre marquee, May 1977.

Page 49

The Ice Show company. Back row: Gordie McKellen, Jim Millns, Don Fraser, David Porter, Jack Courtney, Bob Rubens, Brian Foley, Toller. Front row: Kath Malmberg, Colleen O'Connor, Candy Jones, Barbara Berezowski, Emily Benenson, Elizabeth Freeman.

Photo: Gifford/Wallace Inc.

Page 80

At Harvard, 1985.

Photo: Anna-May Walker

Page 94

The finale, Holiday on Ice, Berlin.

Page 101

The Firebird, 1979.

Photo: Cylla von Tiedemann

Page 136

With Japanese skaters in Tokyo.

Page 150

John Curry (front and centre) with Michael Seibert, Judy Blumberg, Ken Shelley, JoJo Starbuck, Tai Babilonia, and Randy Gardner, 1989.

Photo: Michael Anton

Page 159

Rehearsing Ice in Lake Placid with Robin Cousins and Peggy Fleming, 1983.

Photo: Nancie Battaglia, courtesy Gloria Ciaccio

Page 175

"Totally Possessed."

Page 183

In Munich with M.

Page 190

With Minkus.

Page 207

The lost dog.

Page 210

Part of the royal family: Robin Cousins, Rosalynn Sumners, Ken Shelley, Judy Blumberg, Scott Hamilton, Dorothy Hamill, JoJo Starbuck, Toller, Elaine Zayak, and Michael Seibert (the original cast of Stars on Ice).

Page 217

Isabelle and Paul Duchesnay revolutionize ice dance with "Savage Rites."

Photo: Monica Friedlander

Page 219

Off the deep end, Toronto.

Photo: Cylla von Tiedemann

Page 222

Christopher Bowman (the handsome devil, centre) at Skate America, 1990.

Page 243

The San Miguel de Allende estate, viewed from a neighbour's terrace, 1996.

Photo: Martha L. Kimball

Page 256

Miss USA and judges.

Page 266

Colour commentator with CBC Sports.

Page 280

Invitation to the Trump Tower exhibition, May 3, 1994.

Page 282

With Ekaterina Gordeeva and Sergei Grinkov at Trump Tower.

Photo: Marietta de Aubrey

Page 284

In San Miguel de Allende with a broken leg, 1994.

Page 290

Lu Chen in the costume that won Worlds, 1995.

Photo: Lois Yuen

Page 299

Simone Grigorescu.

Page 309

Michael Seibert (left) with Tracy Wilson and Robert McCall.

Photo: Martha L. Kimball

Page 311

At Skate the Dream with Rosalynn Sumners, Katarina Witt, and Brian Boitano.

Photo: BDS Studios

Page 321

Brian Pockar (second from right) two weeks before his death. With him, from left to right: Leanne Pockar, Peter Carruthers, Brian Orser, Toller, and Dena Carruthers.

Page 328

Monte and Stuart Cranston.

Page 333

At the Olympic Museum, Lausanne, March 1997.

Photo: Martha L. Kimball

Page 340

At work in the Queen Street studio, 1997.

Photo: Thom Hayim

Index